WORK, LEARNING, AND THE AMERICAN FUTURE

James O'Toole

WORK, LEARNING, AND THE AMERICAN FUTURE

Jossey-Bass Publishers
San Francisco • Washington • London • 1977

WORK, LEARNING, AND THE AMERICAN FUTURE
by James O'Toole

Library of Congress Catalogue Card Number LC 76-50726

International Standard Book Number ISBN 0-87589-304-X

Manufactured in the United States of America

JACKET DESIGN BY WILLI BAUM

FIRST EDITION

Code 7703

THE AUTHOR

James O'Toole is director of the Twenty Year Forecast project at the University of Southern California, where he is a member of the faculty in the Graduate School of Business Administration. He is well-known for his *Work in America* report, which he prepared for the Secretary of Health, Education, and Welfare in 1972. From 1972 to 1976 he did extensive research on the relationship of education to work.

James O'Toole was a Rhodes Scholar at Oxford University and received his doctorate in social anthropology there in 1970. Following Oxford, he worked as a management consultant with McKinsey and Company, as director of field investigations for the President's Commission on Campus Unrest, as a special assistant to the Secretary of HEW, and as director of the Aspen Institute Program on Education, Work, and the Quality of Life. He has addressed many major organizations and has published numerous magazine and journal articles. He is principal author or editor of *Watts and Woodstock: Culture and Identity in the United States and South Africa; Work in America; Work and the Quality of Life;* and *Energy and Social Change.*

Born in 1945, he lives in Los Angeles with his wife Marilyn, a lawyer, and with their two children.

75031

Preface

This book is born of frustration. When I finished editing the *Work in America* report in 1972, I confidently expected that others would build on that initial effort and create a coherent and consistent philosophy of human resources development. Unfortunately, with one or two notable exceptions, the entire issue is mired where it was five years ago—still without a theme, a goal, or even a thrust. The broader and more important issues of how society should develop and use its most valuable resource have been lost in nit-picking debates over such narrow topics as job satisfaction, job enrichment, overeducation, and career education. Although these issues are important, it is now clear that resolving them in a piece-meal fashion will not lead to a greatly improved general level of development of human resources in the society. For instance, despite a decade of promising experiments with various forms of job enrichment, the nature of work for the vast majority of Americans is basically unchanged.

There are many reasons for this anomalous situation, but I keep coming back to one that was the original impetus behind *Work in America:* The job redesigners who dominate the work humanization field lack an ultimate vision of human resources development and seem to act without regard for the consequences of their actions. What kind of world are they seeking to create? On what principles are they proceeding? What is the moral basis of their actions? Do they want to change the role of business in society, to alter the relationship of capital to labor, to effect a change in class structure? Or are they merely pursuing greater productivity through motivational nostrums? They shrug off these questions as "ideological" and charge ahead without regard for the implications of their actions for the future of the labor union movement, the nature of democracy in society, the individual's freedom to decline demanding work, and the possible effects on efficiency and the standard of living.

Many in labor, management, and academia are reluctant to follow the job redesigners because they know not where they lead. And the often laudable efforts of the job redesigners are readily undercut by the same doubters because there are no underlying principles to adhere to, no philosophical or theoretical base to their experiments to serve as a unifying force against the inevitable pressures for dissolution and dispersion. "The American genius— and curse—is always to act, seldom to reflect," as the journalist Georgie Ann Geyer so wisely observes.

Nevertheless, many Americans are uneasy about the absence of reflection about work humanization in this country. This absence of reflection has such obvious implications for central institutions in the society (education, the family, and the community, for example) that those outside the field are demanding more information about where the job design action will lead. Since the publication of *Work in America,* I have received at least a dozen appeals from concerned groups, particularly from educators, for explanations about the goals and the implications of the quality of working life movement for the broader society. The chapters of this book have grown out of my earnest, if not fully successful, responses to such appeals. In brief, I have responded by arguing that the issue at hand is not simply job dissatisfaction or how to redesign jobs or how to make education a more relevant preparation for work. Rather, the issue is how to make the development of human resources a prime aim of the key institutions of society. The immediate challenge is to provide some guidance to government agencies, workplaces, schools, and colleges as to how they might develop the potential of the nation's most plentiful but least-tapped resource—the intellectual, creative, and spiritual energy of the people.

My hope is that this book can make some contribution to an overarching philosophy of human resources. My principle contribution to such a philosophy is an analytical perspective that is future-oriented, humanistic, and multidisciplinary. I attempt to show that the traditional, narrow economic way of thinking about the relative roles of land, labor, and capital in productive activities is inappropriate to an advanced, postindustrial society. The economic paradigm is not dynamic or flexible enough to account for the rapid and qualitative changes that characterize our era. Changes in the size and power of technology, in resource availability, in environmental constraints, in levels of educational attainment, and in social values and expectations transcend the concerns and capabilities of the established economic discipline. Consequently, economics (whether in the mold of Adam Smith or Karl Marx) is not conducive to creating the flexible, dynamic, and holistic social inventions needed to make education and work satisfying and rewarding in the future. Instead it leads only to the regurgitation of tried and untrue public policies and private practices.

Nevertheless, I do *not* argue that economics is unimportant. For example, market mechanisms provide the most efficient allocation of goods and services in the short run; stimulate needed entrepreneurial activity and technical creativity; and, most important, they are a necessary (although not sufficient) condition for political liberty. My goal, then, is to free the analysis of education and work policies from the crippling constraints of the discipline of economics not to propose a self-defeating rejection of all the manifest advantages of the economic market. Admittedly, this is

a fine and difficult line to walk, but I suggest that failure to execute
such a feat will lead to the continuation of current inadequate work
and education policies.

Readers who have followed my thinking in the periodical
literature will find in this book some ideas that I discussed in less
detail in articles (listed in the bibliography) in *Change,* the *Journal
of Occupational Medicine,* and *Worklife.* Much of the material in
Chapter Four appeared in *The Annals* of the American Academy
of Political and Social Sciences for March 1975, and much of Chapter Five is derived from "Lordstown, Three Years Later," in *Business and Society Review* for Spring 1975. Some material stems from
my recent book *Energy and Social Change,* published by the MIT
Press in 1976. Part of Chapter Two began as a report of a 1973
Aspen Institute project on "Education, Work, and the Quality
of Life." I gratefully acknowledge the contributions of Martin
Kaplan to that document, and many of his words and ideas have
found their way into this chapter.

Throughout all of the chapters I draw freely on the ideas,
writings, and inspiration of a group of mentors and friends, including Mortimer Adler, Hellmut Becker, Ivar Berg, Howard
Bowen, Selwyn Enzer, William Herman, Elliot Liebow, David
MacMichael, Beatrice Reubens, and W. Willard Wirtz. It is with
pride that I acknowledge the grand larceny of their insights into
the problems of work (I assume full responsibility, however, for
my zany interpretations of their ideas).

This book is divided into four parts. Part One identifies and
defines the major problems of work and education to which the
entire volume is addressed. (The first chapter, in particular, introduces the issues of human resources development and the futurist
perspective that guides the analyses that follow.) Part Two dis-
cusses the role of government in securing full employment and
the roles of employers and unions in improving the quality of
working life. Part Three outlines alternative ways in which education might be made more relevant to the future world of work
while not becoming a passive handmaiden of industry or the
economy. With less confidence, Part Four teases out several un-
tried policies that might lead to fuller utilization of the nation's

human resources. My major purpose here (and, indeed, a major purpose of the entire book) is to illustrate that there are many more alternatives available to society than has been commonly assumed. It is not only desirable but possible and practical to pursue some of these new forms of work and education.

Los Angeles   JAMES O'TOOLE
December 1976

Contents

Part Three: Role of Education

Part Four: The Quality Society

WORK, LEARNING, AND THE AMERICAN FUTURE

1

The Case for Change

This book advocates significant changes in the public policies and private practices that will determine the future of the institution of work. The purposes of this first chapter are to introduce the arguments for such changes and to present the assumptions and values on which these somewhat unusual and difficult arguments are based. Only if these underlying premises are stated clearly and candidly can the reader fairly judge whether to reject or accept the proposals for change. Let me begin, then, at the roots of the current concerns about work and workers.

In this increasingly complex and complicated world, some things remain pristinely basic and simple: for all that our social and material inventions have altered the planet, there are still only three categories of resources from which people may draw in order to produce what they need to sustain life. These resources are *land* (including energy and all other natural resources), *capital* (including machines and all other man-made sources of wealth), and *labor* (including all aspects of human skill, intelligence, ingenuity, and other abilities). Significantly, the first two of these "factors of production" may be reaching the point of maximum exploitation. By the end of the current millennium, it is unlikely that great increases in productivity will still be wrung out of natural resources (unless power from the sun—or sunlike fusion power—can be effectively harnessed). But even if we make the risky assumption that there are no immediate limits to natural resources, it is not clear that humankind will continue to benefit from greater use of capital-intensive machines. The kinds of machines that industrial societies (and would-be industrial societies) seem bent on producing often bring pollution, waste, inefficiency, cheap and shoddy goods, unemployment, and a general diminution of the quality of life. But economic growth, per se, is not at fault. Rather, growth pursued in the traditional mode of the industrial revolution seems inappropriate for tomorrow's constrained environment—both in the advanced, technological societies and in the overpopulated, underdeveloped countries.

It would seem, then, that improvement in the quality of life will occur mainly through making better use of the third factor of production—human resources. And by "better use" I mean not *harder* work but *smarter* work. Humankind's puny muscle power is not a potential source of greater progress; rather, it is the intellectual powers of the race that constitute an immense reservoir of productivity and advancement.

In *Small Is Beautiful* E. F. Schumacher explores policies for more fully tapping these human resources. Unfortunately, his bold approach to the issue is appropriate only to *pre*industrial countries. In this book, I show why and how these resources should be more fully developed in the world's most advanced *post*industrial societies—particularly in the United States. My approach differs from Schumacher's in one other important respect. Schumacher seems to conclude that a more humane, just, and technologically sane society cannot develop in a free market economy. I believe, however, it is possible and desirable to achieve the humane purposes he advocates while preserving the individual liberty, economic efficiency, and standards of scientific and professional

excellence and of quality of goods and services that socialism seems
to preclude. Thus, this discussion of human resources is placed in
the broader context of developing a just alternative to socialism.
To ignore this broader question is simply irresponsible, for the
reasons I discuss below.

The Liberal Alternative

The first step toward the development of human resources is to
increase the quantity and quality of jobs. In the United States,
educators, employers, economists, and legislators have traditionally
approached this task by advocating programs from a time-honored
laundry list that includes vocational and technical training, public-
service employment, increased manpower planning, and manipulation of monetary and fiscal policies. Although such actions are
not intrinsically bad, they are unlikely to successfully create plentiful
and rewarding jobs in the future. They will be not only ineffective, but inappropriate for the conditions likely to prevail in postindustrial societies—a future in which there will be restraints on
the uses of energy and natural resources, in which the demand for
cheap, mass-produced goods will be reduced, and in which there
will be a highly educated work force looking for satisfying, challenging jobs.

My approaches to producing more and better jobs will appear
utopian, even quirky, to many observers because work is not the
only concern that guides my analysis. There is no doubt that the
problems of too few jobs can be solved—at the expense of freedom.
And the problems of boring jobs can also be solved—at the expense of efficiency. But my goal is to avoid such trade-offs. Any
work-oriented solution that does not contribute to the *overall*
welfare of the society, that does not make the society in its *totality*
more just, is rejected here as being no solution at all. This view is
not shared by those on either the ideological left or the right of the
political spectrum.

The policy alternatives suggested in these pages are designed
for a "liberal society" that does not yet exist in the United States
and may never exist. I mean *liberal* as the word is used by liber-
tarians: to refer to a society based on individual freedom rather

than on governmental command and control; in short, a society
committed to both broad personal civil liberties and a free-market
economy. But I also mean *liberal* as the humanists use it: to suggest
a society in which progressive social goals are set by democratic
processes, one in which limited government powers are used to
realize a high quality of life and to minimize human suffering and
injustice.

   This democratic marriage of humanistic, quality-of-life principles with economic freedom may appear to be a shotgun union.
Those on the right, of course, find progressive and humane goals
"uneconomical" and "impractical," and those on the left are ap-
palled by the "naivete" of suggesting that such goals can be achieved
using "the tools of exploitation."

   Clearly, the liberal approach is inconsistent with the way politics has been conducted in this country. While the right has pursued liberty at the expense of equality and social justice, the left has
pursued equality at the expense of freedom, quality, and efficiency.
Such painful trade-offs have been destroying what little consensus
on social values remains in the nation. Increasingly, national debates are being waged in extreme either/or and win/lose terms:

> inflation vs. employment
> jobs vs. a clean environment
> equality vs. quality
> freedom vs. order
> equality vs. efficiency
> economic growth vs. the quality of life

Such a formulation of issues not only polarizes debate, it narrows
the range of policy options that are considered. It may even lead
to Solomon-like compromises between the two extremes which
overlook innovative alternatives that might have better satisfied
both of the conflicting parties.

   Consequently, this book looks for ways to develop work
policies that avoid the consensus-destroying and politically unacceptable trade-offs that unrealistically constrain social choice.
In so doing the book turns its back on the rationalistic assumptions
of the economists, budgeteers, and professional managers who

dominate decision making in the most important public and private institutions of the nation. Their assumptions tend to support certain subsets of the system, while often throwing other and more important parts into chaos. For example, an economics professor at Harvard has recently caught the attention of the nation's press and politicians with the assertion that the recent college graduates who cannot find good jobs are "overeducated." (Freeman, 1976). His conclusion flows neatly from the constrained perspective of his discipline. Unfortunately, the only answer to the problem (as he identifies it) is to limit access to education—a "rational" solution that would run counter to the American commitment to free choice and equality of opportunity.

A liberal definition of the problem differs from the economist's. Borrowing on the anthropological notion that issues should be analyzed in the context of the whole of which they are a part, the liberal finds it difficult to call most college graduates "overeducated." If he looks beyond simply their employment prospects, he discovers that many of these young people do rather poorly in reading, writing, and computation and that most are ill-equipped educationally for meaningful participation in family, community, and leisure activities. If there is disequilibrium in the system, then, it is not due to too much education but to underemployment. That is, the potential of these graduates for producing the goods and services the world needs is being underutilized. Cutting back on educational opportunities is to throw the baby out with the bath water; it satisfies some of the employment parts of the system, yet worsens the state of the more important other social and political institutions. If the problem is defined as underemployment, the liberal solution is to more fully develop and use the education, training, and talents of youth to serve not only the needs of employers, but the needs of the social system in general. Holistic analyses, then, are needed to find liberal solutions to national problems.

Bursting the Economic Integument

Such analyses must include economics, a fact that infuriates many progressive humanists, who feel that the needs of people must be tended to regardless of cost or efficiency. Equally, these approaches must include humanistic considerations, even though these do not fit into the elegant assumptions about human behavior that guide the thinking of economists (for example, "people work only to make money," and "the sum total of individual preferences adds up to an optimal collective decision"). My purpose in challenging the assumptions of traditional economics is to free our imaginations to develop new and more effective work and education policies. Like a kind of skin or rind, the economic way of thinking encloses us and restricts our vision and maneuverability. Cramped in a cover of economic myths, we cannot see the myriad policy opportunities available to create more and better jobs, different and more rewarding learning experiences. Of course, the discipline of economics is not intrinsically evil, nor even particularly wooly-headed. Indeed, it is the most advanced of the social sciences. The problem is that decision makers in academia, government, industry, and unions *listen* to economists. Most public policies in America are consciously or unconsciously based on the assumptions of the established discipline. It is better that policy makers listen to economists than to anthropologists or psychologists, one might say, but that is not the point exactly. Simply because economics is the most rigorous of the social sciences does not make it a true science. It is not based on natural laws. Unlike the physical sciences, it has little predictive reliability. But we nevertheless misuse economics as if it were a science. Perhaps because the economist is always ready with an answer, we assume that the answer is right.

But many of the confidently asserted answers or "laws" of economics are no more than assumptions (for example, that "people work only to make money" is not empirically verifiable). Moreover, the traditional economic paradigm is simple and static, while the world is complicated and dynamic. Consequently, the models of economics constitute nowhere near a complete view of reality. Qualitative matters, in particular, are seldom included in economic models.

Unfortunately, the reflexive, almost ideological nature of economic thinking distracts us from hard, imaginative and objective thinking about the problems of work and education. Thus, to develop new and more effective policies, we must sunder the economic integument, freeing our imaginations from the constraining dead-hands of economic scribblers from Smith to Marx to Keynes. All that the economists can tell us is what we cannot do to solve our problems, or why if we respond in one area it will create more problems in another area (for example, "if we clean up the environment, it will cost too many jobs").

The liberal goal is to invent policies that will allow the nation to have its cake and eat it, too. Although achieving this trick is often impossible, it is possible in more cases than is commonly assumed, and it is nearly always worth trying. Consequently, we need processes and policies that permit the simultaneous pursuit of such goals as low unemployment *and* low inflation, a high quality of life *and* a high standard of living, freedom *and* equality. The task is to identify our options, examine the consequences of various policies, agree on common goals, and develop strategies for achieving them. Of course, nothing could be more difficult, but nothing is more important.

One who makes such claims might well be considered certifiably looney. Let me then suggest the kinds of policies that I have in mind, if not to establish my sanity, at least to clarify my position. But first a caveat: the purpose of this book is not to advance any specific programs or policies. The proposing and disposing of policy is quite rightly a political process in a democratic nation, and the analysis and planning required for developing effective liberal policies to meet the myriad problems of our society constitute an agenda not for a single book or author but for the millions of citizens of the nation.

With this caveat duly registered, let us look at two public policies that might avoid difficult trade-offs. The first is designed to remove the wedge that has been driven between environmentalists on the one hand and labor and industry leaders on the other. For example, because of pressures from unions and management, President Ford recently vetoed an important environmental bill on the grounds that it would cost many workers their jobs. It is desirable, then, to develop environmental policies that *create* jobs. There is some evidence that the banning of nonreturnable beverage containers would be a small step in this direction. Such a law might simultaneously clean up the environment, create thirty thousand jobs in the aggregate in the private sector, lower dependency on foreign bauxite, and save billions of kilowatts of electricity (Bezdek and Hannon, 1974).

The second example is directed at the inflation vs. unemployment trade-off. In West Germany, the government offers a voluntary retraining program to workers. The program appears to have lowered inflation by moving workers out of declining and into expanding industries, reduced unemployment by opening up the job slots vacated by workers who undergo training in the schools, and increased productivity and job satisfaction by enhancing the mobility of workers (Striner, 1972).

Of course, there are many problems with both of these examples. My purpose in citing them is only to suggest the necessity for breaking with the traditional ways of thinking that constrain our ability to cope with the terrible problems of employment. Like everyone else, I have my pet proposals. But I am not here an advocate of any specific work, education, or training programs. Rather, I am a critic of the ways in which vocational educators, industrial engineers, managers, and manpower economists are framing the issues of work and developing policies for resolving them. It is the dominant set of assumptions about employment that I wish to question, because it is these assumptions that foreclose liberal policy alternatives.

To break with these beliefs it will be necessary not only to undertake holistic analyses, but to engage in more effective long-range thinking. Consequently, another major premise of this book is that a futuristic perspective is needed to develop liberal work policies. What do we know about the future of work?

Work in America's Third Century

Science fiction writers, utopians, and other visionaries often predict that the future will be laborless. In this common scenario, if Ms. X does any work at all in 2076, she is at it for only two or three hours a day. She works not at a plant or an office but at a remote computer terminal located conveniently in her condominium. Her job consists of scanning relevant information on a cathode ray tube and "interacting" with a robot named Hal miles away who does all the work faster and more efficiently than humanly possible. Seemingly, the only people putting in a full day's work in the future are Big Brother and his secret police, who are more than occupied with spying on, dictating to, and brainwashing the blissfully underemployed masses.

Professional futurists have a different view of work in America's third century. In the short period during which futurists have been practicing their craft, they have made one discovery of fundamental importance: *the future cannot be predicted.* Moreover, futurists believe that society is relatively free to choose, and ultimately to achieve, the future it desires. In the long run, the only thing inevitable about the future is that it will be determined by the actions that society takes (or fails to take) in the present.

For this reason the projections of futurists are couched not in terms of certainties but in the less precise language of probabilities and options. The goal is not to predict but to inform the democratic decision making process of the full range of alternatives that might be sought and of the probable long-term and indirect consequences of the policies attendant to each option. The underlying assumption is that society is more likely to arrive at a desirable future if it attempts to think about it in a systematic and formal fashion. For example, futurists often find it useful when analyzing public policies to ask the question "What if?" concerning the various alternatives: "What if Americans choose a four-day work week?" or "What if employers continue to substitute machines for labor?" Thus, although responsible futurists would be loath to predict how Americans will be working in the year 2000 (let alone 2076), they would nevertheless claim that there is considerable value in attempting to identify some of the key trends and events that might shape the future of work. For example, the choices America makes in each of the following areas will determine how we work, where we work, and how much we will work in the future.

Technology. Because machines can be made to do nearly every imaginable noncreative task, the role of technology is a key variable in determining whether America will be a leisure- or work-oriented society. Technology is a bugaboo to many people: one man's leisure is another man's unemployment. Indeed, the fear that machines will replace workers and lead to mass unemployment is not without some justification. For example, if an automatic typewriter is marketed that successfully takes dictation directly from the human voice, America might witness a faster dislocation of human labor than accompanied even the introduction of the tractor or computer. The potential consequences of such a new technology are troubling, especially for American women, who are already bitter over their slim employment prospects (in the past five years the number of women college graduates working as secretaries has increased by about 100 percent). With the introduction of an automatic typewriter, the job prospects for many women might deteriorate from the current absence of upward mobility to the absence of any paid work at all.

Fortunately, we need not be the helpless victims of applied science. Although it has for long been assumed that technology (like the weather) is a given, technology is actually determined by choices made by engineers and managers. For example, Volvo and Saab have discovered that the assembly line came not from Our Maker but from Henry Ford. And E.F. Schumacher (1973) is arguing rather convincingly that there are more technological options in producing cars, computers, and widgets than has been assumed.

Moreover, for over two hundred years it has been an economic tenet that progress occurs when capital (machinery) is substituted for labor. This verity, too, is now being questioned. No doubt technologies of mass production made more and cheaper goods available to millions of consumers than would have been available had they been produced in other ways. But assembly lines and the other middle-range technologies of the industrial revolution are best suited for eras of cheap energy, surplus capital, high consumer demand for low-quality, mass-produced goods, little environmental concern, and a poorly educated work force. Since the American future will probably not manifest these characteristics, it seems likely that industry will slowly begin to move either to the high productivity of high technology or to the high quality of low technology. In the industries that choose the latter course, people will be substituted for machines. This action could improve such things as the availability of capital, resource conservation, the quality of goods, job satisfaction, and rates of employment. And such a change need not entail a return to toil and drudgery: skilled crafts, for example, are highly satisfying occupations. Nor would there have to be a neo-Luddite revolution in which technology was exorcised from the body politic. As Volvo has shown with the 250 individual car-carrying devices that have replaced its assembly line, labor-intensive technologies are not necessarily primitive ones.

If America chooses to move away from the energy-capital-intensive mode of the industrial era, the negative consequences could be increased inflation, lowered productivity, and a cessation of scientific, social, and material progress. Although these outcomes would have been a serious threat in the past, they may be offset by another factor: it appears that America's most underutilized resource in coming decades will be the human skills, training, education, and talent that will be needed to overcome the loss of machine power. Even today, something like 80 percent of recent college graduates are employed in jobs that do not tap their productive potentials. Consequently, the development of these untapped human resources is likely to be the "technological" challenge of the postindustrial era, as the development of better tools and machines was the ultimate source of productivity in industrial society.

Social Values. If the future were to develop along these lines, it would mean working more and not less. Thus, the value-choice Americans may ultimately face is this: Do we want a leisure society or a work-oriented society? In hypothetical form, this question has challenged the Western mind since antiquity, but our children may be the first for whom it will be a practical choice. Surprisingly, there is evidence that they may actually choose work over leisure—Aristotle be damned. The contributions of work to an individual's identity, self-esteem, status, and sense of order and meaning are probably too powerful to make unproductive leisure an attractive alternative. After all, it is through work that one becomes a full participant in society, and such a basic fact is not likely to change in the future. (This is one reason why such great numbers of housewives wish to enter the paid labor force.) Moreover, there appears to be an overwhelming amount of work that needs to be done—ending pollution and poverty, rebuilding our cities, providing food and appropriate technology to the Third World, and solving the mysteries of energy, space, and the seas. Given such important and imposing tasks, a leisure society would probably even seem irresponsible.

At the same time, however, the odds favor a redefinition of work to include some things currently classified as leisure. The current definition of work as "paid labor" is increasingly criticized for being damaging and anachronistic because it excludes such important activities as the rearing of children and the volunteering of one's time and effort in schools, churches, hospitals, local government, and political campaigns. It also excludes the real work of the dedicated, creative artist who labors eight hours a day at a menial job to earn the wherewithal to support what some might carelessly call his "hobby."

But the most difficult value-choice American society will face in the coming decades concerns the most important work of any society: the care of children. How well this task is done is related to the controversial issue of *who* should do it. In almost all societies, women have cared for children, while men have been the instrumental providers of food, clothing, and shelter. Now, this traditional division of labor is under attack because it often excludes women from reaping most of the social, economic and psychological benefits of real (paid) work. Many American couples are attempting to equalize these benefits: both of them take paid employment while their children receive institutional care during the day. The problem with this otherwise unexceptionable solution is that it further downgrades both the status and quality of child care.

What should be done if women want equality with men in the paid labor market, but also feel that the rearing of children is too important to be left to institutional arrangements? No one, particularly not the state, should answer this question for families. What is needed are more options and free choice among these. One option that may develop is for men and women to share work and family roles, each participating equally in child care and paid employment. This is currently a realistic option only for the tiniest minority of families, but it might someday become available to the majority if trends toward flexibility in working conditions continue to develop.

Working Conditions. The frequency with which one hears such phrases as the "humanization of work," "job satisfaction," and "the quality of working life" leaves little doubt that the traditional work ethic is changing. To an immigrant, a migrant from the South, and to almost everyone who lived through the Depression, a good job is one that pays well and offers some security. Young Americans do not share these experiences with their parents, and consequently their work attitudes differ. The under-thirty generation—the future majority of the work force—wants and expects jobs that contribute to others and to society, that are challenging, and that offer the opportunity to learn and to grow. But there are some workers who do not desire these things, and even those who do have individual preferences concerning when, how, and in what mix and quantity they want them. As a result there is no *single* job design capable of providing satisfaction to *all* workers. In the past decade, many employers tried and failed to enrich jobs using one or more of the many set formulas promulgated by management experts. Frustrated in these efforts, some of the most sophisticated employers are now discovering that they can't *dictate* happiness for their workers. Instead, some firms are finding that workers' needs can best be satisfied if the company offers many alternatives and provides the resources whereby the workers can succeed at whichever of these jobs they select. Flexibility and choice—in job design, length of work week, hours of work, form of compensation, career paths, and types of training—are thus the emerging watchwords of employee relations.

Some experts now argue that workers should even have the option of holding two jobs, say as a plumber in the morning and a bureaucrat in the afternoon. This would allow a worker in a dull job to find some intrinsic rewards in a better second job, would allow potentially redundant workers to train half time for a future job, and would allow husbands and wives to work part time and care for their children part time. We aren't there yet—managerial practices and sex-role attitudes are still in the way—but the Pitney Bowes Company now permits pairs of working mothers to split one job, thus freeing them both to spend more time with their children.

Relation of Work, Education, and Leisure. Flexibility at work might complement a broader dismantling of the anachronistic, monolithic, and mechanistic life path that has developed in industrial society. In this rigid path, education is synonymous with youth, work with adulthood, and retirement with old age—thus segmenting lives into age traps and segregating generations into age ghettos. Not only are there few second chances in such a system, there are enormous costs in terms of (a) limitations on freedom of choice and on access to work and learning resources and opportunities, (b) dissatisfaction with life, and (c) poor performance in job, school, and family roles and tasks.

What if flexibility were to become the hallmark of the next century? Willard Wirtz (1975) and others are now arguing that education, work, and leisure should be experienced as continuing strands running throughout each person's life, each strand to be stressed by the individual at the appropriate and desired stage in his or her career. Current moves to break the lock-step in education that keeps many young people out of workplaces until their mid-twenties, to provide continuing education for adults, and to offer flexible retirement programs for the aged (often with an educational component) portend movement toward the flexible integration of lives and generations. Such an increase in freedom might well make work (and life) more enjoyable.

Role of Workers and Citizens. However Americans decide to work and spend their leisure time in the future, the choice must be theirs, and it must be a real choice among practical options. If America's bicentennial celebration is to have a lasting purpose, it can only be realized as a reaffirmation of the nation's commitment to democracy. The importance of the event we commemorated so fabulously is that it marked the first time the political future of a nation was placed squarely in the hands of its citizens. Significantly, after two hundred years of political democracy, it now appears that the future of work will also be determined democratically. American workers are just now beginning to participate in the decisions that most directly influence their day-to-day existence. Although they spend more of their waking hours at work than at any other activity, only a few Americans have participated in such decisions as when they will work, with whom they will work, with what technological tools they will work, and how they will divide the tasks that need to be done. However, some managers are beginning to discover that workers are most satisfied and productive when they are given the rights, resources, and responsibilities of self-management. It is a lesson that was learned long ago in political affairs. Indeed, it permeated the thinking of the Enlightenment that influenced Jefferson and his contemporaries to advocate democracy not only as the most just system of governance, but also as the most practical and efficient (for example "overhead" costs in a democracy are low because there is no need for secret police to be engaged in the impossible task of trying to keep the populace "loyal" and "committed" to the goals of the nation).

Extending this theory to the workplace, Warren Bennis (1966) argues that democracy is not only a more just but also a more efficient *management* philosophy than authoritarianism. Apparently, this insight is belatedly spreading to some parts of American industry. For example, when workers have been organized into autonomous, self-governing teams, managers have needed to spend less time and effort on the "policing" tasks of supervision. How far this movement will go is uncertain, but in companies in Vermont, Indiana, and the District of Columbia, workers have recently become the owners as well as the managers of their firms, even taking seats on their boards of directors. Although there may be many practical problems with such "worker capitalism," some observers argue that it presents a way to further social justice and equality, while preserving the free-market mechanisms that seem necessary to protect liberty and ensure efficiency in the economic system. At any rate, if the major challenge facing Bicentennial America will be to create a just alternative to socialism, then worker capitalism is at least one means that merits consideration.

Two Hundred Million Different Futures

What will work be like at the time of the Tricentennial? That there is no single answer to such a question reflects, I believe, the source of the superiority of democracy over authoritarianism. Consider what the experience of two hundred years of political democracy has given to contemporary America: a system that is pluralistic, dynamic, experimental, malleable, contradictory, unbalanced, and unpredictable. Thus, the beauty and frustration of democracy is that it is not evolving deterministically toward some ideal, final form; rather, it perpetually generates more choices, more opportunities, more conflicts, and more uncertainty. A hundred years of democracy in the workplace will, one hopes, have the same exciting outcome. If all goes well, work won't become fixed in a single, rigid pattern, but will expand into multiple and flexible forms to meet the diverse, changing, and unpredictable needs of American workers. The best to which we can aspire, then, is two hundred million quite different futures of work for 2076, a unique future, chosen freely and democratically, for each American who will be working at that time. Such an eventuality would bring the nation closer than ever to the ideals of 1776.

In the following chapters, I expand these forecasts and analyses. The chapters that follow in Part One begin this process by identifying some of the major problems that face employed, underemployed, and unemployed citizens in the America of 1976 and by exploring some of the problems they are most likely to confront in the future.

2

Misuses of Human Resources

The phrase "misuses of human resources" is freighted with value judgments and assumptions about human nature, the role of work in life, and the purposes and efficacy of private practices and public policy. The most fundamental of these assumptions—one that lies behind all the analyses that follow—is that *work is of prime importance in the lives of most Americans.* I do not argue that work must have or should have such importance, nor do I hold that work is inherently noble or ignoble. The simple fact is that almost all Americans work and that work has significant economic, psychological, and social functions. The most obvious and basic function of work is economic: to provide food, clothing, and shelter. But it also has several less obvious psychological purposes or functions:

● Work contributes to self-esteem; through mastering a task, one builds a sense of pride in oneself. The job tells the worker he

17

has something of value to contribute to society. The workplace, then, is a major focus of personal evaluation.

• Work is also the most significant source of personal identity; we identify who we are through our jobs. We say, "I am a college professor" or "I am a housewife" when someone asks, "Who are you?" A consequence of this work-connected identification is that welfare recipients and the retired become nobodies.

• Work is a prime way for individuals to impose order, control, or structure on their world. From this perspective, we see that the opposite of work is not necessarily free time or leisure; it can be disorder or chaos.

For many people, work is like sex in that it is a source of great personal satisfaction, an overarching purpose for existence, an *élan vital.* In short, work offers the individual self-sufficiency, status, identity, self-esteem, a sense of order and meaning, and often pleasure and fulfillment (O'Toole, 1973a, pp. 1–8). Because it has such power, work can also be an incubus, a source of great dissatisfaction, frustration, stress, and guilt. For a few unfortunate souls it is even a fatal social disease—I once found a tombstone with the one-word epitaph "WORK" in the Aspen, Colorado, graveyard.

Although few of us would share with Freud the belief that the "death wish" is a part of the working or striving instinct, as a society we do take work very seriously. This attitude is attested to by the lack of humor with which the institution is treated. Like death and unlike sex, work is seldom the subject of jokes. One reason may be that work has become part of our subconscious assumptions about reality; indeed, it often defines reality for us. Most of us view it much as we view time—as inevitable and immutable. Work is so much a part of our mentality that we are often unaware that when we talk about other institutions, such as education, we often do so in the context of work. And most of us subordinate other activities, including our family life, to work. In fact, there is no clearer way of demonstrating the importance of work in life, and the social problems that emerge from it, than to review the way it relates to another of the most basic social institutions, the family.

Damage to Family Life

Evidence compiled for the *Work in America* study leads to the conclusion that if the opportunity to work is absent, or if the nature of work is not sufficiently rewarding, severe repercussions are likely to be experienced by the individual worker and his or her family. Several major studies of family life and employment document this relationship:

● Loss of work has been found to produce chronic disorganization in the lives of parents and children. Among the long-term unemployed, attitudes toward the future and toward the home and community have been shown to deteriorate. Family life loses its meaning and vitality for these individuals.

● The children of long-term unemployed and marginally employed workers show poorer school grades.

● Despite the popular notion that unemployed people fill their free time with intensified sexual activities, studies show that the undermined egos of former breadwinners are associated with diminished libido.

● The physical and mental health of the unemployed tends to deteriorate. For example, there is a correlation between unemployment and the onset of schizophrenia.

● There is a demonstrable relationship between a family breadwinner's work experience and family stability. Sociologist Frank Furstenberg reviewed forty-six separate studies of work experience and concluded that economic uncertainty brought on by unemployment and marginal employment is a principal reason why family relations deteriorate (1974).

● Sociologists have attributed the high rate of illegitimacy among poor people to the occupational uncertainty of men. Lee Rainwater (1974) found expectant mothers rejecting marriage if their sexual partners were unemployed or had poor occupational prospects.

● Manpower economist Michael Piore has developed a dual labor market theory that helps to explain the relationship between the nature of employment and the ability to sustain a nuclear family. He describes a secondary labor market that is distinguished by low wages, poor working conditions, considerable variability in employment, little security, harsh and arbitrary discipline, and little opportunity for upward mobility. Poor people are drawn to this market because they do not have the characteristics required for employment in the primary market. Piore has shown that the secondary market does not meet the social and economic requirements of those who wish to establish a stable family (1970).

• Anthropologist Elliot Liebow (1967) has found a relationship between the frequency and nature of employment of men, on the one hand, and their willingness to form stable nuclear families with the mothers of their children, on the other. Liebow's landmark research among ghetto dwellers in the District of Columbia offers the most poignant evidence we have of the correlation between mother-headed families and the subemployment and unemployment of street-corner men.

• My research in Watts in Los Angeles and among the nonwhite population of Cape Town, South Africa, reveals a striking similarity in the family structure of these two geographically distant communities. In both Watts and Cape Town, a high percentage of mother-centered families is found among the poorest people. In both communities, mother-centered families are more common when the father is chronically unemployed, employed irregularly, or employed in a job that will not permit him the social and economic dignity and security needed to assume the breadwinner's role in his family (O'Toole, 1973b).

• Divorce and separation rates for the poor are not greatly different from the rates for the middle class. Significantly, however, the remarriage rate of the poor is considerably lower than that of the middle class. Poor women, once they have been the victims of an unsatisfactory marital experience, tend to be unwilling to repeat the experience with another high-risk mate. For this reason, and not looser morals, the number of mother-headed households is higher among the poor. Unemployed or subemployed men simply are not seen as good remarriage material.

In summary, the evidence is overwhelming that unemployment and subemployment among breadwinners is a primary factor leading to continued marital instability among the poor. The absence of work—or work that fails to offer economic security, self-esteem, identity, and a sense of mastery over the chaos of one's environment—often does not provide the stable basis required to build a lasting familial relationship.

Problems Associated with the Normative Life Path

The work and family problems of the disadvantaged deserve most of our attention because they adversely affect opportunities for full and equal participation in society. Nevertheless, it is worth a moment to analyze the way society allocates access to work across all population groups and across time—if only to put the problems of the poor in sharper focus.

Access to work varies by age, sex, and social class. These variations are not the outcome of preferences of men and women expressed in a free labor market. Indeed, major pieces of social legislation are responsible for the differences or were designed to support existing differences. Let us review what social, psychological, and economic effects the differences in sex, race and generational access to work might have. To analyze these differences, we must first establish the normative life path for Americans, the one followed by white men. The canonical path for this group begins with an infancy of two or three years, during which the family is the controlling presence. As in traditional societies, the family is the basic unit that embraces living, working, and learning. There follows a period of childhood, when peer groups, the school, and, especially recently, the various media compete in influence with the family. During the period of youth—which is more and more being prolonged—the institution of education becomes the salient factor; today, the structure of our society prescribes that youth means schooling. Here, too, but growing less common, are the first passes at employment.

Freed from the educational institution, the new adult embarks abruptly on his career. His work occupies most of his time, and it is sharply set off from his two other prime concerns: leisure (the whole nexus of entertainment, social and civic and recreational activities, and whatever amount of continuing education he decides to engage in) and, most important, family.

And at the end of his working life—which is more and more

being shortened—the adult enters a period of retirement. Free time, either voluntary or enforced or some combination of the two, becomes the key motif. His dependence increases as he becomes older, and finally he may be placed in an institution at the approach of death. Viewed in this manner, life becomes a kind of maintenance path along which we are expected to slide irreversibly.

Which groups is society not prepared to assist along this linear progression? An obvious group—suggested by the fact that we use the masculine pronoun when we describe the canonical path—is women. In spite of our egalitarian motives, girls and boys do not receive the same kind of socialization and education. Nor, perhaps, should they. But in any case, girls' expectations are different because they are taught to stake different claims on life. Sex stereotypes and the role they play in encouraging widely divergent life choices have only recently begun to be understood. On the whole, it is still very much the case that the careers girls are supposed to pursue are meant to be secondary to the careers men pursue. John will grow up to be a lawyer, Jill his secretary. And the labors in the home and with their children that adult women engage in are not "really" work, because they are not rewarded financially. Moreover, a lifetime of housework does not provide eligibility for retirement.

Disadvantaged minorities, too, are not well served by the accepted path. They receive inferior educations, and they experience difficulty in entering and staying in the work world. At the end, they often find themselves without adequate retirement funds. Other outgroups—the insane, the chronically ill, the involuntarily unemployed—spend their lives in warehouses designed to contain them. Adulthood, for them, is not a period of earning that follows education. It is not a period in which work supports family and leisure activities.

There are, then, certain readily identifiable problems associated (a) with the ways we divide the time of our lives, (b) with the ways we provide access to institutions like work, education, and the family, ways that validate our legitimacy as contributing members of society and (c) with the ways our national programs and policies support the current structure. As a society, we can organize life paths in any ways we see fit. Seemingly natural divisions are actually the artifacts of one particular society. For example, the length of adolescence is as arbitrary as what we eat for breakfast. That adolescence does not exist in many cultures comes as a surprise to many Americans, but it is as true as the fact that not all peoples eat eggs and bacon for breakfast.

But that we can change life paths around relatively at will does not argue that we should. For example, is it clear that young people should work for a time before entering college, or that middle-aged adults should draw on some of their "retirement credits" and take a year or two off work for education or leisure purposes? The number and kinds of constraints necessarily operating on any society are poorly understood. It is crucial to distinguish between those societal features that are essential to the running of our society, and should not or must not be changed, and those features that can profitably be altered. Great questions of personal values and individual freedom are involved in making these determinations. Given the myriad alternatives before us, and the lack of consensus in favor of any one alternative, thorough analysis becomes all the more imperative.

Nevertheless, the profound problems that accompany or result from the artificial divisions of lives compel an analysis of policies that might help to reduce the dissonance between work and other institutions. The following list of five key problem areas does not attempt to be exhaustive or rigorously taxonomic. Rather, its purpose is to be archeological, to focus attention on the undergirding reasons for the existence of commonly cited problems related to work.

Segmentation of Lives. Several problems result from dividing life into discrete, age-graded functions:

Because work is "the badge of adulthood," the only fully legitimate activity of maturity, there is "something wrong" with someone who is not working: the adult nonworker is considered to have and to be a social problem. Women who take care of their children, the unemployed, the dropouts, the elderly—all lack full "working identities." They suffer both economically and psychologically from their second-class status and so are excluded from some of society's rewards.

By segmenting life functions, we make the activities of education, work, and leisure *less* meaningful than if they were interwoven strands throughout our lives. Many individuals observe that education is more meaningful if it has a work component; that work is more meaningful if it has elements of education and leisure; and that leisure is more meaningful if it comprises some aspects of work and education (and by "meaningful" I refer to the individual's perceptions of value, not simply to imposed societal norms).

Family activities are segregated from other activities. In the middle years of life, particularly, the worker is separated from his or her family for many hours during the day.

A segmented life means that the individual often has only one chance for success or satisfaction. Education once missed or misapplied in youth will likely cause untoward consequences throughout life. Only with difficulty can one escape from the track established by early educational experience. Those trained in vocational education shops, for example, are likely to be blue-collar workers for the rest of their lives—particularly if they are black or from a working-class background.

Segregation of Generations. Education, the activity of youth, occurs at schools, which become youth ghettos. Work, the activity of adulthood, is performed in similarly age-segregated institutions. Retirement, the activity of the aged, occurs increasingly in "leisure communities" cut off from the rest of the world, both spiritually and physically. As a result, the segregation of generations becomes a corollary to the segmentation of lives.

Young people seldom, if ever, see adults at work. As James Coleman (1973) and Urie Bronfenbrenner (1970) have noted, this omission leaves youths improperly socialized in relation to the work world and prolongs their adolescence. Cut off from older generations, from aspects of the essential guides of experience, tradition, and history, young people face a special difficulty in coping with important value questions in our rapidly changing society.

Another result of segmentation is that we have age-graded expectations of behavior, expectations that may run counter to economic necessity. For instance, it is considered deviant for an adult working-class male to go back to school for a year. To cite another example, we have institutionalized the cultural expectation that people should retire when they are sixty to sixty-five. Although the rationale we offer for this practice is that retirement is a reward, a primary reason we retire healthy old people arbitrarily at sixty-five is a shortage of jobs. But in the near future, demographics may require that individuals work until they are seventy to keep participation in the labor force high enough to support our productivity needs. What will then happen to the cultural notion that older people shouldn't work?

Limited Access to Work. One of the clearest social problems in the society is the scarcity of jobs due to the apparent national reluctance to pursue a full-employment economy. But this scarcity is not equal among the demographic groups of society; indeed, for middle-aged white males the problem is minimal. To keep the problem at bay for this group, we have kept young people out of the labor market until they are older and we have retired workers at an earlier age. To create employment for middle-aged women in answer to recent demands, we have increasingly excluded the young, the old, and minority men from the work force.

Institutional Inflexibility. Most jobs are organized in an inflexible, authoritarian fashion: they follow a model of set and simplified tasks, rigid schedules, and tight discipline and control. Most of us work from nine to five for fifty weeks a year, from ages seventeen to sixty-five (for the poor and working class), or from twenty-six to sixty (for the upper middle class).

Most schools are also organized, by custom or by design, in an authoritarian fashion which instills conformity and obedience. They too have strict schedules, as well as standard texts and patterns of examination and grading. Students go to school from 8 A.M. to 3 P.M. for nine months of the year, from ages five to sixteen (for the poor and working class) or from three to twenty-five (for the upper middle class).

These forms apparently suit some individuals. But poor school performance and low work productivity are signs that many persons find something wrong with the present structure. Increasing numbers of people are demanding greater choice in the *form* of education: they are asking for self-mastery courses, flexible time schedules, and on-the-job and in-the-field training. They want a greater range of curricular content, from pottery to phenomenology, from coping skills and risk taking to Zen and the media. They demand greater flexibility from their jobs: in educational opportunity, in clothing, in personal autonomy, and in job design. And they want the freedom to drop out of school and into work, out of work and into school. Surely a balance must be struck between complete institutional flexibility and maximum societal productivity, but at present the pendulum seems too far to one side.

Lack of Work–Education Interrelations. Many of the sorest spots in our society are at the nodes where education and work meet. One glaring problem is the failure to achieve productive relationships among those in the world of work (business and labor union leaders), those in the world of education, and the citizenry. In Europe, no meeting of educators would be complete without representatives of business and labor in attendance. In the United States, only at the level of the local school board do we find those responsible for work institutions mingled with educators. And much of even this association is unproductive because those from business and labor who serve on school boards usually represent their own political interests rather than the needs of their work organizations.

Another cluster of problems at the nexus of education and work includes the difficulties of making transitions between stages of life. There are few means to facilitate the change from school to work. Exploratory jobs and apprenticeship programs are in short supply. Counseling, guidance, placement, and valid information about employers and jobs are inadequate. There are few institutions to help adults who wish to change jobs or to be retrained for another job—although many demonstrably need counseling, information, placement services, and occasionally financial assistance. Then there is the transition from work to retirement, perhaps the most painful one in life; after over forty years of work, people are abruptly sent out to pasture. No attempt is made to smooth the transition, for example by allowing the worker to taper off by working part time before full retirement.

Moreover, little or no academic credit is offered for work experience, and so workers, especially those in blue-collar jobs, have little incentive to put in the long hours in classrooms to earn a degree. And although employers often encourage continuing education for managers and professionals, such practice is discouraged for lower-level employees if it entails stepping out for more than a month.

These are only some of the problems resulting from the delicate relationship between work and other institutions in America today. There are equally important problems, including access to education for all age groups and all classes and overcredentialing, underemployment, and undereducation (discussed in the next chapter). Then there is also the controversial issue of job dissatisfaction.

Job Dissatisfaction

In *Working* (1974), Studs Terkel presents the actual words of 130 American workers—everyone from a supermarket checker to the president of a corporation, and including a bookbinder, fireman, doorman, housewife, elevator operator, salesman, and spotwelder—from a series of remarkable interviews about their jobs. One worker tells Terkel, "I'm caged"; another says, "I'm a machine"; and yet another says, "You can't take pride any more." Emotionally, the workers tell Terkel how they repress their resentment, how they cope with bad jobs, and how they rebel through alcohol, violence, and even sabotage. They want something from their work that isn't there. "Most of us," as one woman worker puts it, "have jobs that are too small for our spirits."

No available index of job satisfaction and dissatisfaction is as reliable or objective as 98.6° on a thermometer. But what is clear from all available survey research data as well as "soft" data such as Terkel's is that the design of jobs tends to be monolithic, too limited to meet the wide array of changing human needs. Each individual requires something slightly different to be satisfied with work: as young people put it, "Different strokes for different folks." Because there is no single source of job satisfaction, there is no single way for employers to provide it. What is required is more variety in design, more flexible working arrangements, and freer access to and information about jobs.

The monolithic structure stems from the assumptions of economists and engineers about the "one best way" to design a job. Moreover, managers make many assumptions about their workers' capabilities, based upon the workers' race, sex, age, social class, or educational credentials. Using such criteria, employers assume, for example, that blue-collar workers are incapable of accomplishing tasks that require much intelligence, and they therefore design jobs for the less-educated to be repetitive, simple, and unchallenging. But facts about the labor force belie these employers' stereotypes. The IQ range of workers, for instance, challenges the wisdom of giving simplified tasks to many blue-collar employees (Rigby, 1970). As the figures below show, there are few dull Ph.D.s, but there are many bright laborers. (In fact, because there are many more laborers than Ph.D.s, *three times more laborers than doctorate holders have IQs over 130.*)

Occupation	IQ Range	Mean IQ
Ph.D. (Professor)	100–169	130
Engineer	100–151	127
Clerk	68–155	118
Laborer	26–145	96

Unfortunately, we design most laborers' jobs for the mean I.Q. of 96 (or lower), an action that leaves many exceptionally bright laborers in jobs that are unchallenging and, *for them,* demeaning. It is possible, even probable, that these intelligent, dissatisfied workers are often the ones responsible for defects, failures, accidents, and errors in the workplace. Most important, it is clearly a waste of human resources to place bright people in bad jobs because we fail to recognize their potential. Thus, at least some of the problems of job dissatisfaction might be lessened through better identification of worker talents and a better fit between person and job.

Since the publication of *Work in America,* scholars have been engaged in a bitter and fruitless debate about how to measure the nature and extent of job dissatisfaction. The academic mind often seems attracted to the unresolvable. But job satisfaction is too basic and too complex an attitude to measure unitarily. The endless rounds of bickering exemplify the point that social science methodology is still too primitive and its subject matter—us—too complex to lend itself to the kind of quantification possible in the hard sciences. If the findings of a particular study do not square with the preconceived values of a critic, he can always pull some arrows from his methodological quiver and shoot holes in the quantitative basis of the study. Its sample was too small, the questions were misleading, the control group was contaminated, and the conclusions were not supportable by the data. Thus, there are few important human issues of which I am aware that have been finally resolved by social science in the manner of the hard sciences.

But even if hard data about the nature and extent of job dissatisfaction could be agreed on, the divergence of expert opinions about the *meaning* of these data would be one more of values than of fact. If we accept Bertrand Russell's conclusion that questions of values are not susceptible to scientific resolution (such questions as, Are workers *legitimately* dissatisfied? *Should* employers attempt to improve working conditions?), we can see why some scholars of the workplace see the glass as half empty and others see it as half full, no matter what the data show. In the final analysis, social scientists and economists cannot remove the necessity for value choice from our shoulders through presenting us with irrefutable facts. Even if their facts indicated that fewer workers are dissatisfied with their lives and their opportunities than Terkel's interviews suggest, the question would still remain, What benefits could accrue to society at large, and especially to the few unhappy individuals, if we improved the quality of working life? One beneficial result might be better health.

Ill Health

In about the year 200, the Greek physician Galen wrote that "employment is nature's physician and is essential to human happiness." It might be called an achievement of modern science that several dozen recent studies have now "proved" what Galen so brilliantly intuited. They have shown rather convincingly that various aspects of work account for many of the factors associated with heart disease, including tension, high cholesterol, and above-normal blood pressure and blood sugar. Work problems also correlate highly with symptoms of poor mental health (such as low self-esteem), although not necessarily with mental illness (such as schizophrenia).

Although we are largely ignorant of the causal factors, the correlational, case-history, and anecdotal evidence relating work conditions to both mental and physical health problems is too convincing to dismiss. Particularly convincing is evidence linking occupational stress to physical health. One of the most interesting findings is that workers who are motivated by extrinsic rewards (such as pay and security) are more likely to have heart disease than those motivated by intrinsic reward (such as job challenge and self-actualization) (House, 1974).

The famous studies of "type A" and "type B" personalities show that competitive, ambitious individuals with a sense of time urgency and aggressive drive are likely coronary candidates (Friedman and Rosenman, 1974). An important lesson of this research is that thoughts can kill—and they can keep you alive. This conclusion is buttressed by a fifteen-year longitudinal study of aging in which the best overall predictor of longevity was work satisfaction (House, 1974). Less well-documented, but potentially as significant, is the marked increase in the death rate of employed men between the ages of thirty-five and forty. Identified by Elliott Jaques (1965), this "mid-life" crisis perhaps claimed the lives of Mozart, Raphael, and Chopin. And there is reason to believe that the rationalized bureaucratic design of office work that came into ascendancy in the 1950s has heightened the effects of this crisis for many contemporary male workers.

Coinciding with the male climacteric (marked by a reduction in the intensity of sexual behavior), the mid-life crisis is characterized by Jaques as the fear that one's creativity has ebbed and that one's best work is in the past. According to a California Institute of Technology study of more than four thousand individuals, five out of six workers undergo the crisis, and one out of six never fully recovers. This study shows that a prime cause of the crisis is a gap between their expectations of work and the realities of the job. The design of most white-collar and middle-management jobs seems to intensify this crisis because individuals in these positions tend to peak in terms of salary, promotion, and responsibility at about age forty. And cardiovascular disease among men about this age and in these occupations increased greatly between 1900 and the mid 1950s—paralleling the apotheosis of the "organization man." Significantly, as women have begun to move into these same job categories, they have begun to demonstrate some of the same kinds of coronary patterns.

Stress probably compounds the effects of the mid-life crisis and helps to explain the health problems of middle-aged, middle-level workers (as it helps to explain their growing interest in mid-career change). These are the employees who suffer most from the role stresses that have been shown to correlate highly with heart disease. Among such stresses are role ambiguity (not knowing what is expected of one or what constitutes adequate performance); role conflict (being caught between two sets of demands); and role overload (not having enough time, equipment, or authority to do a job). In a study of one hundred young coronary patients, "prolonged emotional strain associated with job responsibility" preceded the heart attacks of 91 percent of the patients, but such strain was evident in only 20 percent of a "healthy" control group (House, 1974).

A recent study conducted by the University of Michigan's Institute for Survey Research concludes that dissatisfaction is the major cause of stress on the job and that stress is the major cause of occupational health problems. The study (Caplan and others, 1975) concludes that people in undemanding jobs are often under more stress than those in demanding jobs because the latter more often like what they are doing. The issue is not simply whether a job is intrinsically good or bad—although in most cases a good job is demanding—but whether it fits the person who does it.

What all of this means is that work organization probably can save the lives of many employees through such structural changes as:

● Redesigning jobs to *reduce* conflict, territoriality, excessive competition, and role stress and to *increase* autonomy, authority, and resources.

● Providing better fit between worker and job; for example, by guiding "type As" away from potentially "suicidal" jobs.

● Providing greater access to midcareer change or to mid-career educational sabbaticals.

● Incorporating techniques that offer greater emotional and peer support for individuals in organizations (for example, the Japanese "godfather" system in which older workers guide and counsel their juniors throughout their careers) (Drucker, 1974).

The methodological obstacles to greater knowledge in the field of work and health are great, but intervention may nevertheless be warranted, for we presently know about as much about the effects of work-related stress on the body as we know about the physical factors on which we are spending millions of dollars to reduce heart-disease risk.

Clearly, several aspects of the relationship of work and health are germane to public policy. First, workers and society appear to be bearing medical costs that have their genesis in the workplace, and many of these could be avoided if preventive measures were taken. Second, work can be transformed into a singularly powerful source of psychological and physical rewards, especially for those who have health problems. Finally, a good job can also be "therapy" for those who are free from such problems—and who want to avoid them.

Conclusion—Why Not Education, Too?

The complex relationships between the quantity and quality of jobs and the quality of life forced themselves into the public consciousness in the early 1970s. Many of us now recognize that unemployment is a misuse of human resources, that family life is affected by employment conditions, that jobs can make workers healthy or unhealthy, and that a better utilization of young, old, minority, and women workers is a potential source of increased national productivity.

Little wonder, then, that making education relevant to work is fast becoming a national concern, almost an obsession. After all, we tend to measure almost everything else, at least in part, by its effect on work, so why should we not do the same with education?

Indeed, to many, education presents the best policy fulcrum for developing human resources.

The assumption inherent in this line of reasoning—that there is an unquestionable, integral, natural, and beneficial relationship between education and work—has long been a part of national policy in America and has become the guiding, if not sole, principle of educational reform in this decade. Without doubt, there is and must be such a relationship, but evidence presented in the next chapter indicates that what that relation is or should be is far from clear.

3

Promises of Education
and Realities of Work

Education is society's most future-oriented activity. Children entering kindergarten in the last half of this decade, for example, will spend about 80 percent of their working lives in the third millennium. They will be preparing for adult life and working between the years 1985 and 2040. Yet, the American system of education seems bent on training young people to meet current, ephemeral employment demands and cyclical economic circumstances—conditions that normally pass by the time the student is ready to enter the labor market. There is little doubt that the training students now receive will become anachronistic over the long haul of their forty to fifty working years.

Is it possible to create an educational system that is geared to the future and not to the past? Choosing future-oriented educational policies requires some notion of the environment in which people will be working in coming decades. Since no one has a crystal ball, policy makers recently have been turning to futurists to help them to identify the probable characteristics of life and work over the next five to twenty-five years.

Although futurists speak not of predictions, they do offer two kinds of forecasts—exploratory and policy. A navigational analogy (for which I am indebted to my colleague Selwyn Enzer) is helpful in differentiating between them. The exploratory forecaster can be visualized as a sailor sitting in a crow's nest. He scans the horizon to identify factors in the environment that are likely to impinge on the ship and perhaps upset its course. He looks for icebergs, signs of storms, other ships, and he even examines the passing flotsam and jetsam (because what may seem trivial to an untrained observer may actually contain profound signals). Exploratory forecasts attempt to identify external events likely to affect some future course, whether that of a school, a city, or a nation under study. Exploratory forecasters typically examine long-term shifts in demographics, political and economic indicators, values, and behavior.

The policy forecaster, on the other hand, is like a ship's navigator. The navigator is told by the captain that the ship's goal is a specific port, and he is charged with finding the optimum course for getting there. The navigator says, "If we steer course A, at this speed and in these wind conditions, we'll arrive at our destination on Thursday." He identifies for the captain the many possible routes and spells out the unique advantages and disadvantages of each. Policy forecasters usually examine a particular objective and attempt to discover the direct and indirect consequences of the various programatic paths leading to it. For example, if the aim is to provide the nation with abundant energy, the policy forecaster would try to specify the costs, benefits, and trade-offs involved in developing such sources as nuclear, solar, and fossil fuels. For each such technological option, there are many accompanying social and economic consequences, and some of the most important ones are frequently obscured in the short term. Thus, the policy forecaster must clarify as many of these potential and unintended results as possible to help the decision maker choose the most appropriate and effective means of achieving a desired goal. This level of analysis often involves normative considerations, and this is what makes policy forecasting more controversial than exploratory forecasting.

Recognizing that a ship's captain needs someone in the crow's nest as well as a navigator, this book offers both exploratory forecasts and policy forecasts. In this chapter, I outline several exploratory forecasts of how the future of work might develop and how current education policies might be either compatible or incompatible with these developments. (Chapters Six to Ten contain normative, policy forecasts of these same issues.)

The Reserve Army of the Underemployed

Society should seek to anticipate potential disjunctions between education and work in order to develop congruent, proactive policies that might prevent severe social, political, and economic problems in the future. The most disturbing of these potential disjunctions is *underemployment,* the underutilization of education, training, skills, intelligence, and other human resources. Unlike unemployment, the official rates of which are basically cyclical in nature, underemployment appears to be a chronic and growing condition in advanced economies. This condition, which has both objective and subjective dimensions, is probably at the root of many of the most severe problems of industrial society, and it is certainly a major cause of job dissatisfaction and increasing demands for improvements in the quality of working life.

In socialist and capitalist nations alike, increasing numbers of highly qualified workers are unable to find jobs that require their skills and training. Thus, many individuals are forced to take jobs that can be performed just as adequately by workers who have far lower levels of educational attainment. Examples of this phenomenon are not startling—indeed, they are becoming commonplace. In England, a young Oxford graduate finds that the only job open to him is as a salesman in an electronics firm. A Stanford Ph.D. takes the best post available upon graduation, that of a middle-level bureaucrat in a regional office of the U.S. Department of Labor. In Sweden, a young woman with a B.A. in chemistry finds that the highest status job that is vacant is a secretarial position. In Poland, a university graduate is a clerk in a state industry.

And the effect trickles down the occupational scale: in Germany, a graduate of one of his nation's finest technical high schools works as a machinist in a job that fewer than five years ago was held by a worker with only a primary school education. Finally, and predictably, this process of job displacement reaches its full force at the bottom of the occupational ladder, where poorly educated workers are often knocked off the last rung. In California, a black dropout is told that a high school diploma is required to box groceries.

From 1945 to about 1965, labor markets in the industrialized nations were porous enough to soak up the ever-burgeoning supply of educated workers. Indeed, it seemed that industrial society's appetite for educated workers was insatiable. To meet this seemingly unquenchable demand, all the stops were pulled out in the early 1960s and public policy was geared to forestall dropping out of high school, to increase the number of college graduates at almost any cost, and to turn out teachers, engineers, and scientists in abundance. In this country, such activity was justified by patriotic appeals to beat the Russians to the moon. America responded to the challenge with characteristic enthusiasm and overkill: demographer Ben Wattenberg has calculated that during the sixties America built a new two-year college every ten days.

But no socioeconomic trend runs on eternally. It is now becoming clear that the growing body of educated workers is hitting a ceiling of job demand, as Ivar Berg became one of the first to discover in 1971. This effect is most pronounced in the United States. Today, about 80 percent of American college graduates fill jobs that were previously held by workers with lower educational credentials (Berg, 1971). Japan and several European countries, notably Sweden, show signs of replicating the American experience.

Thus, the most industrialized and progressive nations are fostering what might be called a "reserve army of the underemployed." In a turn unanticipated by Marx, who contended that countries with free-market economies are unable and unwilling to reform themselves, governments whose ideologies are as diverse as those in America, Spain, and Denmark are attempting to provide greater equality of opportunity for all social classes by increasing the availability of education, extending the years of mandatory schooling, and prolonging the length of educational programs. But their very success is having contradictory results: to the extent that developed countries are solving the centuries-old problems of providing freer access to education, they are creating a situation that threatens their efforts to achieve greater equality and political stability. No industrialized nation has been able to produce an adequate number of jobs that provide the status, and require the skills and educational levels, that their work forces are achieving. By way of analogy, the situation is nearly Malthusian in its proportions: levels of educational attainment have tended to grow in almost geometric progression, while the number of jobs that require highly qualified persons has risen much more slowly. The evidence for this statement comes from quantitative comparisons of data presented below concerning the educational attainment of the work force on one hand and labor-market demand for educated workers on the other.

Supply of Educated Workers

Manpower economists know a bit about a lot of things, and what they know best are the demographic shifts likely to occur in the work force over the next twenty years. Their margin of error in forecasting broad work force trends is quite small, not because their techniques are terribly sophisticated, but because their raw data exist in a quite comprehensible and convenient form. That is to say that almost every nose they will have to count over the next twenty years is currently alive, wiggling, and countable *now*. Thus, they know with a rather high degree of certainty such things as the distribution of the various age cohorts in America's future work force, the race and sex components of each cohort, and, with a little less reliability, the levels of educational attainment of each cohort.

The statistics of the educational explosion over the past quarter century are so familiar that they no longer shock. In 1947, about 33 percent of students completed high school; today nearly 80 percent graduate. In 1960, only 26 percent of white skilled and semi-skilled workers had a high school education, but by 1969 the figure had reached 41 percent. The median educational attainment of all blue-collar workers rose from 9.2 years of schooling in 1952 to 12.0 years in 1972.

Even more dramatically, college enrollment expanded from 2.6 million in 1952 to 8.4 million in 1972 (an increase of about 250 percent). In 1955, 380,000 young people received first and advanced degrees; in 1970 the figure was close to a million (Simon and Frankel, 1972). In the mid-1950s America produced 8,000 new Ph.D.s annually; in 1975, 43,000 new Ph.D.s received degrees (Coleman and others, 1973, pp. 73–74).

Can this exponential growth in education continue? Surely, as the post-war baby bulge passes through the age chart, the exponential growth in school enrollments will slow: elementary school enrollments will show a slight drop in this decade of about 6.8 percent and high school enrollment will also dip (but by only about 0.4 percent because of lower drop-out rates). Rates of higher education attendance will continue to climb, but at a slower rate: enrollments will increase about 14.3 percent in this decade as against more than 50 percent in the 1960s (Simon and Frankel, 1972).

Although there are a few dramatic examples of private colleges' falling into bankruptcy as the result of declining admissions, college enrollment in the aggregate reached a record high in 1974, having increased 19 percent since 1970, according to the Bureau of the Census. This trend is likely to continue because this growth is not dependent on the dwindling pool of so-called college-age youth. Much of the increase in enrollment is due to a phenomenal rekindling of interest in education among older learners. Between 1970 and 1974, for example, enrollments of people aged twenty-five to thirty-four increased by 63 percent, and in 1974–75 alone, enrollments of people thirty-five and older increased by 30 percent. Much of this new educational interest no doubt reflects the growing trend in the economy toward multiple careers and dramatic mid-life occupational switches. The government now estimates that a twenty-year-old man will make 6.6 job changes during his life, and at least one of these will entail formal retraining.

Thus, a temporary slump in primary and secondary school enrollments will occur, but the demographers at the Bureau of the Census (not known by temperament to be a bullish lot) are forecasting *increasingly* high enrollments at all levels of schooling for the next twenty-five years! They hedge their bets, of course. But under any of the three most reasonable assumptions about the future, school attendance will continue to grow through the year 2000 (see Table 1).

For reasons I discuss below, it is unwise to place too much faith in such projections. But for what it is worth, the U.S. Bureau of Labor Statistics (1973) forecasts that one out of four people in the work force will have some kind of a college degree in 1980

TABLE 1. Projections of Fall-term School Enrollments under Three Assumptions

Level of School and Assumption	Enrollments (in millions of students)			
	Actual 1970	1980	1990	2000
Elementary School				
B-1		44.9	52.6	55.5
E-2	36.7	35.8	38.1	36.9
E-1		36.1	38.4	37.3
High School				
B-1		14.6	19.0	25.3
E-2	14.7	14.0	15.5	17.2
E-1		14.4	16.0	18.0
College				
B-1		11.9	12.8	20.7
E-2	7.2	10.2	10.4	12.6
E-1		11.9	12.5	15.9

Assumptions:

B-1: Highest level of population and highest proportion enrolled in school.

E-2: Lowest population level and lowest proportion enrolled in school.

E-1: Lowest level of population but highest proportion enrolled in school.

Source: Goldstein, and others, 1973.

(the figure was one in eight in 1970). In 1950, there were fewer than a million college graduates in the twenty-five to thirty-nine age cohort; by 1985 there will be nearly five million. Of the men in the twenty-five to thirty-four age group in 1990, about 20 percent will have had one to three years of college, and thirty percent will have had four or more years (15 percent with a B.A., and a like percentage with five or more years) (U.S. Department of Labor, 1973c, p. 357).

Americans take great pride in this record of educational achievement, feeling that in this area, at least, our nation knows no peers. Remarkably, however, other nations have been quietly catching up to the United States in providing access to education. Sweden, Japan, Canada, and the Netherlands, for example, have educational profiles that will closely resemble ours in the next decade. The accomplishments of these countries are all the more remarkable in that they have had further to come than the U.S. (lacking, as they did, its tradition of universal free public education and hundreds of universities open to all social classes). Sweden provides a startling illustration of how much Europe has accomplished in the past decade: about two-thirds of the *adult* Swedish population have only six to seven years of schooling, while 90 percent of *young* Swedes have at least eleven years (Reubens, 1974a). In Japan, only 55 percent of the school-aged population attended high school in 1959; by 1971 the figure was 85 percent. By the end of the decade, it is expected that 38 percent of Japanese high school graduates will go on to higher education (Reubens, 1973b).

The Organization of Economic Cooperation and Development (OECD) figures for full-time school enrollments show that Japan and the industrial countries of Europe no longer lagged far behind America in 1970. Although the figures in Table 2 are the latest official data available, it is certain that the gap between Europe and America has been narrowed over the last six years. And the spread between the United States and the other developed countries appears even less pronounced at the level of higher education, where America has traditionally excelled (see Table 3). In short, the level of educational attainment in all the industrialized nations is rising with startling and unprecedented rapidity.

TABLE 2. Percentage of 16-to-19-Year-Olds in Educational
Institutions, All Levels, Both Sexes, Selected Countries,
Recent Year, 1966–72

| | | | Age | | |
Country	Year	16	17	18	19
United States	1970	94.1	86.9	58.1	45.4
Australia	1972	54.9	36.3	18.0	10.7
Belgium	1969	70.8	52.8	36.7	25.6
Canada	1970	87.1	69.0	45.5	30.3
France	1970	62.6	45.5	30.6	21.8
W. Germany	1969	31.3	19.2	12.9	9.6
Italy	1966	33.6	27.4	19.7	11.0
Japan	1970	80.0	74.8	29.5	22.0
Netherlands	1972	68.7	46.3	28.8	18.3
Norway	1970	71.0	50.3	40.6	28.9
Sweden	1972	73.7	60.7	40.7	24.0
United Kingdom	1970	41.6	25.9	17.4	13.7

Source: OECD, *Educational Statistics Yearbook,* 1975.

TABLE 3. Entry to Higher Education as Percent
of the Relevant Age Group in 1970

U.S.A.	46.5%
Canada	33.6
Sweden	32.0
U.K.	29.3
Japan	26.8
France	22.4

Source: OECD *Educational Statistics Yearbook,* 1975.

Increased Expectations. Concomitant with the worldwide rise
in educational attainment is the increasing desire among young
people for even *more* education and for *better* jobs. It is beyond
the state of the art of the social sciences to identify whether higher
levels of education cause higher expectations or whether higher
expectations lead people to pursue higher levels of education.
What is known is that there is a clear and persistent positive correlation between educational attainment and rising expectations.

A recent American College Testing Service study showed that 65 percent of eleventh graders were planning to attend two or more years of college, and 46 percent planned to attend for three or more years (Prediger, Roth, and Noeth, 1973). In a study of college freshmen, Alexander Astin found that 56.9 percent planned to go on to graduate school (Trombley, 1974).

Equally measurable and conspicuous is the increasing desire of young people for good, high-status jobs. The Equality of Educational Opportunity Survey found that 41 percent of all twelfth graders desired to enter professional or technical occupations (Jencks and others, 1972, p. 184). A more recent U.S. Office of Education survey found the job desires of high school seniors to be even more skewed, with more than 54 percent desiring professional, technical, or administrative jobs (see Table 4).

Not surprisingly, students at higher educational levels have higher expectations. For example, Schrank and Stein (1972) report that in California's community colleges 64 percent of the students aspired to jobs at the professional or managerial level (even though only 32 percent of the students came from families in these occupational categories). And such rising occupational aspirations are not limited to America or to capitalist societies. As Daniel Bell reports, "A number of studies by Soviet sociologists indicate that in the land of 'workers and peasants' few of the children of the

TABLE 4. Kind of Work Plans of High School Seniors

Professional	44.7%
Clerical	14.7
Craftsman	7.7
Technical	6.6
Service	4.1
Manager, Administrator	3.0
Homemaker or Housewife	3.0
Sales	3.0
Laborer	2.5
Military	2.4
Operative	2.3

Source: Gilford, 1974.

proletariat want to be workers, much less peasants, and that the great majority want to go to college and be members of the 'intelligentsia'" (1973, p. 103).

New Values. The surveys of job satisfaction conducted over the past few years agree on one important fact: young workers are more dissatisfied than older ones (O'Toole, 1973a). Why this should be so is best explained by studies showing sharp differences in their attitudes toward the value of work: there has been a measurable shift from the past primacy of economic considerations to an ascendency of quality of life concerns. This change reflects the economic well-being of most American workers, who can now take for granted that tomorrow they will have meals on their tables, shirts on their backs, and roofs over their heads. Nevertheless, it would be incorrect to assume that people will be indifferent to money in the future—there will continue to be a marginal shift in values, not a change in human nature. Specifically, it would seem that money will not be the *prime* consideration in life for most Americans. In the past, the typical worker was by necessity primarily concerned with securing the basics of life. To an immigrant, a migrant from the South, and almost everyone who lived through the Depression, a good job is one that pays well and offers some security.

Young Americans do not share these experiences with their parents, and, consequently, their attitudes and expectations differ. Daniel Yankelovich has been polling young people for nearly a decade, and he finds that male and female, white and black, white-collar and blue-collar members of the under-thirty generation want and expect jobs that are meaningful (contributing to others or to society), challenging, and offer the opportunity to learn and to grow (1974).

The phrase *the quality of life* has come to symbolize the apirations of this generation. Since people spend more than half their waking lives on the job, the quality of working life is thus the most obtrusive manifestation of the overall quality of life. As a result, young people to a great degree look to realize a good life on their jobs. Yankelovich's major finding in 1974 was that these "new values" (held by only a minority of college students in the late 1960s) have spread to about two-thirds of the college-age cohort, including a large portion of noncollege and blue-collar youth.

The new attitudes toward work are most clearly expressed in a desire for self-fulfillment on the job. Significantly, the desire for jobs offering intrinsic rewards has increased over the past five years, even in the face of a tightening job market. Although young college people have become more career-oriented during this period, Yankelovich finds that 80 percent of them say they "would welcome less emphasis on money"; 68 percent are looking for jobs in which they can express themselves; and 77 percent are looking for challenge on the job. Some of the work-related attitudes of young people are probably in marked contrast with the feelings of their elders and their employers. For example, 53 percent of youth feel that Americans are "entitled as a social right" to participate in job decisions.

In the past, attitudes changed slowly with each generation. Today, it seems that almost a generation of attitudes separates each graduating *class* of high school seniors—and each one appears more committed than its predecessor to the new work values. The U.S. Office of Education study referred to earlier revealed attitudes similar to those found by Yankelovich, only more pronounced: just 18 percent of high school seniors ranked "having lots of money" as being of first importance in their lives. When it came to choosing a career, their first choice was finding a job that was helpful to others or useful to society. As in the Yankelovich study, factors related to learning on the job and throughout life were ranked consistently high (Fetters, 1974). Although in 1975 Astin found some renewed interest in money on the part of college freshmen, the desire for good jobs has apparently not abated.

In sum, young workers and students differ markedly from their parents in feeling that money, status, and security are less important than self-fulfillment and interesting and meaningful work (Survey Research Center, 1971). It is common for those in authority to dismiss such findings with the truism that "kids will grow out of these ideas." Indeed, Lipset and Ladd (1971) demonstrate that people *do* become more conservative in their values as they grow older, but each generation ends up more liberal than its predecessor. Young workers will no doubt moderate their views, but even as they mature, self-fulfillment is unlikely to disappear as a major workplace desire. In 1980, the post-war "babies" (born between 1946 and 1962) will be adult workers and will constitute

42 percent of the total U.S. population. What are the chances that these young people will find the challenges they desire on their jobs?

Demand for Educated Workers

Although a good deal is known about the new work force, there are clearly many things about the future supply of workers that cannot be flatly predicted. For example, the attitudes of the next generation might shift as suddenly and as radically as did those of the current generation in the 1960s. Too, the ever-accelerating desire for higher levels of education could reach a plateau. These changes are *possible*, but they are unlikely, because the trends are running too powerfully in the opposite direction. Some trends—like the desire for greater social equality—never seem to reverse themselves. It is safe then, to forecast (but not predict) that the new work force will probably have higher educational qualifications and expect more from their jobs in terms of intrinsic satisfactions than did their elders.

Can as much be said with confidence about the kinds of jobs that will be opening in the next quarter of a century? Probably not, because many positions that will open have not yet been created and because labor market forecasts are based on the following kinds of shaky assumptions: (1) continued high levels of employment; (2) energy availability; (3) continuation of economic trends; (4) continuation of the pace of scientific and technological change; (5) peace; and (6) no significant reduction in defense spending (U.S. Department of Labor, 1974b). These are rather large "ifs." The number of unpredictable variables involved in projecting the future supply of jobs is staggering. The list includes changes in markets, technology, products, materials, foreign competition, interest rates, inflation, and government spending patterns.

Nevertheless, the complexity of forecasting has not deterred a great many manpower economists and decision makers. With great determination, these well-meaning individuals continue to pursue the unattainable: accurate long-term projections of (a) the demand for workers broken down by specific occupation, industry, and region and (b) the supply of workers disaggregated according to levels of skill, training, and education. In their efforts to help policy makers turn out the "right" numbers of workers for the jobs that will be available, the forecasters have shown dismal marksmanship. Not only have these economists, demographers, and statisticians failed to score many bull's eyes with their various projections, in some areas they have so missed the mark as to seriously mislead those who make public policy (the classic example being, of course, the inflated projections made during the sixties of the future demand for schoolteachers, which contributed to a painful oversupply in this decade).

Attempts to forecast supply and demand are complicated by the so-called cobweb effect. For example, a reported shortage of engineers will draw so many trainees that a surplus of qualified workers is produced when they graduate from engineering school three or four years later. Ironically, when this surplus is reported, potential engineers stay away from training in droves, thus producing another shortage a few years later. Moreover, it is becoming increasingly difficult to estimate the qualifications for the ever-increasing number of occupational titles. As the economists put it, these qualifications are highly elastic. That is, there are literally dozens of ways of becoming qualified for most jobs, and people trained in one field can be quickly substituted for those trained in a related field.

The madness of the situation is that forecasters take only fairly reliable data about the supply of workers, run these against unreliable demand data in a process complicated by the cobweb effect and the substitutability of labor, and, lo and behold, produce "the truth." It is no wonder that manpower planning efforts to match the exact supply of workers with specific job openings simply have not worked in the past (and are unlikely to work in the future). Because of the large number of variables involved and the large number of assumptions that must be made, no one can predict with any accuracy, for example, the number of anvil salesmen who will be needed in Chicago in 1980 or the number of openings for tennis pros in Schenectady in '82.*

---

*Nevertheless, many of America's most costly manpower training and vocational education programs continue to be based on these unscientific projections. Western Europeans have long since abandoned these methods. An only partially fictional story has it that the leading Soviet manpower expert was recently asked how he accounted for the egregious Russian failures at manpower forecasting. "The reason is simple," he replied, "we used all of the latest American techniques."

Yet, it is still possible to make some *broad* and *general* forecasts about the future supply and demand. For instance, the shift to a services economy will probably continue, workers will continue to be better educated, and the basic structure and requirements of the job market will not shift too greatly or too suddenly (for example, the ratio of the demand for professional workers to the demand for unskilled workers is unlikely to alter by even a factor of two).

Significantly, this information is just about all we need to forecast the likelihood of continued underemployment. But even if we are still reluctant to forecast the future, some things are quite clear from the past. Over the past decade, for example, the demand for a more qualified work force has not kept pace with supply. The percentage of those engaged in the highest skill category of professional jobs grew from 7 percent to only 9 percent between 1950 and 1970. Moving down the hierarchy a couple of notches to the occupation that has recently gained perhaps the most attention from college students looking for job-relevant training, we find that the percentage of "managers" increased from 12.9 percent in 1948 to only 13.6 percent in 1973.

If the economy isn't creating professional and managerial jobs in great abundance, what kinds of jobs are being created? Although the answer is not "bad jobs," most of the new positions are not the kinds that college students have been promised or expect upon graduation. To help put this conclusion into perspective, it is useful to analyze the two fastest growing industries in the economy: government and "miscellaneous service." In 1955, 10.5 percent of all jobs were in government; by 1975, the figure was 15.5 percent. In 1955, 15.9 percent of jobs were in service industries (cleaning, maintenance, health care support services, and provision of food, for instance); by 1972, over 20 percent of the work force was in this industry (not to be confused with the "service sector," which includes all "white-collar" activities that do not produce goods). Service industry jobs—such as working behind the counter at McDonalds or punching I.B.M. cards—are usually thought of as representative occupations in a postindustrial economy. Some of these may be considered good jobs by some persons. For the worker who has been assaulted day in and out by the re-

lentless clamor of a machine, the opportunity to take a job whose
most salient characteristic is human contact may appear attractive.
But most of the people who take the new service jobs are not transfers from industry; they are young people, many of whom have
had at least some higher education. For them, service jobs appear
to have many of the worst characteristics of blue-collar work (the
jobs are dull, repetitive, and fractionated and offer little challenge
or personal autonomy). Indeed, these new jobs often lack the best
of skilled blue-collar jobs (relatively high salary, security, union
protection, the sense of mastery that comes from producing something tangible and needed by society). Thus, the economy is creating a great number of not terribly attractive jobs. For example,
between 1960 and 1970, the number of orderlies and nurses aides
increased by 420,000; the number of janitors by 530,000; and the
number of busboys and dishwashers by 70,000 (Wool and others,
1973). Characteristically, such jobs offer low salary—nearly 30
percent of all services workers earn less than four thousand dollars
per annum (Goldstein and others, 1973)—and little in the way of
advancement. In hospitals, orderlies do not progress up a career
ladder to become nurses; in hotels, chambermaids seldom advance
to become desk clerks.

Moreover, many of the new jobs that look good (positions as
health paraprofessionals and teachers' aides and the "new careers"
for technicians that require a two-year A.A. or A.S. degree) also do
not have career ladders and are limited in their scope by the prerogatives of the professionals who supervise them. In reality, there
are precious few jobs that make much use of higher-order skills,
training, and intelligence. The Bureau of Labor Statistics estimates
that only about 20 percent of all jobs will require a college education for successful performance in 1980. Even more alarming, the
Office of Management and the Budget found that half of all jobs
do not even require a high school education (Miller, 1971). In the
same study, the O.M.B. found that the average education required
for all jobs increased from 10.0 years in 1940 to 10.5 years in 1970.
How can this be? Some examples may help us to understand these
figures: Berg (1973) reports that office machine operators need
the educational equivalent of 8.4 years of school, electricians need
11.1 years, and bookkeepers only need 10.3 years.

Of course, the methods used to measure what level of education is required are crude at best, and downright misleading at worst. Nevertheless, the conclusion that America is not creating a great many good jobs can still be upheld. For example, one need only examine the fastest growing industry—state and local government. Here, where one of the three new jobs in urban areas is being created, most of the rapidly expanding demand is for service jobs (in hospitals, maintenance, and the like) and for jobs with service characteristics (typing and clerical work, for example) (Berg, 1973). This demand pattern is not apparent at first glance because the largest governmental occupation group is composed of teachers (about 40 percent of the total), who clearly have professional-level jobs. But relatively few *new* jobs for teachers are being created or will be created in the next decade. In 1973, 243,000 teachers competed for 111,000 openings, and most of these positions were vacated by retiring teachers (Newman and others, 1974, p. 23). Thus, the hundreds of thousands of new jobs being created in state and local government are not in the most attractive category, that of teaching. When teachers are subtracted from the total of government employees, the two largest remaining categories contain clerical and service workers, who together account for about 78 percent of all nonteaching jobs. Even if teachers remain in the total, clerical and service jobs constitute about 42 percent of all government jobs, while the comparable figure in industry is only about 28 percent. If one accepts that skilled and semiskilled blue-collar work is often more rewarding than service or clerical work, then the mix of jobs in industry is far more attractive than the mix in government. Even if one feels that blue-collar work is no better than low-level white-collar work, the mix in industry is still better if one subtracts the slow-growing teacher category from the total, as Table 5 illustrates. (The table actually underestimates the percentage of bad jobs in state and local government since it pertains to all government levels, including the federal, where few teachers are employed.) According to Harrison (1972) directors of government agencies report that 60 to 70 percent of the new jobs they are creating are in the categories of aide, attendant and assistant, clerical worker, custodian, and semi-skilled blue-collar.

TABLE 5. Distribution of Employment in Government
and Private Industry in 1972

Occupation	*Government*	*Private Industry*
White-Collar (total)	(67%)	(44%)
Professional, Technical (including teachers)	35	10
Managers and Administrators	8	10
Clerical	23	16
Sales		8
Blue-collar (total)	(14)	(39)
Craftsmen	7	15
Operators	4	19
Laborers	4	5
Service Workers	19	12
Farm Workers		4

Source: U.S. Department of Labor, 1974b, p. 788.

Supply and Demand

Thus, it is my conclusion that as a consequence of the disjunction
between the supply of educated workers and the demand for
workers with high levels of educational attainment, there is *now*
massive underemployment in the United States. Although what
we know about *future* demand is not as clear as what we know about
past and present demand, it would be difficult to make a logical
and convincing case that the labor market can respond within the
next decade or so to the rising supply of credentialed workers.
It is improbable that the structure of the job market will be suddenly altered after having established a fairly predictable pattern
of evolutionary change over the past three decades. Thus, when
the Bureau of Labor Statistics (BLS) forecasts that fewer than 20
percent of all jobs will require a college education in 1980, it would
be unwise to dismiss this figure out of hand.

Furthermore, the data collected by the BLS portend even
greater underemployment in the future. In the next decade, for

example, the demand for blue-collar workers will expand very little (what openings there are will largely be due to retirement). Between 1972 and 1985, however, there will be a demand for about forty-eight million white-collar workers (of which more than sixteen million will be in new jobs). Composing this forty-eight million will be about seventeen million clerical workers, twelve million professional and technical workers, nine million service workers, six million managers, and four million salesworkers (U.S. Department of Labor, 1974b). Thus, there will be about eighteen million job openings that tend to have high status: the professional, technical, and managerial positions. Indeed, jobs in these categories could easily come to more than 20 percent of all employment by 1985.

Viewed in this dimension only, this news would be sanguine indeed. Unfortunately, in the period between 1972 and 1985, there may be as many as twenty-two million people with graduate and undergraduate degrees competing for the eighteen million professional and managerial posts (Simon and Frankel, 1972). But this potential shortfall of four million jobs is also grossly misleading. It assumes that all of the jobs in the two top categories are potentially attractive to college graduates. In reality, many of the technical and lower-management positions included in these categories offer little in the way of job satisfaction, status, or salary—5.4 percent of the professional-technicals and 7.0 percent of the managers earned less than four thousand dollars in 1971 (Goldstein and others, 1973). Moreover, as many as eighty-five percent of the replacement jobs in these categories were formerly held by high school graduates and others without a college degree. And competition for the few really choice jobs is further exacerbated by the 120,000 trained professionals who immigrate to America annually (U.S. Department of Labor, 1973c).

In short, by 1980 there may be as many as two and a half college graduates competing for every choice job. This view of oversupply is shared by even those most conservative of researchers, the statisticians and economists at the Bureau of Labor Statistics. They estimate an annual excess of one hundred and forty thousand college graduates per year in 1980. Using nearly the same careful methods as the BLS, economists of the National Planning Association (NPA) estimate that the annual surplus of college graduates will grow up to seven hundred thousand by 1985. In the shorter run, between 1970 and 1980, they forecast a total demand for thirty-nine million choice white-collar jobs and a supply of forty-five million college graduates (Wool and others, 1973).

Important, the NPA study also notes that the general educational upgrading of the work force has freed many blacks and other disadvantaged workers from the necessity of doing the dirty jobs of society—as laborers, janitors, cleaners, chambermaids, and charwomen, for example. The net effect is that demand will soon exceed supply in low-level jobs, while supply will exceed demand in high-level jobs. No real "shortages" or "surpluses" will occur, of course. There will still be someone to clean the toilets, and Ph.D.s will not be on breadlines. The labor market will complexly adjust itself to make supply meet demand. For the good jobs, the market will adjust by raising educational credentials; for the bad jobs, salaries will be increased and working conditions improved.

On one level, this market balancing of supply and demand appears more advantageous to individuals in lower level jobs than to those in higher-level ones. Indeed, that younger white workers—half of them students—are taking the place of many black workers in unskilled and semi-skilled jobs could be viewed as a stage in the movement toward greater occupational equality (Wool and others, 1973). However, it is probably not racial integration of bad jobs that we are witnessing but the bumping off of the occupational ladder of unskilled blacks by downwardly mobile whites. In this way, underemployment is structurally related to a specific kind of unemployment found more often in the United States than in other industrial nations—that is, the chronic existence of a hard core of unskilled, uneducated people who can't even get a foot on the bottom rung of the occupational ladder.

Moreover, the downward bumping that results from underemployment might someday come to affect the salaries of workers at almost all levels. In the future, as competition grows keener and credential requirements are raised, salaries might become depressed at all sub-professional levels not protected by unions or other forms of labor protection (such as professional licensing).

Over the next decade, skilled blue-collar work is the only

TABLE 6. Supply of and Demand for Workers
Between 1970 and 1980 (in millions)

Occupational Group	Employment Increase (Demand)	Labor Force Increase (Supply)	Difference
I. Professional, Technical	39.0	45.3	+6.3
II. Managerial, Clerical, Sales	21.9	24.6	+2.7
III. Skilled Labor	16.5	15.1	−1.4
IV. Semiskilled Labor	16.9	11.0	−5.9
V. Unskilled Labor	10.6	4.4	−6.2

Source: U.S. Department of Labor, 1974, p. 111.

occupational category for which the supply of people by education and training will be anywhere near demand, as Table 6 indicates.

The problem of the oversupply of qualified workers becomes more acute as one ascends the occupational hierarchy. Speaking of those with advanced degrees (Ph.D.s), Allan Cartter says, "We have created a graduate education and research establishment in American universities that is about 30 to 50 percent larger than we shall effectively use in the 1970s and early 1980s" (Cartter, 1971, p. 132).

Thus the problem of underemployment is not just a forecast, it exists here and now. In 1970–1971, only 63.9 percent of American men were able to find professional, technical, or managerial first jobs when they graduated from college (U.S. Department of Labor, 1973a). More than 13 percent took clerical or service jobs, 12 percent went into blue-collar work, and 11 percent went into sales. There is no doubt that education "paid off" for the 63 percent: in the same year, only 4 percent of high school graduates found choice jobs (U.S. Department of Labor, 1971). In other words, the real brunt of underemployment falls most heavily on the person on the middle to lower rungs of the occupational ladder, the person who once had access to good jobs and is now downwardly mobile.

Richard Freeman of Harvard has recently (1976) updated the data concerning the possible effects of underemployment. He claims that from 1969 to 1975 the starting salaries of college graduates fell from being 24 percent more than those of nongraduates to being only six percent higher and that the relative lifetime-earnings advantage of a college degree over a high school diploma (which was once about three hundred thousand dollars) has all but disappeared. During this period when the supply of graduates rose by about 8 percent, demand fell about 2.8 percent in industries that have traditionally employed many college graduates. During this five-year period, the number of male college graduates working as salesmen increased by 50 percent and the number of women college graduates working as secretaries increased by an incredible 100 percent.

The Quintessential Reservist. In the army of the underemployed, the ranks of women are legion. Women, as a group, are overrepresented in some of the worst jobs in the economy—more than 90 percent of all receptionists, secretaries, telephone operators, sewers, and stitchers are women. Women are overrepresented in the worst jobs in the apparel and textile industries and on assembly lines in light and medium industry (O'Toole, 1973a). At the same time, women have nearly the same educational qualifications as men. Many women secretaries, for example, have higher levels of educational attainment than their male bosses. This underemployment of women is reflected in the fact that women in jobs they consider below their qualifications are, along with young blacks, among the most dissatisfied members of the work force (Survey Research Center, 1971).

Some women use their educations in the most important work of society—rearing children. But because this work is not recognized by society as being equal in value to paid employment, as we have already seen, a regrettable sense of underemployment often exists even among caring and committed mothers. And their problems of underemployment do not stop after their children are grown. Mothers returning to the paid work force find that their educational and life experience is undervalued by employers. If fortunate enough to land a job, most find their skills underutilized.

Women used to be docile workers, willing to do dull, repetitive, unchallenging, and even potentially demeaning jobs. They

did these jobs, and were largely undamaged psychologically by
them, because they identified themselves as mothers and wives,
not as blue-collar workers. Work was purely instrumental—and
not a source of identity, as it was for blue-collar men. Today, however, women want the same rewards for work as men do—a sense
of identity, self-esteem and mastery; and that they have been
largely denied these satisfactions has led to the most important
and far-reaching social movement of the age. The desire for *good*
jobs, as opposed to *any* jobs, has become a hallmark of the women's
liberation movement. Hell hath no fury like that of a woman
underemployed.

One of the sources of frustration in the women's movement
is that women are demanding good jobs just when such positions
are becoming scarce. Because of a down cycle in industry, the
economic growth that was to have opened new jobs for women has
abated. A long-term barrier women face is that the phenomenal
economic growth of the past decades may never be seen again.
Consequently, women will be pitted against men and minorities,
in competition for the few good jobs available. Underemployment,
then, exacerbates the already delicate relations between the sexes
and between the races.

Limits to Growth. If economic growth is to be permanently
limited for environmental and other reasons, as is now a serious
possibility, the problems of underemployment for all educated
workers, particularly women in the short run, are likely to be
exacerbated. The primary reason why underemployment was not
a serious problem during the 1950–1970 period of rapid educational expansion was that the economy was undergoing a period
of tremendous growth and new, good jobs were being created at
almost the rate college graduates were being turned out. Thus, any
future public policy that limits growth will have to deal with a
chronic oversupply of highly qualified workers, men and women.

Zero growth might require a reduction in federal spending
for defense and space—industries that use great amounts of
energy and other natural resources. These are also industries
that traditionally have employed large numbers of highly trained
workers. Federal spending might increase in such fields as health,
welfare, housing, transportation, communications, and educa-

tion—fields (with the exception of education) that have been disproportionately composed of middle- and lower-level jobs. As productive and extractive industries were allowed to shrink, and as services were encouraged to grow, national productivity would fall. The employment consequences of this scenario have not been fully analyzed, but on first blush it would seem to further complicate the problems of unemployment and underemployment. On the plus side, human labor might well replace machine labor in some fields, notably agriculture and crafts, which could provide employment (and possibly satisfying employment in the crafts) (Mankin, 1973). But since the net effect of a policy of limited growth on employment is unknown, such a policy is a wild card in forecasts of the future of work.

"The Overeducated American"

Curiously, Richard Freeman (1976) and other manpower economists review the same data about supply and demand that I have offered here and come to a quite different conclusion: they say that young American men and women are not "underemployed," they are "overeducated." This is not a mere semantic quibble. I believe as I stated in Chapter One, that the problem should not be construed as one of overeducation, because alarming numbers of high school and even college graduates cannot read or write, and most are unprepared for meaningful participation in family, community, and leisure activities.

If the problem is "overeducation," the solution is to cut back the opportunities for education. Indeed, when the issue of underemployment was identified in 1973 in the *Work in America* report, Michael Moscow, then Assistant Secretary of Labor, responded that the matter could easily be resolved if we at HEW just quit wasting billions on education. (Although I begged to differ with Mr. Moscow at the time, he had the last word and was last seen moving up the hierarchy of the federal government.) Because of the traditional American commitment to freedom of choice and equality of opportunity, I argued that underemployment should be handled *not* by reducing educational opportunities but by addressing the unmet expectations created by selling education almost solely as the passport to good, well-paying jobs. Young Americans are not overeducated, they are suffering from disappointment with the nature of the jobs to which they find themselves relegated.

This argument fell on deaf ears then, and continues to receive little shrift in policy-making circles. The problem is not that the Richard Freemans and Michael Moscows of the world are evil, it is just that the issue of underemployment is devilishly difficult for policy makers to take the time to understand (and, impossible for economists to understand because of its qualitative nature). Underemployment is not so concrete and readily measurable as unemployment. We cannot simply count the number of underemployed as we count the unemployed in the queue waiting for their checks at the state bureau of human resources.

Underemployment has two dimensions, separate but often overlapping. On the one hand, it is capable of being objectively measured. A qualified engineer with a Ph.D. who can only find work as a dishwasher is clearly underemployed. On the other hand, underemployment is also a subjective state of mind. An M.B.A. who aspired to an executive training job but who could only find work as a first-line supervisor may also be underemployed. Objectively, we might say there is nothing socially unjust or economically inefficient about an M.B.A.'s working as a first-line supervisor, but the young person may still *feel* that his or her abilities or talents are being underutilized or underappreciated. In this subjective sense, the job does not meet his or her expectations, and consequently the individual becomes dissatisfied with the position. Now, what is important is that there is a very high correlation between objective and subjective underemployment. My interpretation of recent survey research data is that it indicates that people who express dissatisfaction at work because their talents are underutilized are most often also objectively underemployed in that they are in jobs below the level usually associated with their educational attainment. This is not always the case, of course, but it is true often enough to warrant some concern on the part of policy makers. Nevertheless, economists often dismiss attitudes as being unimportant or at least ephemeral ("Some people are chronic *kvetches*," or "Give them time and they'll adjust"). Although there is more than a grain of truth in saying that actual behavior is more important to social policy than the attitudes expressed to survey researchers, these attitudes can and do have potentially profound consequences for the society, polity, and economy, as I illustrate below.

The Contradiction and Its Effects

Educational systems serve the selecting, sorting, and certifying functions in hierarchical, competitive societies (Green, 1968). Indeed, in most advanced societies, these systems are seen as the prime instruments for achieving stratification or inequality. Hence, it is natural that these same systems would come to be viewed as instruments to right the injustices of class and status. The recent history of Europe, Japan, and America shows that educational reform has been used as the means to achieve greater equality. In all the industrialized nations, social pressures for equality have overheated the educational systems, building expectations for higher social status that are not likely to abate. Unlike revolutions, which artificially and temporarily titillate the masses with unrealizable expectations, education raises expectations fundamentally and lastingly in a climate of authority and legitimacy. But there is simply not enough "high status" available in modern industrial societies to distribute to all those who feel they have earned it. The potential consequences of this contradiction are not yet fully understood, but there is some evidence that they include some potentially grave social, political, and economic problems in industrial nations. For instance, national policies designed to upgrade work forces educationally seem to be creating frustration and low morale among younger workers—workers who, ironically, have the educational backgrounds to articulate their dissatisfactions.

To make these statements is not to alarm, to forecast revolution, or to advocate unrest. It is rather to recognize that a situation in which taxi drivers have college degrees is not necessarily benign. According to Blumberg and his coauthors (1976), college-educated taxi drivers in New York City have formed a radical socialist Taxi Rank and File Coalition and control fifteen of fifty garages in the city. The coalition garnered 20 percent of the vote in a 1974 union election. On the other coast, U. C. Berkeley graduate Peter Bruno hails the potentially radicalizing side effects of underemployment: "Dissatisfaction is going to come easily, but it can prove useful, for dissatisfaction foments change. It may enhance your desire to examine problems and questions that would otherwise have remained at a distance. Dissatisfaction will heighten your ability to perceive the real villains in our society" (1976).

Although such findings are anecdotal, some evidence about the possible effects of underemployment is strong and unequivocal. Studies undertaken at the University of Michigan, for example, show that people who feel they deserve better jobs than they have come to suffer from what is known as *status conflict* (Kahn, 1974 pp. 203–8). At the extreme, some of these workers come to feel trapped in bad jobs, believing that by rights they should have better, but by circumstances they will probably never achieve more. These feelings are primary sources of dissatisfaction with life and work and correlate highly with problems of poor physical and mental health. Harold Sheppard (Sheppard and Herrick, 1971) has shown that blue-collar workers who supported George Wallace in the 1968 elections were not the dull ones, but the ambitious ones who felt cheated by their low social standing. They displaced their personal frustration by directing hostility toward minorities and toward "the system."

What is clear from almost every study of job dissatisfaction is that the placing of intelligent and highly qualified workers in dull and unchallenging jobs is a prescription for pathology—for the worker, the employer, and the society. Alvin Goulder describes how such a system leaves major parts of the worker's personality "unemployed": "In short, vast parts of any personality must be suppressed or repressed in the course of playing a role in industrial society. All that a man is that is not useful will somehow be excluded . . . and he thereby becomes alienated or estranged from a large sector of his own interests, needs and capacities. Thus, just as there are unemployed men, there is also the *unemployed self*" (quoted in Rosow, 1974).

In his book *Strategy for Labor,* Andre Gorz describes how underemployment has become the prime source of job dissatisfaction and social alienation in the last half of this century: "Industry in the last century took from the countryside men who were muscles, lungs, stomach: their muscles missed the open spaces, their lungs the fresh air, their stomachs fresh food; their health declined and the acuteness of their need was but the emptying functioning of their organs in a hostile surrounding world. The industry of the second half of the twentieth century increasingly tends to take men from the universities and colleges, men who have been able to acquire the ability to do creative or independent work; who have curiosity, the ability to synthesize, to analyze, to invent, and to assimilate, an ability which spins in a vacuum and runs the risk of perishing for lack of an opportunity to be usefully put to work" (1968 p. 106). Although Gorz is a Marxist, the problem of unemployed selves is not just the concern of the radical left. Employers, too, are becoming aware of its existence. Myron Clark, past president of the Society for the Advancement of Management, estimates that 80 percent of all workers in America are underemployed (Bolles, 1973, p. 15). In a recent interview in the *Christian Science Monitor,* Tom Taggert (vice president for manpower planning at the Bank of America) echoes Clark's sentiments: "I would guess that 60 to 70 percent of our employees think they're underemployed; in the company's mind probably 30 to 40 percent are underemployed." A recent study of seven million jobs in eleven industries shows that 34 percent of the jobs led nowhere: eight of nine had no opportunities for promotion and the ninth offered only one step up. Undoubtedly this fact is affecting worker morale: the University of Michigan surveys cited above reveal that about 25 percent of American workers feel they are in dead-end jobs and 35 percent feel overqualified for their jobs.

Social Consequences. Although such evidence is depressing, it is possible that the social disparity between the promises of education policy and the realities of work are creating problems even more acute than job dissatisfaction. Society may be in the throes of establishing a new meritocracy, one composed of the 20 percent of the population that holds almost all the good jobs. In itself, the creation of an elite is not a new phenomenon. Nor is it surprising that this elite, like others that have gone before it, appears to be amassing social and political power to match its weight in the economic order. Yet at the same time there is a noteworthy break from past patterns of social class in the growing refusal of the 80

percent of the population (the "masses" who have bad jobs) to
accept the right of the elite to its special privileges. What is new
in history is that the masses are now almost as well educated as the
elite. Consequently, they look on the meritocracy with envy and,
perhaps, hostility. Although there is little hard data to support this
view, social observers ranging from Daniel Bell and Peter Drucker
to special commissions that have reported to foreign governments
have all seen signs of potential conflict between those who have
bad jobs and those who have good jobs. For example, a Czech
study, prepared during the liberal Dubcek thaw, warns of a new
form of class polarization, one that will afflict even the socialist
states: "the dominant feature in the social stratification starts to
be differentiation primarily according to the content of work. The
long-term existence of two distinct strata working side by side—
people performing exacting creative work and others occupied in
simple operative jobs—will then have to be seen as a serious problem" (quoted in Bell, 1973, p. 10). The Czechs argue that the an-
tagonism will spill out of the workplace and there will be "resultant
disagreements in ideas on life apart from work." Signs of such
emergent, class-based *ressentiment* may also be seen in the evident
ungluing of the traditional left-center political coalitions in the
Western democracies. In the past, Britain, Scandinavia, and the
U.S. had powerful parties composed of liberal-intellectual and
labor-working-class factions. But in Europe and America, antag-
onism between the professional, upper-middle-class liberals and
the workers has surfaced during the past few years. Our own
Democratic Party saw its once solid labor support slip away when
it nominated the liberals' candidate for the presidency in 1972.
In the 1974 British election, the Liberal Party siphoned off much
of the middle-class support that had recently gone to the Labour
Party. (A great number of these voters returned to the fold in late
1974, however.) And in Sweden and Denmark, government officials, teachers, and others who have traditionally supported the
Socialists are becoming increasingly restive as they see salary and
other distinctions between the classes eroded.

Such potential social conflict stems in part from the difficulties that societies encounter in deciding who should get the
relatively small number of good jobs. And when almost everyone

in society has high levels of educational attainment, another, and potentially more disruptive, question arises: Who should do the dirty but necessary tasks of civilization? In Europe, this issue was not faced until Switzerland, Germany, Sweden, and France found themselves with highly skilled native work forces unwilling to do menial jobs and with large groups of low-skilled immigrants (up to 40 percent of their work forces), who cause a variety of social problems. In the U.S., we are "solving" the problem by increasing legal immigration from Asia, Africa, and Latin America and closing our eyes to the presence of perhaps several million illegal immigrants. The moral implications, let alone economic repercussions, of this situation are staggering.

Another social consequence of selling education as the entrance fee for a good job may be a decline in support for higher learning. In the past two decades, universities, corporations, and the government adopted the "human capital" mode of analyzing the economics of education. Human capitalism views education as an investment, with increasing economic returns per each additional year of education or training. These returns are realized by the individual (through higher salaries), by the firm (through higher worker production), and by the society (through increases in the Gross National Product). But as the ceiling on the need for more highly qualified workers is being reached, the increasing supply may actually be driving down the market value of educational credentials. So as people learn that education will not pay off as promised, they may very well experience disillusionment and feel betrayed because they are stuck with a "bad investment."

The refusals of middle-class voters to approve school bonds, the cries of intellectuals for de-schooling society, and the general attack on the irrelevance of education may be the opening salvos of an action to discredit an institution that has failed to meet the false economic expectations that have been created for it. Indeed, the writings of Freeman, although falling just short of recommending reduced support for education, led to alarmist cover stories in *Time* and *Newsweek,* in which the failure of education to pay off in high-paying jobs was used as an excuse to advocate a reduction in support for higher education. Unfortunately, if an entire disappointed generation does not maintain this important social institution, its valuable roles in self-development, leisure activities, family life, and citizenship will all be imperiled.

The Fetish of Credentialism

Paradoxically, as the investment value of education slumps, the importance of its credentialing function soars. Employers have responded to larger pools of qualified workers by needlessly raising the credential requirement for jobs—without upgrading the demands, challenges, or rewards of these jobs. Thomas Green concluded that employers and society are no longer concerned with how much one learns in school, but with whether or not one has the proper credentials: "we have succeeded in transforming the function of the schools from the primary one of education to an emphasis on certifying, sorting and selecting" (1968, p. 154). Lester Thurow argues that it no longer helps greatly to get higher credentials simply in order to succeed, but people are seeking them now in order to defend their current income positions: "the larger the class of educated labor and the more rapidly it grows, the more defensive expenditures become imperative" (1972, p. 79). A 1967 survey in the San Francisco area showed that 17 percent of employers required a high school diploma for *unskilled* jobs (Collins, 1972, p. 176).

Thus, the problem of increasing credentialism not only fosters frustration among the educated, it closes off employment options for the lower classes. Michael Marien (1971b) offers a list of other problems created by a credentials-conscious society:

- Artificial restraints on learning—diplomas are needed as entry passes for many educational experiences.

- Overlooked obsolescence—being certified today does not guarantee competence tomorrow.

- Generational inversion—the young, though less experienced, have higher credentials than their elders.

- The myth of a well-educated nation—Although we are overcredentialed, we are not overeducated; there is much we need to learn and know.

• Artificial social classes—all college graduates are members of the same club, even though they differ greatly in abilities.

There is also some evidence that this inflation of the value of educational credentials may lead to an actual *lowering* of productivity. In the 1960s Gary Becker (1964) and the "human capitalists" argued that investments in education were investments in the gross national product. These economists felt that upgrading the work force educationally would lead to higher productivity as under-qualified workers were replaced by those with greater skills. More recently, however, Berg (1971) has asserted that the process works quite differently. What actually happens is unproductive job dis-location—more highly qualified workers bump slightly less qual-ified workers from their jobs. No increase in productivity occurs because the nature of the jobs is usually such that they do not re-quire higher skills. Productivity may actually drop because the more highly qualified worker is likely to be dissatisfied with the job. In sum, increasing the educational attainment of the work force above a certain level, without concomitant changes in the structure of work to capitalize on the increased capabilities of work-ers, will probably have a slightly negative impact on productivity.

Finally, credentialism is one more artificial tool with which inequality is justified in society.

Inequality, the Underlying Issue. A future in which the supply of highly qualified workers greatly outpaces the number of choice jobs not only brings into question the problems of the well-educated, but raises the spectre of increased inequality for the less educated. Inequality is certain to be aggravated if the educational credentials for low- and medium-skilled jobs are raised. Moreover, in an age in which almost everyone will have at least a high school education, the issue then becomes how society can more equitably allocate access to the best and worst jobs. The problem is not an easy one. Peter Schrag has observed (in Jencks and others, 1972) that schools cannot be equalizers and at the same time sorters, certifiers, and selectors. Are the schools sources of equality or inequality? In either case, should they be changed? How? Should society look to some other institutions to increase equality? To pursue these ques-tions in their natural direction is to become embroiled in a quagmire of regression analyses, prejudices, and politics. I wish to avoid that swampy debate, from which no analyst returns unsullied, and deal with the problem of inequality in traditional terms of social class, a subject on which there is a rather well-defined and accepted literature.

Although liberals are opposed to a society in which all the benefits would be equally distributed, because this aim could only be accomplished through authoritarian means that would destroy efficiency, quality, and individual liberty, they nevertheless are interested in abolishing hereditary social class. Hereditary social class is unjust because it distorts the market allocation of social benefits. That is, unworthy individuals may have access to good jobs in a class-stratified system, while worthy individuals are prevented from making a full contribution to the economy and society and from reaping their just desserts. The full development and utilization of human resources cannot be achieved if a bright individual who is a minority group member, a woman, or the daughter or son of a blue-collar worker cannot get the education and job he or she deserves. In this way, social justice correlates with economic efficiency.

To address the relationship of education to work is to raise the issues of class structure that St. Simon, Marx, Weber, Veblen, Parsons, and all other macro-sociologists have seen as central to discussions of a just society. Social class has been, and remains, one of the overriding considerations of public policy in industrial society because social class is closely related to almost every other important issue: occupation is correlated with social-class standing; education is correlated with occupation; and to complete the cycle, educational opportunity and performance are correlated highly with social class. Because this is so clearly cyclical, what is cause and what is effect is unknown. Moreover, there are many unexplained variables, as there are with the measurement of any significant social phenomenon. Nevertheless, the correlations of education, occupation, and class stand out quite clearly—and it is with what we know that we must work.

Daniel Bell has recently (1973) stated that education is increasingly becoming the primary source of power (and class standing) in the emerging postindustrial society. If this is true, then access to higher levels of education, and learning of better quality, becomes even more critical in the future. Deciding who gets what education greatly determines who gets what jobs. The stakes in this process are high: jobs greatly determine life chances, life styles, the quality of life, and even whom one will marry. The difference between winning and losing is great: the best-paid 20 percent of the white work force earns 600 percent more than the worst-paid 20 percent (Jencks and others, 1972, p. 14). And access to that top fifth of the jobs is greatly determined by education (recall that only 4 percent of high school graduates have access to choice jobs). And access to higher education correlates highly with social class. A study of the 1973 college freshman class showed that 27.4 percent came from families earning more than twenty thousand dollars a year, and only 11 percent from families with incomes of less than six thousand (Trombley, 1974). Jencks's data indicate that a great many bright, poor children go to college, but poor children of average intelligence are far less likely to do so than average wealthy children. But even the brightest children of the working classes are at a relative disadvantage: Martin Trow (1962) reports that in California in the early 1960s nearly half of the top academic 20 percent of high school students who were children of blue-collar workers did not go on to college. And demographic input has a way of imitating occupational output in the system. In the 1960s, 60 to 70 percent of the business "elite" in America came from the upper and upper-middle classes, whereas only 15 percent were scions of the working class (Collins, 1972, p. 183).

What can be said from a review of the evidence, then, is that the academic record of young people—in particular, their years of schooling—bears directly on occupational achievement (Husen, 1975; Jencks and others, 1972). And we know that the rich are more likely than the poor to go on to more years of schooling (whether this is due to parental influence, genes, or some other cause is unknown). Whatever their source, these factors strongly suggest a future dominated by an *inherited* meritocracy, whose members will have the advantages of education and class. Thus, the ties among class, education, and occupation will tend to prohibit a just and efficient society.

This somewhat contradictory situation—in which education

presumably provides upward social mobility for all, but the children of the meritocracy are more likely to rise—has led some observers to conclude that the children of the meritocracy are somehow intellectually or morally superior on the average to the children of the disadvantaged. Being ignorant of genetics gives one an edge in this debate: one can posit at least two purely sociological explanations for why inequality continues to exist even when access to education is relatively open. First, it has been argued by Herbert Gintis, David MacMichael, and others that schools offer class-specific instruction to students (Bowles and Gintis, 1976; Mac-Michael, 1974). That is, they teach two work ethics—the upper middle class learns the Protestant ethic of deferred gratification necessary for success in higher education and good jobs; the children of the poor are taught the working-class ethic of docility, obedience, acceptance, and discipline that is needed in the traditional workplace (MacMichael, 1974).

Thus, even in a system of open access to higher education, the children of the poor are not equipped by the schools to compete equally with the children of the meritocrats. But it is not just the schools that limit the social mobility of the poor and working classes. A major study by Melvin Kohn (1969) shows that working-class families rear their children on values that *lower* their expectations but help them survive in a working-class world. One thing that emerges from all studies of the poor and working class is that the important socializing institutions—family, work, school and church—reduce their expectations of success and instill values that are dysfunctional for competition with the upper-middle class. (In Chapter Six, I return to this issue with an analysis of the ways in which vocational education compounds the injustices of inequality of opportunity.)

The second sociological explanation that can be offered for the persistent inequality of disadvantaged classes is that these people become trapped in a "secondary labor market" that greatly inhibits their mobility. The dual labor market theory is described by Michael Piore: ". . . the primary market offers jobs which possess several of the following traits: high wages, good working conditions, employment stability and job security, equity and due process in the administration of work rules, and chances for advancement. The secondary sector has jobs that . . . tend to involve low wages, poor working conditions, considerable variability in employment, harsh and arbitrary discipline, and little opportunity to advance" (quoted in O'Toole, 1973a, pp. 171–172).

Piore and his colleague Bennett Harrison describe the factors that draw the poor to this market and tend over time to lock in even those who initially had appropriate traits for the primary market, such factors as the low aggregate demand for jobs in the primary sector and racial discrimination. Piore and Harrison argue that there is little skill deficiency in this group because the complexity of the lower-level jobs they aspire to in the primary market has been greatly exaggerated. Thus, education or training is unlikely to lift them out of the secondary labor market. Indeed, according to Harrison, "Not only do black attempts at self-improvement (like education) often lead nowhere, but they may be counter-productive in the long run, since they only produce larger numbers of educated blacks who are forced to compete with one another for a virtually fixed supply of jobs—a competition which could well drive the wages of educated blacks down instead of up" (1972).

The only solution to this problem is to increase the number of primary-labor-market jobs. Increasing the amount of education will not expand the number of such jobs and may, as Harrison argues, "increase workers' expectations and standards which, when frustrated by discrimination, lead to discouragement and non-participation" (in Berg, 1973, p. 9). Here, as with well-educated workers, there is an inherent discrepancy between the expectations and needs of workers and the very shape of the job market.

In summary, the issues of credentialism and underemployment have several important implications for social class inequality in America: (1) The increasing reliance on credentials leaves the uncredentialed and less-educated segment of the workforce without access to the good jobs in the primary labor market. (2) The uncredentialed become locked-in to the secondary labor market, thus rigidifying the class structure of the society. (3) Access to education and training will not greatly reduce this rigidity because the problem is not a shortage of skilled workers. Rather, the problem is a shortage of good jobs in the primary labor market. (4) The mobility problems of minority and working-class youth are compounded by the socialization to work that they receive. Lower-class institutions (schools, families, workplaces) prepare young people for a life in bad jobs. Thus, they are not able to compete successfully with middle class youth even when there is equality of opportunity in higher education or in primary jobs.

Significantly, then, the problem of underemployment is not merely confined to the middle-class college graduates who cannot find jobs that meet their inflated expectations. In addition, underemployment is related to such key issues of justice and injustice in the society as who will do the dirty jobs in the economy, and who will reap the benefits of middle-class social status.

Moving On

In Chapter Two some of the current misuses of human resources were reviewed. The present chapter has offered some exploratory forecasts of how these problems are likely to be exacerbated by the disjunctive relationships of education and work. In the next part, I offer some normative forecasts of alternative policies for dealing with these present and future issues, singling out roles for government, employers, unions, and schools in developing human resources.

In particular, I analyze what can (or should) be done

- to change jobs so that they engage the "unemployed self"

- to decrease the reliance on inappropriate credentials

- to create more good jobs

- to increase equity in access to education and jobs

- to help keep people from being locked in to the secondary labor market

- to reduce the social distance between those with and without good jobs.

- to increase the values of education that do not relate to employment.

I now turn to an exploration of public policies and private practices directed toward putting the reserve army of the underemployed back on active duty.

4

Securing Total Employment: The Role of Government

Full employment without inflation is generally accepted as a primary goal of national economic policy. Legitimate and important differences over definition aside, when the unemployment rate is down around the four percent level, this figure is widely taken as the prime indicator that employment conditions in the economy are healthy.

But full employment does not in itself signify a condition of true health in the labor market, it merely indicates the absence of serious or apparent illness. By way of analogy, a man with tuberculosis is clearly sick, but is another man without visible signs of illness *ipso facto* healthy? Perhaps if we were to conduct a more searching examination, we might find his lungs black and deteriorating from smoking, his heart weakened from stress, or his resistance to all varieties of ailments lowered by mental depression or poor diet. Similarly, no clean bill of health could be granted auto-

71

matically to even a full-employment economy unless the following kinds of latent or seldom diagnosed problems were eradicated from the body economic:

(1) Subemployment: working less than full time, full year (and often for less than the minimum wage) is a chronic problem for many workers. It has serious consequences for the life styles and life chances of families when it afflicts heads of households.

(2) Low-level employment: many disadvantaged and minority workers are trapped in jobs that offer them little in the way of dignity or self-esteem. These jobs are characterized by harsh and arbitrary discipline, unhealthy, unsafe, or inhumane working conditions, low pay, and the absence of a career path.

(3) Involuntary employment: many older people are forced to take jobs because they cannot live on their retirement incomes; many heads of households are forced to moonlight because they cannot attain a decent living standard for their families on wages from primary jobs; and many women who would prefer to stay home and rear their children are forced to take paid jobs in order to be eligible for social services.

(4) Underemployment—the underutilization of skills, training, and education of workers, described in the previous chapter.

The United States has not made much headway against these problems, in part because we pursue other problems that we can more readily measure. The measures used to evaluate public employment policy focus largely on unemployment statistics and the size of the labor market. These indicators are relatively unambiguous, but they tell us only whether jobs are available for all those workers in the *official* labor force.

This official measure of the size of the labor force is both important and controversial. It is a partial guide to how many jobs might have to be created in coming decades, but it excludes millions of people who might want jobs if they were available. For example, it excludes labor-force dropouts who have given up looking for work, students who stay in school because they cannot find jobs, people on welfare, and those who are in sheltered environments ranging from prisons to mental hospitals. The labor-force participation rate is important also because only those who are in the official labor force can be counted as either employed or unemployed. The relationship of the participation rate and the unemployment rate is not a simple one; indeed, it is quite fluid. For instance, when new jobs are created, they are often filled by people who are not in the official labor force. White middle-class women often are attracted into the labor force to take new jobs, while chronically unemployed black men and boys remain unemployed.

Over the past decade, the total size of the labor force as well as the relative size of the force as a percentage of total population have grown remarkably. Paradoxically, as the economy created new jobs at a clip unprecedented in history, rates of unemployment also rose. The primary reason behind this phenomenon has been the entry of millions of women into the paid labor force. In 1950, the female labor-force participation rate was 33.9 percent; by 1973 it was 44.7 percent. Most dramatically, the rate of participation by women with children aged six to seventeen went from 32.8 percent in 1950 to 52.6 percent in 1972. Between 1975 and 1976, the number of women job holders and job seekers increased by nearly two million and accounted for almost all the growth in the entire labor force.

Since rates of unemployment mask such shifts in the demographic make-up of the work force, they are imperfect measures of the health of the economy. Still, unemployment rates are important pieces of information and not to be made light of, especially in the midst of a recession. But recession is not a permanent condition, and the presence of a temporary crisis should not distract us from pursuing more durable, appropriate, and longer-term performance measures for public policy. Although by necessity we engage in "crisis management," we should not forget that the latent problems outlined above are basic and enduring shortcomings in the labor market and will not vanish with the current recession.

Clearly, current labor-policy performance measures are inadequate to the challenges that these complex, deeply rooted problems present. They are inadequate, in brief, because they aggregate and thus obscure such problems as chronic subemployment and the existence of millions of labor-force dropouts. Moreover, the measures lead to the policy conclusion that simply creating more jobs will cure the major illnesses of the labor market. Unfortunately, the simple availability of jobs is often not enough to satisfy the economic, social, and psychological needs that lead people to seek work. Although providing jobs is widely accepted as one of the best public-policy responses to such social problems as poverty, family disorganization, and physical and mental ill health, not just any jobs will do. In order for work to function as a lever on social problems, the right jobs must be made available at the right time to those who need them. This requirement is complicated by the fact that the work needs of individuals change—a job that is good for a young person is not necessarily good for the father of triplets. Moreover, the quality of a job is important in determining its value as an ameliorator of social problems—handicapped, disadvantaged, and other workers need to be able to build their self-esteem on their jobs. These are admittedly difficult demands to cope with because they introduce qualitative measures into an area where problems and solutions seemed to lend themselves so well to quantification.

From the point of view of public policy, these qualitative concerns also lead to two very frustrating conclusions. First, no monolithic program can satisfy the wide range of employment needs. Second, the creation of jobs through either macro-economic stimulation or public service employment are essential but woefully insufficient responses to the latent problems of employment.

Definitions and Myths

In the *Work in America* report, my colleagues and I suggested that total employment is a more appropriate measure of a healthy labor market than is full employment. *Total employment* is defined as a condition in which everyone who desires a job would be assured of finding one that reasonably satisfies his or her personal needs. Clearly, total employment cannot and should not be mandated by government fiat. It can only be achieved by policies designed to create greater freedom of choice for workers. People must have real options among an array of jobs offering different challenges,

styles of supervision, physical working conditions, and working
hours. They must be able to select the appropriate stages in their
lives in which to seek paid employment. Such freedom of choice
does not currently exist because of certain inflexibilities and inequalities in the labor market that restrict its free play. No doubt
a variety of policies could help to remove some of these barriers
and thus permit self-adjustment in the labor force—a process that
may be the only equitable and nontotalitarian solution to the latent
problems of employment.

Unfortunately, such policies are unlikely to be fully or fairly
evaluated in the framework of the current orthodoxy of labor
economics. One simply cannot measure the distance to the stars in
quarts. Consequently, before moving on to a consideration of total
employment policies, we need to examine some myths, fictions,
and superstitions that currently misinform and constrain our vision.

*Myth 1: The problems of unemployment can be solved simply by
creating more jobs.* Economists view unemployment as a condition
in which the demand for existing jobs by those in the labor force
exceeds current supply. This concept is quickly translated into the
less sophisticated notion that unemployment means there is a
shortage of jobs. Thus, when policy makers decide that the shortage has grown to intolerable proportions, they often pursue a
simple and logical course—they use macro-economic stimulation
to create more jobs. Paradoxically, this action may lead to even
higher rates of unemployment because the new jobs attract people
into the paid labor force who previously were not looking for jobs,
as I pointed out earlier in discussing women's entry. Even in the
unlikely event that the United States were to devise millions of
new jobs through massive spending or a program of public-service
employment, because of this "substitution effect" there would still
be many people who would need, but would not be receiving, the
benefits of a good, steady job.

Thus, the notion of shortage is basically nonfunctional in
relation to policy development, which requires an alternative way
of framing the problem. Apparently simple cases of shortages
often can be better understood and acted upon if they are seen
as complex problems of maldistribution and mismatching. Recent
attempts to increase the supply of medical manpower illustrate

this phenomenon. In the late 1960s, American medical schools made a concerted effort to gain a windfall in federal aid by convincing the American public that there was an acute shortage of doctors. This alarmist tactic almost worked—until more thoughtful analyses showed that the apparent deficiency is due more to a maldistribution of doctors both by specialty and geography than to general shortage across the board. There are more than enough psychiatrists in Manhattan, but too few pediatricians in the ghetto; there are so many radiologists in Los Angeles that they have to inflate their fees to keep their incomes above the so-called starvation level (seventy thousand a year), but there are not enough general practitioners in rural Iowa. Thus, what was called for was a system of incentives for the medical schools to correct these distribution problems, and such a program was enacted by the Congress in September 1974.

Similarly, the idea of unemployment itself may not be a valid guide to setting policy. If certain rigidities and blocks were removed from the job market, the total number of jobs might not be far short of the total number of people who want and need jobs at a given time. Here, too, poor distribution is a useful concept. That is, some people who do not want jobs are forced into the labor market because of tradition, laws, or the lack of available alternatives or resources, and such barriers exclude many others who want and need jobs. Those who might be reluctantly employed include: adults who would like to take a year or two off from their jobs to return to school; older people who would like to retire earlier than age sixty-three or sixty-five; welfare mothers who would rather stay home and rear their children than take the so-called incentive of a demeaning, poorly paying job; middle-class mothers who would like to care for their children but feel pressures to work from the woman's movement; and fathers who would rather stay home and take care of their children. Among those who would like to take jobs but cannot find them are the subemployed 20 to 35 percent of ghetto men and boys; teenagers who would rather work than be in school; women who prefer work in the labor market to work in their homes; retired people who would like at least some part-time work; and the so-called expendables of society—addicts, convicts, and the handicapped—many of whom would prefer honest labor to being warehoused in public institutions.

For nearly one hundred years, free-market industrial economies have tried to curb unemployment by increasing the *overall* number of jobs. Regrettably, and often tragically, these noble experiments have failed. A century is a fair test for a policy that does not work. Perhaps it is time to try another tack, one designed to make the labor market freer and more functional. To do this, we may need social inventions that balance the labor supply and demand by allowing unwilling workers to leave the labor force and thereby opening up jobs for people who want and need them. Such policies would attempt to remove the social and legal barriers, such as some social welfare regulations, that force reluctant people to work. At the same time, they would seek to provide opportunities—and, in appropriate instances, income—to people who would like to leave the paid work force and do unpaid work, such as school work, child care, and voluntary social service work.

We are not ready to consider these policies, however, because other myths reflexively force us to raise objections.

Myth 2: Work is paid employment. According to this definition, a housewife and mother does not work. Yet if her services are replaced by a housekeeper, babysitter, and cook, or if she herself performs these tasks for others, both she and her replacements are now considered workers because their salaries are contributions to the gross national product. There are many repercussions of this definition. It forces some poor women to take low-paying, unsatisfying jobs in order to become eligible for government health, welfare, and other social services. Society would benefit more from properly reared children, from lower costs for day care, and from a citizenry whose freedom of choice was preserved than from the fruits of the low-level employment of these poor mothers. The issue is different for the middle classes: women will not be liberated until women *and men* can freely choose to take jobs in the paid labor force, or to stay home and care for their children, or both. This liberation will only occur when child rearing is as highly valued by society as paid employment.

Similarly, much volunteer activity might also be considered work. Working in hospitals, in churches, on school boards, in scouting, and in local government is not paid employment, but it is every bit as important to society as are many activities for which there is compensation—such as much of the make-work of public and private bureaucracies.

Raising the status of child care and volunteer work to that of paid employment would not be easy. It would first involve eliminating provisions that require employment as a prerequisite for social services. It might also necessitate some cash payments or tax write-offs for these activities, as is the case in other nations where there are child allowances, mothers' pensions, and pay or tax breaks for community activities. We are not open, however, to considering such alternative policies, not only because we believe that work is paid labor, but also because of our adherence to the following related myth.

Myth 3: All paid labor is ennobling. Labor and welfare policies reflect the puritan views that any job is better than no job, and no one is too good for any job. Taken to the extreme, these beliefs often lead to an incredible contradiction manifested by many political leaders: they espouse that work is good for everyone, but at the same time they find it necessary to force people to work. If the former is true, why is it necessary to advocate the latter? How is it that those who preach the dignity of work also believe that work should be used as punishment? At the root of this contradiction is the simple fact that not all jobs are good jobs.

Although many jobs provide the social, psychological, and economic rewards that make work so essential and meaningful to life, some jobs offer none of these satisfactions. Not only do they fail to provide the worker with even minimal dignity, challenge, and economic resources, they may actually destroy an individual's self-esteem.

The nature of work, then, is a critically important variable in discussion of total employment. Related to the nature of work is the stage in one's life when one takes a certain kind of job. For example, picking fruit is not a bad summer job for a student, but it is literally lethal for migrant farmers and their families. There is nothing wrong with working in an unsteady, low-paying job if one is young and single, but if one tries to marry and raise a family in such an economic condition, the odds are that the marriage will quickly dissolve.

The devastating consequences of the nature of work experience on family life were illustrated to me in 1967 to 1968 while I was doing research in the black community of Los Angeles and in the Cape Coloured community of Cape Town, South Africa (O'Toole, 1973b). As I mentioned in Chapter One, there was considerable family disorganization in both communities especially among the poor. My original thesis was that the unemployment of fathers was the common cause of the high rates of desertion, separation, and mother-headed households found in both communities. In South Africa, however, I discovered that unemployment was only at the frictional level, and in Watts even the high 12 percent rate of adult unemployment could not account adequately for the extreme pathology in that ghetto. It occurred to me after I had completed my research that the crucial variable in both communities was the *nature* of the father's employment. In neither community were men who worked in unsteady, low-paying, demeaning, unskilled, and dead-end jobs likely to have the self-esteem or social or economic wherewithal to hold a family together. In Watts, I estimated that only 65 percent of the men over age eighteen worked full time, full year, and earned more than the minimum wage. That is, the subemployment rate for Watts was approximately 35 percent. It was not purely coincidental that in about a third of the homes in Watts the father was absent and that about a third of the families were on welfare. Of course, there were not always direct relationships among male subemployment, mother-centered families, and welfare cases, but the three factors correlated far more often than not.

From the point of view of family formation, then, all jobs are not good jobs. Moreover, the person who has paid employment in a family is a crucial variable. In both South Africa and the United States, nonwhite women were more employable than nonwhite men. Nevertheless, the availability of a job for a woman with small children had no positive effect on family cohesion or other social problems related to employment and poverty. It was the fathers of young children who needed paid employment. Ironically, welfare work-incentive programs in the United States are designed to get jobs for mothers instead of finding jobs for fathers of welfare children. Work programs are not directed to the fathers because they are not on welfare themselves, even though they are the proximate cause of their family's welfare status. Punishing welfare mothers by making them take undesirable jobs has little or no positive impact on the familial or employment problems of the chronically disadvantaged. (Of course, these women also need the freedom to take a paid job if they so choose.) Headway will be made in the ghetto only when all men who wish to have families can be assured of good, steady jobs that will enable them to support their families. Such a goal will not be realized, however, as long as the following myth is believed.

Myth 4: Total employment would entail the involuntary mobilization of millions of workers in public-service jobs. Many countries in which unemployment has ceased to be a problem—Russia and China, for example—have achieved total employment at the expense of personal liberty. The specter of such totalitarianism has been raised by the editors of the *Wall Street Journal* and others when arguing the case against *full* employment. But *total* employment is a nontotalitarian concept based on enhancing individual freedom of choice. Its goal is not to force every citizen to take a paid job but to remove artificial constraints and rigidities that restrict the free play of the labor market. Artificial educational credential requirements, discrimination based on age, sex, class, or race, and government policies that restrict educational aid to the young or require employment among the middle-aged are examples of constraints that might be removed.

Moreover, most employment is rather monolithic in terms of the hours workers are required to be on the job. There are not enough part-time jobs or jobs with flexible days or hours to provide workers with any real choice. It is quite possible that providing greater opportunities for part-time jobs through job sharing would reduce some of our most intractable unemployment problems, even with less job-creation effort.

I have interviewed a number of unemployed people and have often come away with the feeling that working conditions are frequently a barrier to their taking jobs. The spectrum of reasons unemployed people give for their status is incredibly wide, but in many cases it boils down to the fact that the jobs that are available do not meet their specific needs and desires. For example, I recall an engineer who didn't want to take a job beneath that status, a

blue-collar worker who wanted a job that was intellectually stimu-
lating, a middle-class woman who wanted a job with training and
promotion opportunities, an elderly man who wanted to work
three or four days a week at a reduced salary in a union shop,
and a young college graduate who wanted "to work in a team situation with interesting people." One wonders how much unemployment would be reduced if these workers and others like them had
greater choice among the kinds of jobs and working conditions that
were available? Even without increasing job creation efforts, it is
probable that a great number of unemployed people could find
jobs. What appears to be needed is the removal of certain legal and
credential barriers to employment, better matching of jobs with
individual social, psychological and economic needs, policies designed to create more diversity and flexibility in the conditions of
work, and easier movement in and out of the labor market. We do
not need a totalitarian concept of full employment. Rather, we
must begin to think of ways to remove barriers that inhibit freedom
of choice and human development.

However, since a free market works well only when its partici-
pants are relatively equal, it may be necessary to create some additional public-service jobs in order to produce greater job diversity
and options for those people not fully served by the free market.
But these kinds of jobs should be kept to a minimum, because they
tend to be inferior to private-sector jobs (despite the denials of
decent and well-meaning people). They quite often pay more, but
in terms of challenge, autonomy, status, and opportunities for
growth, they tend to fall short. As evidence presented in Chapter
Three shows, in the public sector, clerical and service jobs constitute 42 percent of all employment (78 percent if teachers are excluded), while in the private sector such jobs account for only 28
percent of all employment (U.S. Department of Labor, 1974b).
One out of three new jobs is being created in the public sector,
and although these jobs are not exactly menial, 60 to 70 percent
call for the employee to be an aide, attendant, assistant, clerical
worker, custodian, or semi-skilled blue-collar worker. In addition
to these criticisms of public employment, there is at least impres-
sionistic evidence that private employment is more innovative,
flexible, and responsive to the needs of workers. For example,

the kinds of self-management described in Chapter Five and worker ownership described in Chapter Nine are all but impossible in the civil service, which, by necessity, must be first and foremost responsible to the voting public.

Another drawback of creating public-service jobs is that they end up going to middle-class people, not to those in the central cities who are most disadvantaged. The chronically subemployed individual has as much trouble holding a public-service job as he does holding jobs in the secondary labor market. At least with day-laboring jobs he does not need the senses of discipline, punctuality, and cooperation that are needed in jobs created under the Comprehensive Employment and Training Act of 1973 (CETA) and other public-service programs. To find ways to make government employment serve those who most need it, the Manpower Demonstration Research Corporation of New York has begun a series of experiments with alternative working conditions. They hope to identify the conditions under which hard-core unemployables can find success on the job. For example, in some cases the workers are not held to strict standards of punctuality and attendance to start with, but gradually the standards are increased as the workers build their work habits. So far, this is all theory and experiment. Until there are solid findings, public-service jobs will continue to benefit primarily the middle class.

There is also some evidence that public-service jobs do not make the best use of government expenditures for job creation. Apparently, the number of jobs created varies considerably from one government program to another. The following table (drawn from several not terribly reliable sources) illustrates the number of jobs created by spending one billion federal dollars in various ways.

51,000 jobs if spent on highway construction (Bezdek and Hannon, 1974)

55,000 jobs if spent on defense contracts (Babson and Brigham, 1976)

60,000 jobs if spent on CETA-like public-service programs (Wall Street Journal, 1976)

76,000 jobs if spent on public housing construction (Babson and Brigham, 1976)

84,000 jobs if spent on health programs (not construction) (Bezdek and Hannon, 1974)

85,000 jobs if spent on water treatment plants (Porter, 1975)

90,000 jobs if spent on educational programs (not construction)
   (Babson and Brigham, 1976)

The actual numbers here are irrelevant. What is important is that every dollar spent by government influences new employment opportunities, that different programs have different job-creation effects, and that CETA-like public-service programs, while not the least effective, are far from being the most effective job-creation tools at the disposal of the government.

For all their liabilities, public-service jobs are nevertheless popular with politicians and the public because they give the impression of forceful and direct action on the problems of unemployment. It is hard and slow work to create jobs that produce goods and services in actual demand, but it is easy and fast to start up training programs and public-service employment. Yet the latter programs are basically palliatives, and because they do not treat the *causes* of unemployment, they may even be counterproductive in that by alleviating the *symptoms* they remove pressures to act on the root causes. When unemployment reaches 7 or 8 percent, advocates of public-service jobs are able to command a wide audience (and are usually able to get a public-employment bill passed in Congress). Then, when unemployment slips back to 5 or 6 percent for cyclical reasons, the public quickly turns its attention to other areas of concern, satisfied that the prompt and wise leadership in Washington has adequately dealt with the problem. Consequently, true reforms are seldom considered, and the damaging problems of subemployment, low-level employment, and involuntary employment remain and grow worse.

The government does have a role in employment, but it should be more creative in applying its funds and regulatory powers in order to produce not only more jobs in the private sector, but more good jobs. For example, in Chapter One I suggested how a new returnable bottle law might create jobs. In another case government could create either 423,000 new jobs with a health program or 256,000 with a highway program—both for an identical investment of $5 billion. In making spending decisions, government should consider both the number of jobs to be created and their potential for producing steady, challenging work with career mobility. (See Chapter Ten for a development of this notion.) Thus, it is more effective for government to use its power to create jobs in the private profit and nonprofit sectors than it is to create public-service employment. In no fashion does a policy of total employment require either worker coercion or greatly increased government employment.

Myth 5: Total employment requires economic growth. In the future, the rate of unemployment may fall toward zero, even without much economic growth. Indeed, within the next thirty years employment rates may be reported negatively, expressing a situation in which demand for workers exceeds supply. The convergence of five trends makes such a zero-growth, total-employment future a distinct possibility: (1) The rising costs of energy may lead to the increasing substitution of labor for capital. (2) The increasing scarcity of capital in our economy may lead to more labor-intensive enterprises. (3) The continued shift from an industry-based economy to a services base will create more jobs. (4) Environmentalist pressures will exacerbate the shift away from capital-intensive, "dirty" industries (metals and mining, for example) toward "cleaner," labor-intensive health, education, and other services. (5) There will be a demographic shift, culminating in about thirty-five years, which will cause the proportion of retired persons in the population to be greater than ever before in American history. Each of these five trends would have the effect of lowering productivity and economic growth while increasing the demand for workers.

Whereas unemployment in the traditional sense will probably disappear in the United States in the future, the broader issue of underemployment might become more acute for all social classes because trends toward labor intensivity and zero economic growth could lead to a greater number of routine jobs. (These issues are elaborated in Chapter Ten.) Here again, macro-economic policies and public-service employment are ineffective tools. The problem is not a shortage of jobs, but a poor mix of jobs. Looking at employment through these new lenses, we focus our attention on policies designed to remove rigidities in the labor market, to enhance individual freedom of choice, to increase the flexibility and variety of jobs, and to encourage human development. Such policies for

total employment, although devilishly difficult to pursue, are at
least not trade-offs against inflation.

Myth 6: Total employment is inflationary. We are now painfully
aware that *high* rates of unemployment and inflation can exist
together. Does this mean that it is also possible to concurrently
experience *low* rates of unemployment and inflation? The current
contradiction of the Phillip's curve trade-off reopens this possibility for discussion.

It is appropriate here to look at some nontraditional employment policies that either are immune to inflation or are proved
inflation fighters. Obviously, total-employment policies that consider the problem to be maldistribution rather than a shortage of
jobs bypasses the issue of inflation. If one's tool for fighting unemployment is not macro-economic, then there is little problem
of its directly fueling inflation.

A non-macro-economic policy of note in this regard is manifested in West Germany's active manpower planning and training
program, referred to in Chapter One. The German strategy for
worker retraining and job change recognizes that career immo-
bility can be a source of worker discontent and of inflationary
pressures. Although the German program is not demonstrably
associated with that country's relatively low rates of inflation and
unemployment, many economists on both sides of the Atlantic
argue that it has not hurt (Striner, 1972). Several economists
propose for the U.S. a similar program that would decrease over-
supplies of labor in declining industries and occupations by retraining workers for places where they will be more productive
and where critical manpower shortages might otherwise create
inflationary bottlenecks (Holt, 1971). Even at a possible cost of
four billion dollars, such a program is attractive, not only because
it would lower the rate of inflation, but because it would create a
quarter of a million jobs. It also strikes directly at the problems
of underemployment.

Several other employment policies could make lesser, but
still significant, contributions to lowering inflation. The following
measures would tend either to increase the mobility or productivity
of workers or to increase the efficiency of the economy, thereby
helping to reduce the rate of inflation for any given level of em-

ployment: (1) reducing race, sex, and age discrimination; (2) increasing mobility and vesting of pensions; (3) introducing profit sharing tied to worker or small-group productivity; and (4) redesigning jobs.

Alternative Policies

What is important about all of these proposals is that they are compatible with the total-employment approach I've been describing. Although such an approach assumes the importance of using macro-economic policy to keep inflation and unemployment as low as possible, the strategy is not *dependent* solely on macro-economic policy, public service employment or any traditional economic methods for creating new jobs. That is how it differs from what we have, and that is why it probably has a greater chance of success than does the current approach.

In order to create total employment, a series of discrete but compatible private and public programs must be undertaken, many of which can be initiated at the state, community, or plant level. Such programs might do one or more of the following: facilitate the withdrawal from the paid labor force of reluctant workers; help those who need and want jobs to acquire them; increase the mobility of workers; and make the job market more flexible. Possible program strategies might be to:

• Reduce institutional rigidities in the labor market, such as seniority rules. Remove the minimum-wage requirements for those under twenty years of age and unmarried and raise them for persons over twenty and for under-twenties who are married.

• Remove all government regulations in which employment is a prerequisite for social services. For example, make unpaid individuals engaged in rearing children eligible for social security benefits.

• Provide a program of mid-career worker training or sabbaticals that covers school tuition and a substantial part of foregone income.

● Provide programs that allow workers to taper off before retirement: for example, fifty-five-year-olds could work four days and sixty-year olds three days. Conversely, those over sixty-five would be permitted to work without penalty if they so elected.

● Establish a system of domestic "Fulbrights" for people who would like to take a year or two away from their regular jobs to engage in some kind of public service. Xerox has such a program for its employees.

● Provide a guaranteed minimum annual income through a negative-income-tax scheme.

● Stop massive immigration except for political or humanitarian reasons.

● Permit cities to charter and operate banks. These banks would underwrite loans to individuals or groups wishing to start nonprofit or cooperatively owned businesses that met the employment needs of an underserved group or community. For example, businesses would be eligible if they offered meaningful employment to the aged, youth, or minorities, or if they provided such groups with training to do meaningful but rare types of work, such as skilled crafts and repairs.

● Provide human-depreciation tax allowances or employment tax credits linked to the ratio of employment to fixed plant and equipment. Both policies (or others like them) would encourage the use of labor-intensive processes in industry.

● Encourage the creation of community councils designed to: (1) match people with work and education opportunities; (2) counsel employers in the redesign of jobs; (3) lobby for the creation of part-time and flexible jobs; and (4) engage in local manpower planning (Wirtz, 1975).

● Provide more part-time jobs and job sharing. One example is the Pitney Bowes program, mentioned earlier, that permits two mothers to split one job. At some universities, a husband and wife may share a faculty appointment. Britain's Patrick Goldring (1974) suggests that if everyone were permitted to hold two jobs, the worker in a bad job might find some satisfaction in another, better position; stressful executives could unwind in manual jobs; and potentially redundant workers could spend part of their work time in preparation for a future job. Although his proposal is fraught with practical obstacles to realization, it at least offers a response to the way society has segmented the work, leisure, education, and family aspects of our lives, producing workers who hate their work, who find no release in their leisure, and who find little time for their families.

This list of possible programs could be twice as long, and I am not certain that all the items included are either desirable or feasible. What is important is that we can and should start thinking in terms of such alternatives to traditional approaches. Although each such program has a cost, its potential benefits must be considered, not only in economic terms, but in terms of their effect on mental and physical health, crime, family cohesion, and social and political alienation. Moreover, one has to weigh the inflationary aspects of the alternative macro-economic policies and the costs of not acting at all in terms of lost income, taxes, and production.

In sum, total employment can be achieved through opening up the labor market, removing institutional rigidities, and offering people greater freedom to choose when and where they will work. Such a policy is appropriate now and will still be appropriate in the future when employment conditions change. Such a policy is equitable because it favors no race, class, age, or sex. And furthermore, it is compatible with traditional free-market principles.

Many things can be done on the local level using this approach that do not require federal initiatives. In particular, the problems of underemployment do not lend themselves to federal programs but are, as the next chapter argues, the rightful responsibility of employers and unions.

5

Improving the Quality of Work:
The Role of
Employers and Unions

In the spring of 1972, a strike at a General Motors plant put the small town of Lordstown, Ohio, on the map. The landslide of publicity and analysis that followed the strike has made the plant into a powerful symbol of the dehumanizing side-effects of industrialism. This plant—with the world's fastest, most fully automated car assembly line—has become a Promethean symbol of technology run amuck. As such, its name has become the code word of a new movement to improve the quality of working life. To say "Lordstown" is to say that Frederick Winslow Taylor still stalks the plants and offices of American industry, stop watch in hand.

Yet the actual circumstances of the famous Lordstown strike are neither what GM's defenders claim nor what its detractors assert. Like most other symbols, Lordstown doesn't live up to its billing. Nevertheless, it is instructive to look at what actually happened in 1972 and at what has happened since, because the Lordstown phenomenon is illustrative of an attitude that is sweeping American industry: managers, with the unintentional help of behavioral scientists, are blaming workers for low productivity. For example, the United States Steel Corporation is currently undertaking a massive advertising campaign ("At U.S. Steel, we're involved") exhorting American workers to greater productive efforts. But if these managers, and their colleagues at other major corporations, ever succeed in identifying the prime cause of drooping national productivity, they may be shocked to find that, indeed, they are *involved*. At U.S. Steel, at GM and at nearly every major corporation in the U.S., managers have looked every which way in order to finger the foot-dragging culprit who is inhibiting efforts to achieve more optimal productivity; they may someday find that the enemy is themselves. At least that is what I believe they would find at Lordstown if they looked deeply and objectively. A brief bit of history illustrates this contention.

The Lordstown Legend

Just about a year before the strike, the Lordstown workers received awards from GM in recognition of the high quality of their work. Shortly after the awards were presented, GM turned the direction of the plant over to its tough Assembly Division—one of the last management teams in this country still practicing an undiluted version of Taylor's "scientific management." GM views the Assembly Division as its vanguard in heading off the challenge of foreign competition in the American auto market. This no-nonsense team came into Lordstown and concluded that although the line in the plant was fast (104 cars per hour versus an industry average of 55), it could go faster still.

After all, productivity is the name of the game. The government, liberal economists, and even the United Auto Workers (UAW) had been using the auto industry as a whipping boy for faltering national productivity and periodic balance of payments deficits. If Lordstown—the crowning achievement of American industrial engineering—couldn't compete with the Japanese and Germans, well, we were all in for a succession of hard winters.

In order to increase productivity, the Assembly Division did the two things that industrial engineers always do: they cut back the manpower on the line, and they increased the number of separate operations for which each worker was responsible. For example, by doing such things as bringing his stockpile of parts within easier reach, a worker could double the number of parts he could install, screws he could turn, and bolts he could bolt in the thirty seconds or so he had with each car.

The upshot was that many workers couldn't keep up with the increased pace of work. Some workers were falling so far behind that they were riding down the line trying to complete their tasks and *running* back to their stations to start the cycle again. Workers complained, but management held its ground. Joseph E. Godfrey, general manager of the Assembly Division, stated his position on the issue succinctly: "If we can occupy a man for sixty minutes, we have the right." The workers answered Godfrey in kind. First, they sabotaged the cars out of sheer frustration; then, after considering and rejecting a sit-in in which they would take over the entire plant, they struck.

From March 3 to March 24, 1972, approximately eight thousand workers participated in the strike. Agis Salpukas, covering the story for the *New York Times,* reported that it was over two of the oldest issues in American industrial relations—speed up of the assembly line and management's supposed evasion of work rules established in the GM-UAW contract. But Salpukas also reported some other facts, and in so doing created a legend that spread so fast that he still does not know how he created such a furor. What he wrote was this: (1) the workers at Lordstown were very young (the average age was twenty-two on the line); (2) the workers had engaged in rather widespread sabotage (and the company had shipped many damaged Vegas to dealers, who at that time could sell all the cars GM could supply); and (3) the "dumb" workers on the line were saying some rather thoughtful and articulate things (namely, that they would not tolerate the type of conditions in a plant that their fathers had tolerated).

It was this part of Salpukas's story that caught the nation's fancy. Here, many claimed, was a strike over boring, repetitive work. "Not at all," objected the company; "Not quite right," added the union, after initially trying to use the inaccurate and adverse publicity as a lever against the company. Salpukas wrote a follow-up story trying to put the issue into perspective. But all these qualifications fell on deaf ears. Overnight Lordstown had become the symbol of idealistic youth standing up to dehumanizing technology. Actually, these workers were mainly just tired of running their fannies off. But symbols need not be accurate to be appropriate. What actually happened is as much the stuff of industrial myth as what people *thought* happened. To understand why this is so, we might look at how the issue at Lordstown has been "resolved."

Twenty-two days and a hundred and fifty million dollars in lost production later, the parties at Lordstown reached an agreement to at least temporarily go back to the old ways of doing things—that is, in the pre-Assembly Division style. The Assembly Division stayed on, however, and during the next three years tried to develop ways to increase productivity just short of causing the workers to walk out. Although strikes have since been kept to a relative minimum, Lordstown has hardly become a model of cozy industrial relations. Workers still are not happy with the system (they filed five thousand separate grievances in one six-month period). And the company, too, is less than ecstatic about the way things have developed.

What is particularly bothersome to the company is that workers have taken to looking for ways to "beat the line"—in effect, as management is trying to re-engineer the jobs on the line, the workers are responding by redesigning their own jobs. Their favorite method is "doubling." Under this system, four workers might agree to become an informal team, and for a set period of time (fifteen minutes to half an hour), two of the team members will work like the devil doing the work of all four, while the other two workers rest, smoke, or chat. The workers claim that this method improves the quality of their work because it forces them to concentrate on what would otherwise be routine tasks, gives them a chance to rest, and affords them opportunities to socialize with co-workers (the latter being an important element in job satisfaction for blue-collar workers, but one that is all but obviated on a fast and noisy auto line).

Doubling drives the Assembly Division managers up the wall. Workers are paid to work, not to stand around chatting, they say.

The managers respond by disciplining the workers (sending them home for a day or more without pay). The workers, in turn, respond by filing grievances, and when this interaction sequence escalates to an unbearable level, the workers go out on strike for a few days. And so matters stood on December 15, 1974, when the plant was closed as a consequence of the economic recession (and when I ceased actively following the events at Lordstown).

Who's to Blame for Low Productivity?

As the industry and the UAW keep insisting, it is patently unfair to single out the auto industry as the arch villain of dehumanizing work. Auto workers are quite well paid, have one of the best benefit packages in industry, are represented by the nation's most progressive union, and labor under conditions markedly better than those experienced by coal miners or by the millions of unorganized service, farm, and industrial workers. Moreover, as even union officials will admit in private, the new breed of auto workers is a rather disrespectful and recalcitrant lot: they lack self-discipline; they drink, use drugs, and fight on the job to a frightening degree; and they complain about such matters as cleanliness in the plant, while they won't even bother to throw trash in available receptacles.

Detroit's auto workers may well be a scruffy, headstrong and unattractive group, but are they responsible for the low productivity of the American auto industry? Not so, say the managers of Volvo and Volkswagen. In public interviews, executives of these and other foreign auto firms have claimed that American auto workers are the most productive and conscientious in the world. (No doubt part of this enthusiasm for American workers is self-serving: Volvo and Volkswagen will soon be producing cars in the United States and naturally want good relations with the UAW. Still, if American auto workers were as bad as they are said to be by the Big Three, it is unlikely that the foreign auto makers would choose to start production here.) Critics point out that even the once substantial differences in salary between American auto workers and their peers in Sweden, Japan, and Germany have narrowed to the point that this gap can no longer account for the failure of American cars to be competitive in world markets. Even if all the costs due to absenteeism, turnover, sabotage, mistakes, and days lost through wildcat strikes were miraculously eliminated, one would be hard pressed to demonstrate that the American auto industry would be substantially more competitive.

The problem of low productivity lies more with management than with workers. The American auto industry has never admitted to itself that it is besieged by competitors, consumers, conservationists, and the Congress primarily because it is producing unsafe, polluting, gas-guzzling, and poorly designed vehicles. The managers in Detroit—representative of a whole breed of American executives—were reared during the Depression and have evolved a managerial ethos that stresses authority, conformity, security, and distrust of change and innovation. None of these cultural traits appears appropriate for meeting the social and economic challenges of a turbulent and competitive world. Within just a couple of years, the managers of General Motors (1) drove John De Lorien from their ranks because he was an innovator and entrepreneur and not "an organization man," (2) rejected the economy compact car until the eleventh hour, (3) invested heavily in the energy-prodigal Wankel engine, and (4) built the "revolutionary" new plant at Lordstown. Such managerial myopia has been rampant in Detroit for some twenty-five years. For example, Ford's erstwhile chairman, Ernest Breech, was offered the Volkswagen plant in Wolfsberg as a spoils of World War II. In turning down the offer, Breech is reported to have said that it "was not worth a damn." The auto industry may once have been the stomping grounds of Henry Ford and Alfred Sloan, but today a manager with vision is as rare in Detroit as a ring-tailed lemur.

The outdated managerial ethos in the auto industry prevents Detroit from realizing the full productive potential of its work force. For example, it is clear that the success and legitimacy of a manager rest with his subordinates' perceptions of him. The difference between legitimate authority and authoritarianism is crucial in this regard. Legitimate authority depends on a recognition by subordinates of the leader's greater expertise, skill, intelligence, charisma, or ability. If the leader cannot call on any of these sources of legitimacy (for example, if he does not know more about his subordinates' jobs than they do), he must rely on force or manipulation to defend his position—a stance that is decreasingly acceptable to a well-educated work force.

Young workers are no longer willing to believe that the people who are managing from two floors away know more about their jobs than they do. At Lordstown workers have often publicly complained of incompetent juggling of work processes by confused and pressured managers. Such instances of mismanagement at GM are embarrassingly numerous. For example, the Assembly Division has a system of competitive-performance ranking among its production units which, instead of providing positive incentives for efficiency, generates costly "crisis management" practices among those managers who find themselves ranked low in the comparative standings. Although there might be good reasons for some units' not faring so well as others (some units may have older physical plants, smaller budgets, or shortages of materials, for instance), the GM system of negative incentives inappropriately encourages the losers in the sweepstakes to attempt to compensate by such poor practices as quality-cutting, pushing machines beyond the time when they are due for maintenance, and increasing the amount of compulsory overtime for workers. Significantly, UAW vice-president Irving Bluestone (1972) reports that these managers often try to rise in the standings through introducing authoritarian practices designed to squeeze the last ounce of effort from workers. Such attempts invariably backfire, because they lead to retaliatory sabotage, strikes, and work restriction.

GM's management has a perverse knack for adamantly sticking with a method or procedure when its effects are demonstrably negative. For example, for more than forty years GM has clung to a pricing structure for its autos that is profitable *only* in an expanding economy. During recessions, the company is hog-tied by this policy and cannot respond to decreasing demand. Since prices cannot be lowered in response to market pressures, inventories grow, unemployment skyrockets, and the company runs dangerously in the red. The workers, who are aware of management's inability to cope with the vicissitudes of a free market, might be forgiven for questioning the competence of their employers.

The simple fact is that GM has become a bureaucracy, not unlike the bureaucracies of Washington with their built-in disregard for quality and efficiency. Management becomes an end in itself in such an environment. In the publicly held corporate giants of America, the loyalty of managers is not to workers, not to society, but to themselves—their status, their benefits, and their perquisites. And they are more concerned about others' working hard than they are about their own productivity. Ivar Berg (1974, p. 34) concludes that there is a "professional-executive class avowedly and conspicuously underworked" in this country. As partial evidence he cites a Gallup Poll in which 57 percent of a cross-section of Americans admitted that "they could produce more each day if they tried." Significantly, among businessmen the figure was seventy percent.

Moreover, when managers are openly disinterested in making a profit, working hard, and being innovative—as, unfortunately, the managers in our private bureaucracies occasionally are when they needlessly buy executive jets, disregard workers' suggestions for improving procedures, or fail to invest in new technologies—their legitimacy and the legitimacy of their organizations are called into question by those whom the managers should be motivating through example. As Berg sees it, what is wrong with the work ethic in America is that underworked executives with clear records of mismanagement have failed to inspire blue-collar and clerical workers. Because managers are often seen as illegitimate authorities, their productivity in their most important function—getting other people to work—is low.

This problem is compounded today by a growing awareness among workers of their role as consumers. At Lordstown, workers were actually disciplined for undertaking quality-control procedures during the time when all the stops were out on the line to produce cars as fast as they could be turned out. When employers are thus indifferent to the quality of goods they produce, or even push shoddy goods, the moral authority of their positions as leaders is undercut in the eyes of the workers.

An alternative to authoritarianism in the plant, of course, is worker participation in decision making. But instead of joining with workers in an effort to find better ways to accomplish tasks, managers at GM and most other large organizations try to impose theoretically sound systems on workers. The workers, rather uninterested in theory, view such systems as merely being arbitrary. In interviews conducted for the *Work in America* study, the most frequent complaint of workers was that when they tried to suggest better methods for organizing their tasks, their employers invariably responded with indifference, disdain, or contempt. Finally, these workers gave up trying. They began to make the minimum possible commitment to their jobs that would still ensure a paycheck at the end of the week. The literature of organizational behavior is rich with cases of managers who insist on neat, orderly, "scientific" work methods, even at the expense of the higher productivity that might result from looser, more informal methods— like production-oriented variations on "doubling" that could be negotiated with workers. Apparently, the fear of change and of losing authority and status prevents many managers from taking advantage of the full resources that workers offer. But fish gotta swim, birds gotta fly, and managers gotta manage. The result of such outmoded authoritarianism is conflict, which is inevitably resolved in an unproductive way: the manager gets a warm feeling from asserting that he is the boss, but the workers retreat into work restriction.

Is Job Enrichment the Answer?

Many managers have started to realize that such problems exist on the shop floor and have turned to job enrichment as a solution. At GM, for example, more than a hundred social scientists were at one time working on a dozen or more job-enrichment experiments. In nine out of ten cases, the enrichers were either rotating workers among jobs or enlarging their jobs to include more parts of a total task. These are sound and truly scientific management practices, as well as being appealing to many workers. The unfortunate part is that these and similar efforts have been sold to top management as a means for improving productivity, and the record of job enrichment in increasing productivity is mixed. Workers (and even their first-line supervisors) often have little control over the factors that lead to high productivity. It is companywide decisions relating to planning, marketing, finance, and production that determine the productivity of an organization, and workers have some influence on only the last of these factors. And in many instances, technology is what determines the pace of production. For example, the line at Lordstown moves at the same steady pace regardless of whether or not workers are motivated. Only in the extreme case when workers strike and stop the line altogether do they have any direct influence over productivity in an auto assembly plant.

Yet despite these limitations, most job-enrichment efforts, like industrial engineering efforts, aim to increase productivity *directly* by getting workers to labor harder. Instead, they should recognize that workers affect productivity more through *indirect* means, by working more cooperatively, intelligently, and committedly. For example, when workers participate in decision making, they often can find new and more productive work methods. Even if they don't find these themselves, when they are engaged in the decision-making process they will be more likely to go along with management-initiated changes. In all cases, turnover, absenteeism, tardiness, and conflict can be reduced through participation. But these items are seldom disaggregated or identified in the usual economic and industrial-engineering measures of productivity.

Consequently, the measures of productivity (for example, "output per manhour") that are most often used to evaluate job-enrichment efforts are inappropriate. They lead managers to attempt to maximize the sweat and muscle power of workers and to ignore the harder to assess (but potentially more important) indirect contributions of human brainpower and the spirit of worker commitment and cooperation. Thus, instead of creating a participative climate in which these human resources can be most effectively utilized, managers take the easier and less threatening road of using job enrichment as a tool to get workers to labor harder. It is little wonder, then, that job enrichment has so often failed to meet the productivity expectations of management and the satisfaction expectations of workers.

I am grateful to my colleague Larry Greiner for drawing my attention away from the shop floor and toward the executive suite in analyzing productivity in a firm. Greiner has examined this issue within many major U.S. corporations and concluded that if productivity is the goal of an organization, then reform should start at the end of the organization where productivity can be most directly affected—at the top. The tone and style of an organization are inevitably set by top management, and it is these cultural intangibles that ultimately influence whether the company will grow, innovate, and succeed. But because these essentials are hard to identify and to change, job enrichment has often been an attractive alternative to many managers. It provides a simple formula, deals with things that can be easily manipulated, and leaves unaffected those really important factors that managers might find painful to change.

Indeed, many managers have apparently used job enrichment as a salve for their consciences and as a palliative for workers in lieu of real reform. Like GM, almost every major firm in the United States has undertaken at least one token job-enrichment experiment during the past three or four years. Managers point to these in defense whenever they are accused of not being change-oriented or dynamic. Although some of these efforts have improved performance in departments with the worst records of discontent, absenteeism, turnover, and product quality, few managers have tried to spread these changes throughout their firms. When skeptics say the experiments were actually showcases, managers respond that the efforts were serious, but that they did not produce the improvements in productivity needed to warrant their wide-scale implementation.

Managers probably deserve to be let off the hook on this issue. After all, it was we, the social scientists, who sold them job enrichment solely as a tool to increase productivity. Now, with the economy gone sour, some managers feel they have every justification in the world to abandon programs that don't pay off, whether the program is a new computer center or job enrichment.

The extreme advocates of job enrichment said that money, security, and all those nasty things no longer mattered very much to workers—what counted was "the job itself." If workers were given interestng tasks, they would work harder. The recession proved them wrong. Trying to find the lotus in the mud, we might say that the recession had at least one beneficial aspect if it disabused the job-enrichment people of the naive notion that money and security also are not important to workers.

The reaction of some managers to the new economic realities has been extremely harsh. For example, Ford, GM, and Chrysler had letters of agreement with the UAW to jointly explore ways to improve the quality of working life. According to one UAW official, Ford and Chrysler had "diplomatically ignored" the letters before the recession, but once the economy slumped, even the diplomacy was off. GM's joint work-quality committee with the union is still technically in existence, but UAW officials tell me that the recession set the program back several years.

Beyond Job Enrichment

There is a shame in this. The quality of working life is a just and decent cause. It is unfortunate that it might not get a fair test in some companies because a few overexuberant social scientists misrepresented what that cause meant to correct and what it promised to do. Although job enrichment may improve productivity as a result of workers' working more intelligently, it should really be thought of as a responsibility that employers have to workers and to society. Just as industry befouls our air and water, the nature of much work in our society is a kind of human pollution. Poor working conditions are every bit as much "externalities" as air and water pollution. There are high social and medical costs being generated in the workplace that are not being borne by employers. These costs include not only occupational injuries and diseases such as silicosis, but heart attacks due to stress and mental problems ranging from nervousness to drug and alcohol abuse.

The *Work in America* report documents these costs in great detail and further shows how conditions of employment are directly and indirectly related to the lack of participation of many workers in family, community, and political activities. For example, workers in soul-destroying jobs are often unable to compensate for these with recreational activities and are unable to muster the self-confidence needed to take part in adult education, politics, or even the PTA. Traditionally, employers have viewed workers as "free goods," much like air and water; they have felt it was their right to utilize workers for their productive ends and, when finished, to return them permanently damaged to family and community.

Today, many employers are beginning to recognize that they benefit from the resources of society, both human and natural, and that they have a responsibility to return these in a healthy condition to the commonwealth. Many have listened to Peter Drucker, who has counseled that although it is not enough for businesses to do well and it is unrealistic to expect them to do good, society can require them to do no harm. Robert L. Kahn, director of the Institute of Survey Research at the University of Michigan, has stated the issue as a bold challenge to unions and management: "Managements have accepted too long . . . the assumption that every increment of fractionation in a job represents a potential increment of production. Unions have assumed too long that they could prevent workers from being exposed to unreasonable hazards or physical strains but not from being bored to death. And the larger society has assumed too long that there was no such thing as sociopsychological pollution—that the effects of monotonous or meaningless jobs were sloughed off as the workers went through the plant gates to home and community" (1974, p. 224).

Efforts to improve the quality of working life should be intended to make work organizations places where individuals have opportunities to grow, create, and exert some mastery over their environment. These actions may also increase productivity in the bargain, but that cannot be their prime purpose. The willingness to undertake these tasks will require a sense of social responsibility on the part of unions as well as employers. Although such a change in attitude is a great deal to expect, in the years since Lordstown brought the issue to national attention a small number of companies and unions have begun to work seriously on improving working life, continuing their efforts even when the recession offered them an easy way out of their commitment.

Important workplace experiments are under way in both Europe and America. These range from simple flextime (workers choose their own working hours) to the revolutionary notion of full equity sharing (the stock of an enterprise is cooperatively owned by the workers). Although each on-the-job experiment from the simple to the radical has been shown to have its unique limitations, almost all of these workplace changes directly or indirectly ameliorate some problems of underemployment. There is now ample evidence that jobs can be altered to engage the "unemployed self" of many workers. In particular, routine assembly-line and continuous-process tasks have been redesigned to give workers more autonomy, challenge, and participation in decision making.

The most successful of these programs have involved a total reconception of work systems. Here, not only are jobs more interesting, but responsibility and authority over their own tasks are delegated to workers. Characteristically, workers in such programs are divided into self-managing teams that decide how to divide their own labor, when they will work, what methods they will use, who will work with them, and how they will undertake quality control. The nature of supervision is also changed, as is the form of compensation (hourly wages usually give way to salaries, profit sharing, or some other equitable system compatible with the new work environment). General Foods, Procter and Gamble, Volvo, and Saab have pioneered in such total redesign efforts, and the Mead Corporation (the paper company) has followed their lead with a new mill that is the first American workplace whose machinery is specifically adapted to human needs. Although there are probably no more than a half-dozen such total design experiments in operation in the United States today, since 1975 two such programs have been made available to auto workers. As might be expected, these UAW-supported experiments are not going on in Chrysler, GM, Ford, or American Motors plants. It would be counter-cultural for these U.S. companies to break so abruptly with tradition.

In this regard, it is significant that certain characteristics of firms tend to be highly correlated. That is, firms that are (a) highly innovative in their business practices are frequently also (b) active in attempting to provide humane and interesting work for their employees, and (c) concerned with other social responsibilities (such as controlling pollution and hiring minorities). Can these correlations be mere coincidence? The Bank of America and Xerox are corporate examples. There is another large category of such firms in which ownership is either entrepreneurial or controlled by a single family (such as Polaroid, Levi Strauss, and Cummins Engine).

It is not surprising, then, that one of the UAW's most far-reaching efforts to improve the quality of working life is in an auto-accessory plant owned by Sidney Harman, a successful entrepreneur who has long been a public advocate of the social responsibilities of business. At the Harman International plant in Bolivar, Tennessee, the company and the union are working with social scientist Michael Maccoby (1975) to find ways to improve working conditions for workers who make mirrors and other auto accessories. Representatives of all the parties involved, including the workers, recently traveled to Sweden to see what they might bring back to their plant from the pacesetters in industrial democracy. After they returned to Tennessee, about sixty jobs at Bolivar were altered and rotated—in ways suggested by the workers—and the increased productivity that resulted was shared with the workers by giving them more time away from work. As workers have gained more experience and confidence they have begun to suggest ways to redesign other jobs in the plant and have invented imaginative new ways to share in cost savings that have resulted from the changes they have either initiated or supported. Although still in its infancy, the experiment at Bolivar is significant because it is the first attempt to totally redesign the work environment in a unionized and existing facility.

The UAW's second experiment is more typical of job redesign efforts. This is a joint project with Rockwell International, which recently purchased a plant in Battle Creek, Michigan, where it plans to produce components for off-highway construction vehicles. The company has announced that it is working with the union to design a system that will include work teams who will be free to divide tasks and assignments among themselves; worker responsibility for setting production standards; and ongoing training to prepare workers for even wider responsibilities.

Although the potential of job redesign has just begun to be tapped, it will probably never turn out to be a complete antidote for underemployment. Task redesign experts are starting to find, for example, that there is not much one can do to make cleaning toilets interesting to someone with an I.Q. of 130, no matter how much autonomy he or she is given. Many jobs simply cannot be reconstructed to be satisfying for some people. Thus, job redesign is an appropriate but insufficient response to the problems of underemployment.

Wrap Up

In summary, the complex lessons of Lordstown defy easy generalization. First, bored workers did not strike for enriched jobs. Rather, production broke down as a result of mismanagement. Second, although the workers were not specifically demanding more interesting jobs, they and society would benefit from improvements in their working conditions. (And the "doubling" activities of the workers is evidence that they are willing to experiment with job redesign.) Third, since workers are not directly responsible for the low productivity of the auto industry, changes in their working conditions cannot be expected to greatly affect productivity. To increase productivity, a change in top-management philosophy and behavior is needed, especially as this relates to the way human resources are valued and utilized.

Unfortunately, it is unrealistic to expect much innovation from the Big Three auto makers. Even experiments like the one at the Rockwell International plant are too threatening to Detroit's ritualistic and ponderous management practices. Yet the auto industry was unwittingly the catalyst for change in other organizations. At Lordstown, GM's industrial engineers brought the issue of the quality of working life into sharp focus for countless workers, managers, and union officials who previously had only a vague uneasiness about the direction in which our industrial system was headed. If Lordstown was the future, then few people wanted a part of it. Thus, even if Lordstown itself has not changed greatly in the past four years, as a symbol it has been a significant factor in creating a climate conducive to change elsewhere.

Although these experiments do not yet constitute a "movement," the growing problems of underemployment that underlie the Lordstown situation and other aspects of work in America will force most employers to redesign jobs and to involve workers in participative decision making in the future. Paradoxically, these attempts to deal with underemployment are likely to create further dissonance between the institutions of education and work. Whereas employers are starting to restructure jobs to make use of the higher levels of worker education, schools are shifting their focus to prepare youth for the narrow, specialized, inflexible tasks and authoritarian environment that employers are beginning to change. The next section reviews the ambivalent but long-lasting marriage of education and work.

6

Problems of Work and Aims of Career Education

In this period of unbridled cynicism and unremitting skepticism—an age in which even the once-sacred institution of motherhood is subject to organized opposition—it is somewhat reassuring to find an idea that nearly everyone favors. While theorists, administrators, parents, and teachers experience forces of dispersion, segmentation, and divergence on issues ranging from open classrooms to busing, the world of career education remains, by and large, more one of consensus than dissensus. All parties seem to agree: unemployment and underemployment can be treated by emphasizing career education in the schools.

There are two probable explanations for this relative harmony. First, career education may be an idea whose time has come. If such is the case, educators need only stand back and let the golden age sweep in. The alternative explanation is much less charitable, but probably more realistic: no one is opposed to career education because no one really knows what it is. As if the scenario were written by Lewis Carroll, each educator may have defined career education to mean exactly that in which he or she believes, and consequently everyone is for it.

There is some evidence that we are in an educational wonderland—that career education is a slogan in search of substance. In attempting to sharpen its definition, the U.S. Office of Education recently polled leading educators and found widespread support of the career concept. The educators were asked to indicate on a list of more than one hundred ideas, programs, and policies the ones they thought should be included in the career concept. On a checklist that ran the gamut from greater concentration on the three Rs to greater concentration on industrial training, almost all of the respondents checked almost all of the items for inclusion (Hoyt, 1974).

But it is not the contradictory nature of the responses that is informative—inconsistency is, after all, a hallmark of America's pragmatic educational philosophy—rather, it is their consistency that elicits awe. Apparently, career education is all things to all people. Logically, this means that the concept is either everything— that is, synonymous with education and therefore redundant—or it is nothing. If educators believe that career education can or should be something, they must begin clarifying its aims and purposes. Without such a basic clarification, there is likely to be drift and confusion in occupational programs in the nation's schools and colleges, and career educators cannot expect to effectively serve the youth of America. Most alarmingly, the lack of a distinct idea of what career education is or should be has allowed the movement in many states to be captured by traditional vocational educators, thus losing the opportunity for a meaningful reform of the education/work relationship and exacerbating the problem of underemployment.

A Confusion of Goals

Confused objectives are not peculiar to career education. Contemporary criticisms of society are filled with an urgent leitmotiv: institutions are not solving the pressing problems of the day. At least part of the ineffectiveness of schools, government agencies, and private and nonprofit organizations stems from fuzzy planning. Failures to identify issues, set goals, and establish adequate, appropriate performance criteria for programs often lead to actions that are unhelpful at best and counterproductive at worst. I am reminded of a cartoon depicting a king on the balcony of a castle addressing his ragged and impoverished subjects assembled in the courtyard below. The caption reads: "My advisors inform me that the problem in our realm is that the population is undereducated. In response to this problem, I hereby grant to each of you the degree of Bachelor of Science."

Such zany policy making is a familiar story. The confusion of aims and means leads to regulatory agencies that do not regulate but protect the interests of industry; to progressive income tax laws that promote further income inequality; to racial integration schemes that lead to segregation; and to defense policies that encourage wars. The last half of the twentieth century seems to be characterized by institutions that lose sight of the problems they were created to address. Without a clear notion of organizational goals, management becomes deucedly difficult: if one does not know where one is going, one is hardly likely to prepare an effective plan for getting there. And without a plan, day-to-day programs and processes take on an inconsistent, almost arbitrary, nature. This result is not simply a measure of incompetent leadership—as we are often too quick to assume—it is more accurately a reflection of the size and scope of modern institutions, of the complex problems they face, and of the competing constituencies they serve. Although these factors explain, they do not excuse the performance of large and growing institutions. As difficult as the tasks of modern management may be, they are not impossible, and improvement in the effectiveness of our nation's institutions can be legitimately expected by the publics they serve.

Peter Drucker (1974) argues convincingly that the source of much misdirection in large organizations is a failure at the top to identify the objectives of the enterprise. As he sees it, the most important question for the chief executive to ask is, "What business are we in?" He believes that the answer to this question is seldom obvious and that most business leaders cannot arrive at a meaningful response. Drucker tells how Theodore Vail, an early president of A.T. and T., answered "service" and not "communications," and thus spared his organization the fate of nationalization, which overcame similar "natural" monopolies in Europe at the time. Vail saw that a well-served, satisfied American public would be unlikely to demand nationalization of telephones.

We might work through Drucker's little exercise to see whether it is helpful in defining the role of education in the world of work. To discover the business of career education we might begin by identifying the problems in the world of work to which career education might be an answer. Of the dozens of work-related problems, two seem of paramount importance to educators: the quantity and quality of jobs. For simplicity of argument, we might aggregate these complex issues under the headings of unemployment and underemployment. Let us now analyze the extent to which the stated aims of career education are appropriate policy fulcrums for these problems.

Although there is little agreement about the purposes of career education, four broad categories appear with enough frequency in the literature to warrant inclusion in our analysis. These objectives are:

1. To provide skills.

2. To change attitudes.

3. To provide information.

4. To provide work experience.

The Provision of Skills

It seems rather widely accepted that skills training will play at least some part in career education. For example, Sidney Marland, the former U.S. Commissioner of Education who spearheaded the recent promotion of career education by saying that "all education should be geared to the world of work," writes that "All education is Career Education, or should be. And all our efforts as educators must be bent on preparing students either to become properly, usefully employed immediately upon graduation from high school or to go on to further formal education" (Grede, 1975, p. 117). The Superintendent of Public Instruction in California,

Wilson Riles, recently announced the state's commitment to career education with the pledge that every high school graduate will have a marketable skill upon graduation. And Marland's successor as Commissioner of Education, Terell Bell, would extend this pledge to the liberal arts colleges: "I feel that the college that devotes itself totally and unequivocally to the liberal arts today is just kidding itself. Today we must realize that it is our duty to provide our students also with salable skills."

Although not all career educators favor specific skill training in the schools, enough do to have convinced the U.S. Congress to subsume career education in a new vocational education act that will permit the financing of the kinds of programs that Messieurs Marland, Riles, and Bell seem to advocate. But before hundreds of millions of dollars are spent on realizing the aim that all high school (and college) students should graduate with a marketable skill, it might be worth asking *why* they should. What are the assumptions underlying the increasingly popular notion that the schools are the proper locus for specific vocational training?

First assumption: the problem underlying teenage unemployment is a shortage of skills. Since the early 1960s, between 20 percent and 25 percent of all unemployed workers in America have been teenagers (Wolfbein, 1975, p. *ix*). Among black teenagers, a 40 percent rate of unemployment has not been uncommon in some areas. Unemployment is a source of considerable frustration for most youth and a source of misery for the most disadvantaged, particularly for those supporting a family. For all youth, unemployment is clearly an undesirable introduction to the world of work. It is as if society introduced idealistic and impressionable youth to the glories of the economic system with a tour of its slums and dumps. Because of unemployment's singular influence on the attitudes and life chances of youth, it is natural to assume that the efforts of vocational/career education should be directed toward its eradication.

But let us be careful not to slip too easily into this obvious conclusion. There are many causes of teenage unemployment. Most clearly, demographics has played a role: the coming of age of the postwar babies has taxed the economy's ability to create enough new jobs. And during the same period, millions of middle-aged women have entered the work force, often taking jobs at the expense of teenagers. Union restrictions and minimum wage laws have also limited the opportunities for meaningful employment, as have the attitudes of some employers that "kids have no place in the grown-up world of work."

Not all the effects of teenage unemployment are signs of a failure of the economic system. Young people have more options today than ever before; hence, they take more time in their career searches, often exploring and rejecting a series of options after rather brief tests. The higher incomes of parents and the ready availability of welfare and unemployment insurance have taken much of the risk out of unemployment, making it easier for youth to refuse jobs and to quit ones that are not fully acceptable. For example, a high percentage of teenage unemployment is due to the fact that many teenagers will accept only part-time or part-year jobs. And perhaps most important, the new values of youth demand more leisure time. It is not uncommon for unmarried young men and women, many as old as thirty, to work and save for six months and then to take six months off on a holiday supplemented by welfare or unemployment benefits. Since most entry-level jobs offer little in the way of upward career mobility, challenge, or responsibility, job attachment has grown rather weak among the under-thirty generation. Thus, there are many reasons for teenage unemployment, and not all of them are negative—at least not in the eyes of America's restless middle-class youth. Thus unemployment, as important, visible, and measurable as it is, may not be the primary problem that career education can or should address.

In short, many causes of teenage unemployment are beyond the influence of education. Yet parents still complain to legislators that their children are unemployed as a result of inadequate preparation in the schools for the world of work. They point out that students with specific vocational skills are often hired before those who have not had vocational training in high school. They then argue that vocational training should be spread, giving to all the benefits that are now received only by a fortunate few. But this argument contains the logical fallacy of aggregation; that is, it concludes that something that works for a few will work for all. Certainly, vocational training affects the relative position of a young person in the job queue. If there are ten people in line for one semi-skilled machine operator's position, the one with the high school vocational certificate will usually go to the head of the line if the other nine applicants have no vocational training. But giving a certificate to the nine other young people will not greatly enhance their chances, because it will not affect the length of the queue. There will still only be one job available. History shows that teenage unemployment rates are not correlated with the skill attainment of youth. During World War II, for example, teenage unemployment disappeared when employers quickly and easily trained unskilled youth in order to overcome the existing labor shortage (MacMichael, 1974b). It would seem, then, that the problem of teenage unemployment is a shortage of jobs, not a shortage of skills.

Although the provision of skills does affect the relative position of young people in the queue for entry-level jobs, it is not clear that the public interest is served by launching a major and expensive training effort to give some young people a competitive advantage over others. In fact, in some ways vocational education is the least justifiable form of public education. The liberal might well question the rationale behind public school expenditures for a program that is geared completely to the private goal of securing a well-paying job. Milton Friedman (1962) argues that public education is justifiable only in so far as there are public benefits. These include the preparation of the citizenry for their roles as voters and leaders in the political system, but what are the public benefits of helping one individual make more money than another? The same argument can, and should, be applied to public support for professional education in such high-paying fields as law, medicine, and dentistry.*

---

*Since I sound like an economist here, let me expand on the reasoning behind this assertion. Clearly, these professionals often provide necessary services which might constitute "public benefits" warranting public expenditures. But these expenditures would be warranted only under the enormous assumption that the services would not be forthcoming if the state did not provide free professional education. For example, one would have to assume that there would be a shortage of doctors or lawyers in California if the state university system charged full tuition at its numerous law and medical schools. As long as there were scholarship provisions for the disadvantaged, I cannot see any reason why medical, law, and business students should not be forced to go to a bank to borrow tuition and living expenses against their incredibly high future incomes. Tuition-free professional education is simply welfare for the rich and soon-to-be-rich.

This argument has been dismissed by vocational educators with the assertion that unskilled youth are virtually unemployable in today's world of advanced technology, and to leave them without a specific skill is to abandon them to a lifetime of unemployment.

Second assumption: technological change is creating a labor market with increasingly high skill demands. This view is derived from the so-called human-capital approach to manpower planning. Economists argue this position in the following manner: (1) technology in industry is changing rapidly; (2) new technology requires more highly specialized and skilled workers; (3) education and training is the source of this new breed of worker; (4) if education provides the economy with the proper mix of skilled workers, the economy will prosper and grow; and (5) through better planning, future job needs can be identified in advance and workers can be trained to fill these slots. These statements were convincing to legislators during the economic boom years of the 1950s and 1960s, and the resulting enormous public investments in education were justified as investments in the gross national product. The beauty of this argument, and every other elegant economic theory, is that it is accurate by definition *if* one accepts its basic assumptions.

Today, however, many observers are questioning the basic assumptions of the human capitalists, for the following reasons:

(1) Technological change does not appear to be terribly rapid in the United States at this time.

(2) Most American workers are engaged in providing services, anyway, and don't work with machines. It is true that there is demand for highly skilled people—professional and technical workers—but these are people with advanced university training that is totally unrelated to high school or even undergraduate college vocational training.

(3) With the exception of those with professional or technical college degrees, most workers learn their skills on the job, not in schools. And this training can be given in a relatively short period of time.

(4) Upgrading the education of the work force no longer seems to increase the G.N.P. Perhaps we have reached the point

of diminishing returns in this regard and now have begun to actually lower productivity through putting educated workers in jobs they find frustrating.

(5) Better manpower planning is all but impossible in a free society with a free market. Specific labor market forecasts by industry, job, or region are difficult to make more than a year in advance. Short of following the Soviet model of authoritarian manpower planning, we can only make marginal improvements in our forecasts.

For these reasons, the human-capital approach (and, interestingly, the Soviets are more capitalist than the capitalists in this regard) is under increasing attack from humanists. They feel that the concept inverts proper ends and means. In the human-capital approach, machines are the given, and humans are the flexible factor in production who must be arranged to meet the needs of technology. Contrariwise, the humanists start with the quantity and quality of workers as the given, believing that technology should be adjusted to fully employ the work force.

It should not be inferred that this schism is of recent origin. In the early part of this century, George Herbert Mead, Owen Lovejoy, and other humanists attacked the willingness of vocational educators to allow their goals to be set by industrialists. According to Arthur Wirth (in press, p. 11), Lovejoy criticized the Captains of Industry who said to the receptive vocationalists, "Here are the jobs: what kind of children have you to offer?" Lovejoy said the educators should respond, "Here are your children: what kind of industry have you to offer?"

Third assumption: vocational education works. Some career vocational educators will admit that these first two assumptions are faulty, yet defend their program on the practical grounds that it works. According to the record, they argue, vocationally educated youth have marketable skills that are in demand, and their training allows them ready access to good, well-paying jobs. Recently, a number of scholars who are independent of funding from the vocational establishment have reviewed the evidence and found that the achievement of vocationally trained students is quite different. These scholars, including Beatrice Reubens (1974b), John Grasso (1975), Wellford Wilms (1974), and David Rogers

(1973), have found that the employment record of vocational graduates in terms of income, job status, turnover, upward mobility, job satisfaction, and unemployment is initially not much better than that of students in liberal programs and is much worse in the long run. Although vocationally trained students fare better than those who follow the dumping-ground "general curriculum" for noncollege-bound youth, that finding is hardly a ringing endorsement of vocationalism. Given a choice between a cold and pneumonia, the timid and unimaginative will take the cold; the bold and perspicacious will insist on a third option.

The record of vocational education was so weak that in the late 1960s major efforts were made to improve it. These efforts were indeed successful, but in a curious way. Vocational educators "upgraded" their enrollments by substituting downwardly mobile counter-culture and other middle-class youth who wanted to "work with their hands" for the disadvantaged youth for whom the expensive training programs were originally intended.

Vocational programs at the college level have a better record than those in the high schools, but even here there is a basis for considerable criticism. For example, in the San Francisco Bay area, Wilms studied the effectiveness of vocational training in community colleges and proprietary schools and found such training not vastly superior to high school vocational education. He found that only 16 percent of graduates who pursued semiprofessional or technical courses ever got jobs at that level. And eight out of ten graduates who succeeded in landing low-level clerical or service jobs barely earned the federal minimum wage. Wilms concluded that postsecondary vocational education, like its high school counterpart, "maintains class and income inequalities rather than overcomes them." Significantly, then, vocational programs are not compensatory. If they are not compensatory, what is the rationale for their existence?

That vocational education "works" seems also to be belied by some observations that several employers have made to me in discussing the value of specific skills training in the schools:

● Most entry-level jobs do not require specific skills. Since most jobs can be learned on the job in a matter of a couple of weeks, many employers would prefer to do the training themselves. The skills employers actually look for—the ability to read, write, compute, learn, and interact cooperatively with others—are not successfully imparted to vocational graduates.

• Work in vocational shops is make work; it lacks the pace and discipline of real work. Work is apparently like sex in this regard—it cannot be satisfactorily simulated.

• Vocationally trained workers have poor records in terms of receiving retraining opportunities on the job and participating in continuing education programs in schools. Because these individuals have not learned how to learn, or learned the theory behind vocational practices, there is little base for employers to build on with continuing training. Thus, high school training is often the terminal educational experience for many vocational graduates.

• Vocational graduates are often trained for jobs that don't exist. Because vocational programs depend on highly unreliable forecasts of labor demand (see Chapter Three), they frequently mistrain youth by giving them obsolete or unneeded skills.

Nevertheless, vocationalists argue, there is *demand* for vocationally trained youth.

Fourth assumption: employers demand school graduates with specific skills. Many vocationalists offer the following kind of argument in defense of their programs: "Employers tell us that they have unfilled jobs and that there is a shortage of people with the requisite skills to fill them. Wouldn't we be doing a disservice to youth not to train them for these jobs?"

There is little doubt that *some* employers feel they cannot find qualified workers to do certain tasks. Particularly in heavy industry, small firms, and declining industries, employers are often heard to complain of a shortage of skilled workers. But when one visits these factories, one might be perplexed by the employer's claims, because the unfilled jobs seem relatively simple to perform. To the casual observer, it would seem that a person with a 70 I.Q. could learn to do such tasks with a few hours of instruction and a week or two of practice. I offer myself here as an example of the least common denominator. I am totally unmechanical. I am all thumbs and can barely change a light bulb. Still, I have suggested to many employers that I could do most of the jobs for which they claimed there is a shortage of trained labor coming out of the high schools. The managers usually laughed incredulously at my suggestion: "No, you couldn't do these jobs because they require special skills that you don't have."

This is an important point to pursue. If vocationalists could only identify these missing special skills, could they not make good on the promise of Marland, Riles, and Bell to provide every young person in the schools with a marketable skill? To pursue this lead, let us move on to the second aim of career education.

The Provision of Proper Work Attitudes

I have pressed employers further on the subject of the shortage of trained workers. What are these missing skills? Are American youth all hopeless *klutzes* like me? Exasperated with my inability to understand what was to them a very obvious and simple situation, at least a couple of employers have reduced the problem to language I could understand: "You must see that it takes a certain skill to stand at these machines for eight hours a day, five days a week, fifty weeks a year, and for, perhaps, thirty or forty years. Most young people try it for a couple of weeks, then they get fed up and quit. The schools do not prepare young people with the skills needed to do an honest day's labor on jobs like these. The kids expect fun and games. They don't have realistic attitudes about work."

Apparently, many employers mean something quite special when they talk about "a shortage of skills." The manual dexterity, technical virtuosity, and competence with machines that employers look for are plentiful. *What is missing is blue-collar virtues.* To many industrialists, to be "skilled" means to be willing to tolerate narrow, boring, and repetitive jobs.

Because of the American school system's commitment to mobility and equality, there is now a shortage of working-class people, individuals socialized for an environment of bureaucratic and hierarchical control and of strict discipline. Employers are correct in their observations that the schools are failing to provide enough men and women who are passive and compliant, who seek only extrinsic rewards for their labors, and who have the stamina and stoicism to cope with the work technologies and processes developed during the industrial revolution. Of course, not all work and not all employers are like this. Sophisticated firms such as IBM, Xerox, and Sears are not looking for robots to fill the jobs they offer. Unfortunately, however, the generalization is most true for the few starting-level jobs that are available to high school graduates—jobs in small, marginally profitable companies or in the relatively shrinking heavy-industry sector of the economy.

Andre Gorz and other Marxist critics go so far as to say that the purpose of technical schools cannot be skills training, because it is in the interest of firms to keep the skill demands of jobs low in order to keep salaries low and to permit rapid lay-offs and re-hirings during business cycles. Moreover, the technologies that managers choose, according to Gorz (1973), are those that permit the most control over workers. They do not choose technologies with high skill demands, because skilled workers are less inter-changeable, replaceable, and tractable. They lack the "flexibility" that is the desideratum of the industrial system. Thus, the Marxists conclude that the purpose of technical or vocational training can only be to imbue a set of attitudes, to socialize working-class youth to a world of submission and subordination. Indeed, they argue that the technical rules and procedures of the schools are designed to mirror the authoritarian social relations with which work is organized.

I think it is possible to reject the simplistic Marxist line that the educational and industrial system Gorz describes is attributable to the greed of capitalists. As far as we can tell, blue-collar life is every bit as unchallenging and authoritarian in Eastern Europe as it is in the United States. Still, we might ask whether there is not at least some truth in Gorz's argument. We must ask what it is about the vocational credential that makes it attractive to employers when (1) they are not looking for technically competent workers and (2) they must retrain almost all young hires from scratch in any event? No answer to this question, particularly not the Marxist aspect of it, is obvious. But could it be that the vocational credential signifies to managers the possession of those skills that are seen to be in such shortage—passivity, submission, and acceptance?

Class and Vocationalism. The value of Gorz's observation is that he dares to raise a common European concept that is increasingly taboo in polite discussions in America: social class. Speakers are greeted with adoration, approbation, and encomium when they engage in tasteless and graphic discussions of homosexuality, drugs, and the other prurient topics so characteristic of the age, but let the topic of social class raise its ugly head, and American audiences will begin to fidget, the ears of children will be covered, and the hiss of disapproval and censure will arise in the hall. Unfortunately, since the schools function as society's primary sorters, selectors, and certifiers, the subject of career education cannot be divorced from the subject of class ascription. Let me risk social censure by placing the issue of proper work attitudes in the perspective of social class antagonisms of other times and other nations.

The shortage of people with working-class virtues is not new. In the nineteenth century, during a time of high unemployment, employers complained of a shortage of skilled workers (Heilbroner, 1961, p. 45). Arkwright, for example, could not get enough workers to man his spinning throstles. So, in the humanitarian name of ending youth unemployment, he turned to young children, "their small fingers being active." In his "dark, satanic mills" he worked these children from twelve to fourteen hours a day, six or seven days a week—easing his conscience, no doubt, with the reassuring notion that he was keeping them out of trouble in the streets.

Robert Heilbroner reminds us that among managers of Arkwright's time, "the most common complaint was the ineradicable sloth of the pauper, and this was mixed with consternation at the way in which the lower orders aped their betters. Work people were actually drinking tea" (p. 45). Parallels today are not difficult to adduce. Many managers claim that poor blacks lack the attitudes and discipline to hold a job, and yet these same disadvantaged people want to drive big cars and drink expensive scotch.

To American revisionist historians of education, the problem facing industrialists is to preserve the necessary gradations between the classes, offering enough in the way of rewards to get labor from the working class, but not so much as to spoil them. These radicals argue that, in this regard, the schools struck a kind of early bargain with industrialists in America: in exchange for support for free public education, they would provide workers for foundries, mills, and, later, assembly lines (Bowles and Gintis, 1976). It has been proved by history that governments can render entire social classes docile and obedient through education. Traditionally, in Europe and America (and, today, most clearly in South Africa) second-class education for second-class citizens has lowered the expectations and self-esteem of the disadvantaged and left them willing hewers, drawers, and toilers. H. G. Wells put the case quite clearly: "The [British] Education Act of 1870 was not an Act for common universal education, it was an Act to educate the lower-classes for employment on lower-class lines, and with specially trained, inferior teachers who had no universal quality" (in Landes, 1972, pp. 72–3).

Vocational training was thus a product of the needs of nineteenth-century industrialism. As such, it is correctly viewed today as an undemocratic anachronism, a way of preserving a dual form of education—one type for "gentlemen," the other for "ruffians." Torsten Husen writes: "This dualism is a product of a society that was almost entirely ascriptive in its allocation of social status. The selection and/or transfer at an early age to academic secondary education by and large determines the subsequent occupational career, decides whether it will fall within the blue-collar or white-collar bracket. The built-in flexibility is almost nil" (1975, p. 45).

In the United States, one school of educators (following in the line of Horace Mann, Owen Lovejoy, and John Dewey) has viewed education as the great equalizer. Although this school has had its innings, on balance it has lost out to the vocationalists (represented by David Snedden and Charles Prosser). Arthur Wirth states the ascendent vocationalist position on tracking: "As Snedden saw it, scientific testing instruments combined with vocational guidance would make it possible for schools to do what Charles Eliot had suggested in 1907—differentiate children into programs according to their "probable destinies" based on heredity plus economic and social factors. The new junior high schools would perform the task of sorting students into differentiated courses with prevocational offerings in commercial subjects, industrial arts, and agricultural or household arts for those "who most incline to them or have need of them," (1976, p. 7).

Promises and Realities: Equality and Tracking. The attraction of career education, of course, is that it promises to break with the traditional schooling function of creating invidious distinctions between the classes. In the past, children who were considered incapable of completing secondary schooling were relegated to technical schools, with little prospect for social or economic advancement. Career education, in distinction, is said to be education about the world of work for all students, regardless of class. Will or can this promise be met in practice? Ideally, there is some reason to hope that a class-free form of education about work is possible. The overriding constraint is that the world of work is itself class stratified, and it is difficult to imagine a realistic curriculum that would not import this characteristic into the classroom.

On a practical level, experience indicates that career education is being taken over by vocational traditionalists at the federal and state levels. Funds allocated for reform are being funneled through traditional sources. What promises to emerge from the new career emphasis is the same old vocational programs, only better funded and given bright, shiny new names. In California, for example, career education has been captured by vocational educators who have defined career education so as to do exactly what they have been doing for decades. It is proudly claimed that the State Advisory Council on Vocational Education has issued a plan to infuse the career concept throughout all of education— thus appearing to eliminate tracking. Indeed, the Council visualizes that career education will provide socialization for the world of work for all students up to the tenth grade. (We are not told whether this socialization is to provide the working-class attitudes of submission that some managers find in such shortage; there is, at least, no sign of *tracking* through age fifteen.) Beginning in the tenth grade, however, there is to be a process of "career orientation" in which, presumably, all students begin the process of choosing their careers. In the next two years those who choose professional careers will pursue college-preparatory courses, which also have some sort of career orientation. Another group will choose technical careers and will be given pretechnical training in grades eleven and twelve in preparation for further training in junior colleges. The rest of the students will be prepared for entry-level jobs. Specialization for all will thus begin to occur in the tenth grade.

If this system sounds familiar, it is because it closely resembles the systems found in Germany, England, and other European countries. We are thus able to anticipate its consequences, because Europeans have been living with it for nearly a century. The tracking that is part of such a structure leads most often to invidious class inequalities. At the extreme, it may even pose a threat to democracy. For example, Albert Speer (1971) suggests that the Nazis' ability to hold power in Germany was strengthened by an educational system that "aimed at separatist thinking." No one was to concern himself or herself with anything outside his own narrow occupation. In this way, Speer argues, no one was able to criticize the overall goals of Hitler or the party. To this day, Germans speak of *fachidioten*—specialist idiots. It is perhaps significant that liberal education as it is known in the West (and, in particular, in Britain and the United States) is unknown in Eastern Europe.

I am not suggesting that vocational educators in the U.S. are dupes for extremist political parties, but rather that a consequence of specialized vocational training is often the inability to think critically about broad social issues. Moreover, vocational educators in America have often been too willing to succumb to majoritarian pressures. Again, let us listen to Wirth on Snedden: "On the question of which social values the teacher should advocate, Snedden said the teacher should remember that he was a public servant and as such had the obligation to teach the 'opinions and valuation of the controlling majority.' A teacher interested in minority views should either surrender them to majority opinion or leave" (In press, p. 9).

While I do not expect that vocational education will lead to the demise of democracy in America, I do worry that vocationally educated youth will not be prepared for full participation as citizens and workers in what is becoming a more participative system. For example, they are not trained to act confidently in the new democratic, team-oriented workplaces (instead, they are taught to follow directions without question). Moreover, working-class people—so many of whom are products of vocational tracking in the schools—all too often have their natural love of learning extinguished to the point where they show little interest in leisure activities in the home or schools and have their self-esteem so lowered that they fear participation in community and political affairs.

But the arguments for tracking in the United States are different from those in Europe. The problem here, we are told, is race and not class. A school administrator from San Francisco once asked me, "How are you going to teach Shakespeare to a dumb black kid? The only thing you can do for him is to teach him a skill." This is an astringent, almost shocking, statement. I choose not to think of it as racist. Rather, it represents the reality of education as seen from the perspective of, I am sure, more than one practitioner.

Never mind that no one is suggesting that all young people must or should read Shakespeare, only that they should be able to read well enough to have access to Shakespeare if they desire to read him. What is important to analyze is the argument that middle-class kids are different from (if not smarter than) working-class or minority youth, and this view not only justifies, but requires different educational programs. Indeed, to argue that all youths should have similar educations is elitist in the eyes of vocationalists because it assumes that all young people share the interests and values of the white upper middle class; moreover, it is impractical because some youth simply cannot pass muster intellectually. Again, before accepting what appears to be a hard-headed, practical conclusion, it might be worth reviewing the assumptions on which it is based. We might begin by asking about the hundreds of thousands of blue-collar workers who have I.Q.s as high as those of many doctors, lawyers, and other professionals. Perhaps they have poor jobs *not* because they are dumb or have aspirations different from those middle-class people, but because of race, sex, class, or educational discrimination that limited their occupational mobility. As Quintillian recognized nearly two thousand years ago, "Those who are dull and unteachable are as abnormal as prodigious births and monstrosities, and are but few in number."

But why is it that middle-class people *appear* smarter, or at least appear to do better in school? There is no single answer to this, as Christopher Jencks has demonstrated, but an interesting study from England sheds some light on the relationship between class, education, and occupational mobility. This study (described in Jackson and Marsden, 1966, p. 232–235) found that working-class speech patterns emphasize description, whereas middle-class speech is given to abstraction. Abstraction, of course, is closely linked with the ability to cope with new situations and to learn new things. For this reason, a primary aim of middle-class schools is to develop the ability to engage in abstract reasoning. Vocational training, in distinction, is specific and descriptive, abstraction and generalization being viewed as impractical in the lives of workers.

Could this be an instance of self-fulfilling prophecy? Working-class youngsters are seen as incapable of abstraction, hence we put them in schools where the ability to abstract is not valued, whence they graduate incapable of abstraction. Are we limiting the social mobility of youngsters by making false assumptions about their capacities? Are attitudes toward the abilities of youth based on incorrect but easy criteria—their color, sex, or social-class standing? These, again, are not questions that elicit ready answers. Nevertheless, they probably deserve a thoroughgoing examination and reexamination by those who are designing career programs.

I am not suggesting that educators should assume that all young people have equal talents—clearly, they don't. Nothing is lost to the individual or to society if a person with an I.Q. of 60 drops out of school after the tenth grade and spends the rest of his life sweeping streets. But there is a terrible waste of human resources if a bright child follows the same course as the result of a lack of opportunity—opportunity denied because of race, sex, or social-class tracking. A system that discriminates on the basis of talent is fair, and all other forms of discrimination are unjust. And since we cannot identify talent accurately in youth, justice is probably best served by eliminating all tracking.

Behavior for Success. Nevertheless, work attitudes are very important. In the final analysis, I believe, we will find that attitude is the best predictor of employment success. Unfortunately, attitude is such a nebulous yet pervasive concept that it is difficult to isolate and measure. It can be demonstrated, however, that the people who seem to do well in work are not the smartest, the most skilled, the most talented, the most ambitious, or even the most manipulative or scheming. Except in top professional jobs, and in a few crafts where highly skilled workers do their tasks in isolation from other workers, the people who get hired and promoted in most modern corporations and in the burgeoning services sector of the economy are people who are able to get along with other people. Attitude, then, would seem to be a crucial variable in occupational success. For example, young people—regardless of race, sex, or class—are not likely to remain for long in unemployment lines if they are perceived by employers as being polite, personable, friendly, and cooperative. If they are also minimally articulate and the kind of people whom peers and supervisors would like as company at lunch, they will probably find themselves on the fast track to success. Even in positions requiring skill or training, the decision to hire seems often to be based on the nebulous attitude variable. Perspective employers ask: Does this person's behavior conform to the norms of the organization? A lawyer summed up her firm's hiring criteria for me in the following way: "It is hard to tell whether one candidate is more skilled as a lawyer than another. Grades are some indication, but in any event the differences in abilities are rather marginal. Ultimately, we are checking to see whether the candidate can hold a fork."

In the final analysis, employers hire people with whom they are comfortable. Surprisingly, this seems to be the case even for such highly skilled occupations as engineering. Lester Thurow (in press) argues that a university like M.I.T. is better seen as a "charm school" than a vocational school. What separates M.I.T. grads from the masses of engineers is not their technical ability— good engineers are in plentiful supply—but their capacity to sell themselves and their ideas. Employers are searching for people who look like them, but not necessarily those who are their physical twins or share their taste in dress or go to the same church (these factors do play a role in some instances, however). More often, employers are consciously or subconsciously looking for people who share their values, attitudes, and world view. Since one spends more time with one's co-workers than with one's spouse, employers are unlikely to hire anyone whose values are openly unsympathetic to the prevailing culture of the organization. Even blue-collar positions are difficult to acquire and hold for people who are perceived as defensive, sullen, or arrogant.

Having said this, a working definition of proper work attitudes is nevertheless elusive. The attitude is what statisticians call a basket variable: it includes too many factors to be fully identified and isolated. However, some career educators are getting close to defining it, I believe, when they discuss the notion of basic career competences. This set of skills includes such things as the capacity to engage in good human relations, problem-solving and analytical skills, the ability to cope with conflict, ambiguity, and complexity, a willingness to change, to be flexible and adaptable, and the ability to communicate, to lead, and to follow. And certainly not all the eggs in the basket that is career competence have been identified.

Although educators have not discovered how best to provide these attitudes to students, it is rather certain that traditional vocational training does not provide them. Clearly, submission, passivity, and compliance are not only anachronistic in a fast-changing white-collar world, but opposed to the true spirit of education. Although a few industrialists still demand these traits, they are a dying breed in dying industries, and I believe that their overtures should be resisted by educators for the sake of preserving the long-term life chances of working-class youth. It would seem that such employers should be forced to change their processes to meet the needs of the young workers, rather than that educators should restrict the vision and expectations of youth to fit the perceived demands of an outmoded industrial order.

The provision of proper work attitudes is, undeniably, an appropriate and necessary aim of career education. The challenge is to identify *which* attitudes to provide and *how* to provide them. As I see it, career education is at a rather primitive state in the development of a response to this imposing challenge. Since this development is unlikely to be rapid, educators may be tempted to slip back into the comfortable and convenient mold of providing traditional working-class virtues. We seem to have the problem in sight yet lack the means to solve it. But because of the necessity to act, the danger is that we will act unwisely.

The Provision of Information

Economists agree that the market mechanism provides the most efficient allocation of goods, resources, and labor in a society. When the invisible hand of the market is not functioning optimally, economists become suspicious that its efforts are being cramped by (a) government intervention or (b) structural imperfections such as monopoly, uninternalized costs, or a constricted flow of the information needed for buyers and sellers to make the most rational choices. Labor-market economists are particularly concerned with unblocking information channels because workers are woefully ignorant of their options, and this lack of knowledge contributes to unemployment and underemployment. In a world of perfect information, economists posit that there would be a nearly optimal fit between people and jobs. Because people would be aware of the full range of employment opportunities available to them, unemployment would be reduced to frictional levels through the greater mobility of workers' moving into industries, occupations, and geographical regions of labor shortage and away from areas of surplus. Underemployment, too, would be greatly reduced because workers would identify the jobs with the characteristics that matched their social, psychological, and economic needs and desires.

Career educators, heavily influenced by manpower economists, have made the provision of information about work a cornerstone of their efforts. (Wolfbein, 1975) No doubt better labor-market information is a desideratum of career education, as it is of labor-market reforms in general. Nevertheless, it may be rash to assume that career education can or should make a major contribution in this area. There are several devilishly difficult issues underlying the apparently straightforward challenge of providing better information. For example, there are not ready answers to how the information should be provided to youth, when it should be provided, or at what economic *and* social costs.

The possession of information about work correlates with social-class standing: Middle-class, college-educated people have a fair knowledge of the opportunities open to them; poor, undereducated people are woefully uninformed (Parnes, 1975). This much is clear. But the lower classes also have less information than the upper classes about health, education, welfare, and other government services available to them and about such basic survival items as how to shop for bargains, what is nutritional to eat, how to avoid V.D. and pregnancies, how to file for an income-tax refund, and how to get a driver's license. Thus, the lack of essential knowledge appears to be a general problem, and not just specific to labor markets. What we need to do, then, is adjust our priorities and develop processes and programs for an entire system of providing life skills, rather than merely stress a single part that might not be the most important one for immediate survival.

Equally as fundamental, there is reason to believe that better information would not greatly reduce rates of unemployment. The search time between jobs could be reduced, thus affecting the duration of unemployment, but better information does not create jobs. To believe that "there are plenty of jobs out there going begging" requires a faith matched only by that of the cargo cultists of Melanesia who believe that, if they dress like Europeans, planes and ships will land on their islands, bringing them the technology, wealth, and power of the West. Jobs will not be magically provided by adherence to ritual or process—even adding a computer will not make the magic more efficacious. Certainly there are unfilled jobs in the economy—highly skilled slots for such professionals as actuaries, accountants, and engineers often remain open for some time, as do jobs for those who do the unskilled dirty work of the economy, such as dishwashers, janitors, and day laborers. But information does not help much with the former category, because three or four years of education are required before one could make use of the information, and jobs in the latter category go vacant not because people don't know about them, but because these are psychologically and economically uncompetitive with welfare, unemployment compensation, and standing around on a street corner chewing the fat (Liebow, 1967).

We should not confuse better information as a solution to the problem (identified in Chapter Four) of finding jobs for people that meet their individual needs and desires. The information solution incorrectly assumes that available jobs are flexible and varied enough to meet the range of worker needs. In short, better information does nothing to meet the fundamental structural causes of unemployment and underemployment.

Another problem with the information solution to manpower problems is, simply, that the future cannot be predicted. For the reasons outlined in Chapter Three, accurate long-term projections of the demand for workers broken down by specific occupation, industry, and region and of the supply of workers disaggregated according to levels of skill, training, and education are probably unattainable. We just do not know enough to accurately assess the dynamic needs of individuals or to match these with job requirements. Part of the problem is cost: literally billions of dollars would be required to measure the content of every job in the society and to put this information on a computer in a usable format.

Again, we should return to the basic question: what business is career education in? To some, the goal of providing information is to facilitate better manpower planning. Experience in Britain after the Second World War, and in the socialist states today, indicates that such planning is effective only when accompanied by restrictions on free access to education and training. The tradeoff has been rather clear: to achieve the benefit of reduced surpluses and shortages in the labor market, a nation must bear the cost of considerable infringements on individual freedom of choice.

The aims of most career educators, of course, are more modest. They wish to provide information only to help young people

• learn about their interests and abilities;

• learn about the requirements and opportunities of the full smorgasbord of jobs; and

• learn decision-making skills (that is, how to choose the right job).

As innocuous or benign as these goals may be, they, too, raise some difficult issues. First, the assumption that seems to underlie them all is that the goal of career education is to adapt people to fit work roles—a kind of 1970s variation on life-adjustment education. The second assumption is that the existing hierarchy of jobs is just and that educators should willy-nilly fit youth into the available slots. The third, related assumption is that the demands and characteristics of jobs are fixed and cannot be molded or redesigned to meet the needs of workers. Finally, there is the heroic assumption that occupational decision making can occur in an atmosphere free of class, race, sex, or other pervasive social biases. Should efforts that encourage career choice in the elementary and junior high schools be considered beneficent reforms? At the worst, they may be creating an American mutation of the British system of early tracking. At the least, early decision making runs counter to what seems to be characteristic of many of those who succeed in the fast-changing occupational milieu: the most successful individuals, in general, are those who are able to postpone specialization.

One other aspect of the information argument is worthy of note. Vocationalists argue that better information about what people do all day would reinstill respect for blue-collar workers and the dignity of manual labor. No doubt this is a laudable goal. But vocationalists seem bent on responding to the lie that blue-collar work is dumb work for dumb people with the equally audacious lie that technology and crafts are a higher order of *knowledge* than science and literature. Booker T. Washington, the most influential vocational educator in the history of our nation, once justified the vocational curriculum with the statement that "an ounce of application is worth a ton of abstraction." In the face of such views, it seems futile, even "elitist," to point out that most practical applications today are based on theoretical abstractions and not the other way around. Engineers did not first shoot a man to the moon while scientists waited to theorize post hoc why it worked.

One cannot deny that Archie Bunker stereotypes are unjustly applied to blue-collar workers, but a great deal of research has shown that the prestige or status of occupations is based almost solely on their intrinsic characteristics. That is, one cannot improve the status of street sweepers by calling them maintenance engineers or by requiring an M.A. degree to qualify for the job. One can change the status by improving the job—but that is not the interest of vocationalists.

Let us move from this emotion-charged subject to the least controversial aim of career education.

The Provision of Work Experience

Although there are more questions than answers in this area, too, there is some reason to believe that experience is the best source of labor-market information. Consequently, career educators have established another broad aim: to give young people actual work experience. This approach directly addresses the problem of youth unemployment. It also seems to ameliorate some of the problems of underemployment by helping young people to establish realistic expectations about the world of work and by permitting them to try on various work roles before settling into one for a lengthy period. To use another analogy, work experience permits young people to engage in a little comparative shopping before making a major purchase.

Erikson, Coleman, Bronfenbrenner, and other students of childhood and youth have shown that work experience between the ages of fifteen and seventeen is valuable in identity formation, in learning how to make decisions, and in breaking down the artificial barriers that segregate adolescents from adults. During this exploratory period of youth, young people examine jobs and careers in terms of their interests, abilities, values, opportunities, and the requirements of the work itself (Coleman and others, 1973, p. 103). The closer this experience is to a real-life situation, the more effective it is in bringing about a smooth transition to adulthood (Shore, 1971). Hence, work experiences are not easily simulated in the schools. Coleman and his colleagues offer an explanation for why this might be the case: "The essential difficulty of schools in handling activities other than academic learning is the position of the child or youth within the school. He is a dependent, and the school is responsible for shepherding his development. Yet, if youth is to develop in certain ways involving responsibility and decision making, then the responsibility and dependency are in the wrong place. To reorganize a school in such a way that young persons have responsibility and authority appears extremely difficult because such reorganization is incompatible with the basic custodial function of the school" (1973, p. 142).

If Coleman is right, work experience must occur outside the schools, and the value of games, simulations, and workshops is limited because the educational purpose of these techniques is different from the educational purpose of work experience. As Coleman says of placing the young in work settings: "The aim of such programs should not be primarily to 'learn a skill,' but to give experience in responsible, interdependent activity" (1973, p. 158). Viewing education as experience means that students can learn about jobs, even try jobs, without committing themselves. Indeed, among high school seniors who work, only one-third feel that their jobs lead to work they would like to do in the future (Fetters, 1974). This is neither a good nor a bad sign in itself; there is no doubt something educative in experiencing jobs that are unsatisfactory as well as those that are satisfactory. What is quite important is that young people seem to be able to make this distinction after only a couple of weeks on a job. What seems desirable, then, is to provide a series of short and varied experiences rather than one job that lasts for a school year or longer.

Cooperative and work-study programs, of course, are seldom formal education programs; the two merely occur at the same time in the lives of young people. Although many attempts have been made to consummate a marriage between classroom experiences and work experiences, these efforts have been terribly frustrating and perhaps unnecessary. The mere opportunity to work is, in itself, a means to learning.

If there is a major problem with cooperative education it is to find enough part-time jobs for youth. Again, the fundamental realities of the labor market seem to overwhelm what little leverage educators possess to help young people make the transition from school to work. There is no simple way of creating enough jobs for youth (and certainly educators cannot do the trick by themselves), but former Secretary of Labor Willard Wirtz has suggested (1975) some promising first steps, including the creation of community councils composed of employers, union officials, educators, and other civic leaders who influence the problem.

Possibly there is even more work for young people than is commonly assumed. One study found that nearly three-fourths of high school students work in their senior year—44 percent of the boys and 29 percent of the girls work twenty hours or more per week (Fetters, 1974). Only 12 percent of high school youths have never had a regular paying job outside the home (Prediger, Roth, and Noeth, 1973). And a recent survey of three cities found enough jobs so that every fifteen- to twenty-year-old could have at least three hours of work-learning experience per week (Kiernan, 1972). Although it is difficult to calculate, the cooperative education movement appears to be spreading; the U.S. Office of Education now lists more than a thousand active programs in American high schools.

Part of the appeal of cooperative education is its parallels to apprentice programs. Apprenticeships are perennially popular in America, because they seemingly give young people reality-based, cost-effective, practical training that is sensitive to the actual demands of the labor market. Thus, it is often argued that an expansion of apprenticelike programs would present an attractive alternative to potential or actual school dropouts. But again, the obvious solution may not be an appropriate response to the twin problems of unemployment and underemployment. In Germany, where fully 60 percent of the high-school-age population is apprenticed to industry, the outcomes of the program are not necessarily what one would predict or desire for American youth (Reubens, 1973b). On a recent trip to Europe, I found many Germans growing increasingly critical of their system, which, in all too many cases, has simply provided employers with a source of cheap labor. For all the Germans' vaunted efficiency and ability to control behavior, they have been unsuccessful in efforts to cajole or force employers to provide high-quality training. Indeed, most of the employers who are willing to accept apprentices are in small and declining industries (successful firms don't need cheap labor). Class segregation is accentuated by the programs, and educational researchers conclude that the major effect is merely to demotivate working-class youth. Another counter-intuitive finding is that apprenticeships do not stem dropouts. About 10 to 20 percent of German youths drop out of all formal education programs rather than trying an apprenticeship at about age fifteen. Even then, of those who choose the apprentice route, about 15 percent drop out before completing the three-year certificate program. We need not accept the German model, of course. But the argument that we could administer such a program more effectively than the Germans is not likely to be all that convincing.

A Choice Among Extremes

A review of the major career-education aims of providing skills, attitudes, information, and work experience suggests that these are likely to have only a marginal impact on the problems of unemployment and underemployment. Because the schools have so little leverage to create jobs, unemployment can be addressed only tangentially by education programs. Underemployment, although a more promising case for educational treatment, may actually be exacerbated by career education. Underemployment, we recall, is largely created by overselling education as a passport to a good job and by driving out of the schools all but the work-preparation function. How can career education respond to the frustration and dissatisfaction of youth created by the overemphasis on work and work credentials in the schools? The answer seems to be: by doing more of the same. Unfortunately, as E.F. Schumacher (1973, p. 38) has pointed out, societies "always tend to try and cure a disease by intensifying its causes."

Paradoxically, vocational/career education is experiencing renewed vigor just when we are recognizing that most employers are not really looking for specific abilities, that most job skills can be learned quickly on the job, that the teenage unemployment rate is unrelated to the lack of vocational training, and that working-class virtues will be anachronistic in a participative democracy.

Many decision makers at the state and local government are like the king in the cartoon in feeling that social problems are best addressed by frontal attacks on their symptoms: if people are sick, give them more doctors; if people are poor, spend more money on welfare; if people are uneducated, spend more money on schools; and if they are unemployed, give them training. The lessons of the war on poverty—that social problems are complex and that effective solutions must be indirect and systemic—have not yet reached the state and federal legislators who are pumping money into vocational programs to meet the political pressures to do *something* about unemployment, even if that something has nothing to do with the problem.

Many states have clearly chosen to adhere to a traditional vocational philosophy to improve the fit between the institutions of education and work. In California and Utah, for example, the preferred solution to the problem of unemployment and under-employment is greater vocationalism. In Utah, where state law already dictates that no less than 75 percent of all courses in vocational institutions must be directly related to the provision of specific job skills, vocational educators are attempting to remove as many of the remaining nontechnical courses as possible. They have begun with an attack on one junior college's courses in physics and English, even though all the general courses constitute much less than 25 percent of the total offerings.

Still, much of the support for vocational education is a response to real problems in the education-work nexus. There is probably a deep understanding on the part of a large segment of high school youth that further education will not guarantee them good jobs, and hence they grasp at a program that promises them early and easy occupational success. This promise of a well-paying job at high school graduation is especially seductive to minority, ethnic, and other working-class young people, who have been taught to believe that they cannot succeed in middle-class institutions. In effect, they are told that vocational training will get them a better job than they deserve.

I have not answered the question, "What business is career education in?" I have only illustrated the businesses I think it should not be in. Pursuing the most frequently stated aims of the career/vocational education movement promises only to fuel the problem of underemployment by further exaggerating unfulfillable promises for good jobs. Thus, what *not* to do is manifest. But what should be done (the subject of the next chapter) is less evident.

7

Fusing Liberal
and Technical Learning

Aristotle declared: "Should the useful in life, or should virtue, or should the higher knowledge be the aim of our training? . . . no one knows on what principle we should proceed." In so saying, the normally self-confident philosopher unabashedly admitted his failure to resolve the tension existing between liberal education, on the one hand, and technical training on the other. Indeed, because the chasm between the two philosophies has remained so conspicuously unbridged for so many centuries, it borders on hubris to even attempt to engineer a span. Nevertheless, the time seems propitious—even urgent—for one more effort at closing this enduring fissure between educational philosophies.

Such a potentially arrogant effort should begin as humbly as possible. I propose no simple answer to Aristotle's question. As we have seen in the last chapter, vocational education is not a useful means of coping with underemployment and unemployment. Unfortunately, the solution at the other end of the spectrum—liberal education—also seems inappropriate given current social conditions.

Liberal education, as good as it is in its purist form for those aspiring to professional careers, does not appear to be generally applicable to all students in an age of mass education and open admissions. In their two reports to the Secretary of Health, Education and Welfare, Frank Newman and his associates found that the traditional liberal arts curriculum did not meet the needs of the expanding clientele of America's colleges, particularly students from disadvantaged classes. The social, economic, and political environment has changed drastically over the past hundred years, but American liberal arts programs have remained in a static mold. Although liberal education was once successfully career-oriented, providing the job skills needed by the clergy, teachers, and other professionals, today only a small percentage of the total number of college students are planning to pursue these traditional careers for which liberal education was designed as preparation. Most damaging, liberal education in the colleges and schools has been scored for its failures to meet the goals it has set for itself. Few graduates today can claim to be broadly or liberally educated and all too many can scarcely read, write, or compute.

Consequently, in recognition of the shortcomings of both liberal and vocational education, a growing number of reformers have attempted to embrace the enduring and relevant from both models, while rejecting adherence to a pure form of either. In nearly every major industrialized nation, efforts aimed at such a fusion are being made in order to respond to such problems as underemployment and social-class inequality.

Beginnings of a Reform Movement

The industrial nations are starting their processes of educational reform from systems remarkably divergent in tradition and function: some systems are elitist, others open; some stress vocationalism, others are more liberal. Beatrice Reubens (1973b) observes that we should look beyond these obvious and clear divergences of the existing systems and notice an important and growing convergence of aims. In the western democracies, at least, the goal for the future of education is strikingly similar in all countries: *each is seeking to integrate academic and vocational education.* Countries with an excess of vocational education (such as Germany) are beginning to stress more general education, and those that have focused on general education (including the United States) are now leaning toward greater vocationalism.

The Germans, for instance, are actively considering a plan for their upper-secondary schools in which college-bound students will be exposed to the world of work, and in which vocationally oriented youth will have greater exposure to liberal studies. The stated purposes of the German proposal are to remove the low esteem of blue-collar work, to break down invidious distinctions between forms of credentials, and to create a freer flow between institutions of work and education for all social classes.

One danger inherent in this reform movement is that it will fail to achieve a union of equality. Successful marriages among equals are rare; usually the most powerful partner comes to dominate. Thus, there is the real possibility, especially in America, that the purpose of all education may come to be seen as serving the world of work. This vocational orientation is, in part, a backlash caused by the problems of underemployment. Because higher (and liberal) education was sold solely in terms of its investment value, when this return started to decline, there was a 180° shift to support for vocational training. But, as we have seen, vocational education is not a real solution to such problems as underemployment and inequality. Indeed, if career education lived up to its promise of training millions more young people in specific skills, the problems of unmet expectations would soar, since the labor market shows little demand for more highly skilled workers.

Career Education—An Alternative Model

There is, however, an alternative model of career education. In the words of Kenneth Hoyt, it is "a response to the call for educational reform." Most clearly articulated by such Europeans as J. R. Gass, Hellmut Becker and Torsten Husen, this model is not vocationalism by the back door. The Europeans do not even talk of "career education"; rather, they speak of creating a "learning society." To achieve this, they propose the following kinds of goals for education and work:

• the integration of education, work, and leisure

• the integration of theory and practice, of liberal and technical education

• the integration of social classes in education and at work

• an emphasis on continuing education or lifelong learning

• an emphasis on education for leisure as well as for work

• preparation of youth for the world of work acquired through actual work experience

• a deemphasis on educational credentialism

• a focus on learning and individual growth as the goals of life

• an emphasis on school as a joyful place where one learns how to learn

• the integration of age groups

These aims are not yet realized in any country, but in one form or another they seem to run through the writings of educators, planners, futurists, and philosophers in Western Europe. In the United States, however, these goals are less well-received, smacking, as they do, of progressivism, humanism, and national planning. Still, they do appear consistent with an American definition of career education that may be becoming competitive with the vocationalist approach. Kenneth Hoyt (n.d., p. 3) writes that "career education is . . . an integration of learning and doing that merges the worlds of the home, the community, the school, and the workplace into a challenging and productive whole."

In this formulation, a career is more than a job or a series of jobs; it is the course of events that constitutes a life. (Indeed, *career* comes from the Latin word meaning *course* or *road*.) It is now widely accepted by psychologists that most people find life rewarding and satisfying when it is experienced as a continuous course toward fulfilling one's individual potential—both on and off the job. Beginning with John Dewey, a small number of American educators have built on this notion and have tried to make human growth the essential goal of education. There are usually about thirty years between the introduction of a social idea and its wide implementation, and Dewey's concepts seemed about ready to achieve acceptance in the late 1960s, finally having shaken off the crippling effects of three decades of misinterpretation and misrepresentation by his friends and foes alike. Then the economy turned sour. Now, with unemployment increasing, vocationalism has again reared its atavistic head, and learning for life again is attacked as an unrealistic luxury. The shame of the situation is that education for growth is not a luxury. Indeed, in a time of unemployment and underemployment, it becomes a necessity.

The small band of humanistic vocational educators suggests the need for a curriculum and pedagogy that would deal with the important and terrible problems of underemployment by imparting to students the tools they will need to develop throughout life. In this view, career education can deal with the unemployed self by encouraging learning through experience. This means that the schools would prepare youth for their life careers by building a basis for future growth. With such a background, as one grows older, one knows how to look for stimulation and how to find rewards both in leisure and in work. In other words, one has learned the joys of learning and how to realize these. One has learned how to put one's unemployed self to work in any situation.

To Dewey, education must help "to carry a person over dead places in the future." He called this process the "experiential continuum" and said: "The most important attitude that can be formed is that of desire to go on learning. If impetus in this direction is weakened instead of being intensified, something much more than mere lack of preparation takes place. The pupil is actually robbed of native capacities which otherwise would enable him to cope with the circumstances that he meets in the course of his life" (1963, p. 48).

Dewey sought to prepare young people for an unpredictable future (a goal that differs greatly from that of vocationalism,

which assumes a predictable and steady-state future). But unlike
the vocationalists, he did not want to *lower* the expectations of
young people through teaching them that bad jobs are their assigned lot in life; he sought to instill *realistic* expectations. For
in practice, Dewey wanted to equip youth to find educative experience even in the worst jobs. He felt that each worker should
have "the education which enables him to see within his daily work
all there is in it of large and human significance."

To achieve this end, Dewey and his contemporary Alfred
Whitehead argued that education should be based on experience
or self-discovery. They showed that acquiring a specific skill without understanding its theoretical background was not learning,
because the knowledge could not be used later when a problem
was presented in a slightly different context. At the same time,
theoretical knowledge is useless and quickly lost by all but the
brightest if it is not acquired through practical experience. Like
Dewey, Whitehead believed that the proper goal of education,
self-development, occurs through "discovery" (experience, in
Dewey's terminology). To help the child to discover, Whitehead
felt that ideas "should be thrown into every combination possible. . . . From the very beginning of his education, the child should
experience the joy of discovery. The discovery which he has to
make is that general ideas give an understanding to that stream
of events which pours through his life, which is his life" (1961,
p. 88).

That "stream of events" is close to what is meant by a career.
But the parts of that career must be integrated for life to be meaningful. Whitehead advises teachers to "choose some important
applications of your theoretical subject and study them concurrently with the systematic theoretical exposition" (p. 89). For
Whitehead, this melding of theory with practical applications is
what gives vitality to education. In short, "the problem of education
is to make the pupil see the [woods] by means of the trees" (p. 92).

How can this notion be translated into terms that would be
helpful for, say, a contemporary college or high school teacher
in California? Apparently, Whitehead would counsel against teaching such things as physics, ecology, politics, law, and sociology as
separate, theoretical courses. Rather, he would pose a problem
for students to solve: for example, should California halt the

spread of nuclear power plants? The teacher would encourage the students to interview businessmen, conservationists, labor union leaders, scientists, journalists, politicians, and whatever other stakeholders or experts could help them to define the issue and to see its complexity. As they explored the issue, they would find that they needed to know some theoretical physics. The teacher would help them gain this understanding and show them how libraries contain answers to real problems. In this way, they would quickly, eagerly, and successfully learn, and they would retain a great deal of theoretical knowledge because they would have learned it experientially and would have had a practical hook to hang it on.

Because of his firm belief in the value of integrating practice with theory, Whitehead was no critic of technical education (something quite different from vocational training, which has no theoretical basis). The "ideal of technical education," according to Whitehead, is the Benedictine vision of life (as expressed here by G.B. Shaw): "It is a commonwealth in which work is play and play is life" (Whitehead, p. 101). If discovery becomes education, and work becomes discovery, then this ideal is realizable. And the task of making work into discovery "is in the hands of technical teachers, and those who control their spheres of activity."

Whitehead felt that education and work must be transformed by making discovery (learning) the goal of both activities. To fail to do so is to encourage underemployment and its many discontents: "Is it likely that a tired, bored workman, however skillful his hands, will produce a large output of first-class work? He will limit his production, will scamp his work, and be an adept at evading inspection; he will be slow in adapting himself to new methods; he will be a focus of discontent, full of unpractical revolutionary ideas. . . . If, in the troubled times which may be before us, you wish appreciably to increase the chance of some savage upheaval, introduce widespread technical education and ignore the Benedictine ideal. Society will then get what it deserves" (p. 102).

In order to achieve a technical education that does embrace the Benedictine ideal, Whitehead counsels that it must be fused with liberal education. Alone, technical training only "emphasizes manual skills and the coordinated action of hand and eye, and judgment in the control of the process of construction. But judgment necessitates knowledge of those natural processes of which manufacture is the utilisation. Thus somewhere in technical training an education in scientific knowledge is required" (p. 106).

The goal of the marriage of technical and liberal education "is to see the immediate events of our lives as instances of our general ideas" (p. 108). But to achieve this aim is not easy. In Whitehead's day, as well as in ours, vocational educators assumed that they were fusing at least some liberal education with the technical. Most often, however, liberal education is merely tacked on, not fused or integrated. This failure of union results from specializing vocational training in the mistaken belief that it will make a young person more employable. Whitehead warned about this consequence. "Above all things it should not be too specialised. Workshop finish and workshop dodges, adapted to one particular job, should be taught in the commercial workshop, and should form no essential part of the school course. A properly trained worker would pick them up in no time. . . . I am only asserting the principles that training should be broader than the ultimate specialisation, and that the resulting power of adaptation to varying demands is advantageous to the workers, to the employers, and to the nation" (pp. 111–12).

Whitehead felt it was possible to find scientific and literary courses that "would illuminate most occupations" and that these should be offered to workers not only for job-related consumption but for leisure as well. Whitehead fully recognized that not all workers were fit for the life of the mind and that the economy would require some people to work with their hands or in other dull types of work. Nevertheless, Whitehead felt that for all people there was value in "linking together knowledge, labour and moral energy" (p. 115).

Equality vs. Quality—An Avoidable Trade-off

Apparently, the ultimate goal of Whitehead and Dewey was what we call today "equality of educational opportunity." They believed (perhaps a bit naively in light of what we know from the Coleman-Jencks data) that equality of educational opportunity would help to reduce the greatest injustices in workplaces, in occupational status, and in society in general. Even if they were a bit too optimistic, they nevertheless served a purpose by warning of the costs to an egalitarian democracy of teaching down to the lower classes. Rather, as Matthew Arnold suggested, the goal of education should be "to do away with classes." He wrote, "This is the social idea; and the men of culture are the true apostles of equality. The great men of culture are those who have had a passion for diffusing, for making prevail, for carrying from one end of society to the other, the best knowledge, the best ideas of their time; who have labored to divest knowledge of all that was . . . difficult . . . professional, exclusive; to humanize it, to make it efficient outside the clique of the cultivated and learned, yet still remaining the *best* knowledge and thought of the time" [in Jackson and Marsden, 1966, p. 244].

Currently, such an ideal seems unrealizable because many schools assume their primary purpose is to meet the demands of workplaces. These schools see their role as providing workers in appropriate proportions to fill slots in the hierarchy of labor. In effect, schools sort out and select the correct ratio of professional to skilled to nonskilled workers for the labor market. Indeed, the educational system historically gained its legitimacy from this selection function. The difficulty today is that this function runs counter to the emerging goals of human development and greater social justice. Ironically, at the same time that the nation is using schools to desegregate society, it is also stressing the vocational functions of the school that promote class inequalities.

The challenge for career education will be to develop the talents of all workers to the full, recognizing that some are brighter than others and that even a few are hopelessly dull. We must take it on faith, however, that a system designed along the lines suggested by Arnold, Dewey, and Whitehead would uncover many supposed dullards who have much to contribute at work and to society.

Still, a dilution of standards of quality may accompany efforts to provide greater equality of educational opportunity, particularly when the means to this end is a policy of greater access to higher education. This problem is often overstated, however, especially by critics who overlook the counterbalances built into the American educational system by virtue of its diversity. What the United States has done is to open the *base* of its system to all comers, while at the same time trying to eliminate sex, class, race, and age discrimination that bars *qualified* people from moving up to the more prestigious institutions that compose the peak of the pyramid. Using merit (not open admissions) as the basis for progression up the hierarchy does not seem to have seriously compromised the standards at Harvard or Stanford. Unhappily, because of class, race, and sex discrimination, and educational tracking in secondary education, all too many qualified people are still not moving up the hierarchy.

Into Practice

Practically, how can education bring the best of the culture to all citizens? Clearly, such a form of education would entail more than just the provision of practical skills. As Schumacher (1973) argues, "know-how is no more a culture than a piano is music." The transmission of know-how is nevertheless important. It would thus be necessary to fuse theory and practice in a single curriculum, without permitting one to become dominant, and without sex, race, or class tracking. To be acceptable to parents, employers, and politicians, this form of education would have to lead to decent jobs—ones with low rates of unemployment, decent income levels, and high rates of satisfaction. To be appropriate to the real problems of work, the skills learned would have to be problem-solving skills and others that permit adaptability and coping with change in an unpredictable environment. The skills learned would also have to be in continuing demand from a broad variety of employers. Is this vision a pipedream? Are there existing models of such practical-liberal, theoretical-applied, vocational-liberal forms of career education? I suggest we look to the professions in search of a model. The law, although far from being the perfect or only paradigm, is an example of what I have in mind.

There is no involuntary unemployment among lawyers, little underemployment; and the skills acquired by lawyers in school are applicable to a wide range of occupations from business and government to journalism. The goals of legal training are five-fold: (1) to develop the capacity for rational thought and decision making; (2) to develop a problem-solving capacity; (3) to develop communications and interpersonal skills; (4) to develop an understanding of our system; and (5) to develop the capacity for continuous learning. The method for achieving these goals is experiential. Students are given real problems—cases—and are encouraged to seek solutions to these on their own. The search takes students into the domains of anthropology, economics, sociology, religion, philosophy, politics, ethics, literature, psychology, and the sciences. Since most pressing problems in this society can be addressed from a legal perspective, "Law may be considered the laboratory where the interdisciplinary synthesis of the social sciences may take place" (Appel, 1957, p. 158).

But legal training is not what I propose—particularly not as it is provided in American law schools, in which the principal model of success is the corporate lawyer earning a six-figure income in a Wall Street firm. I have more in mind the traditional Oxford and Cambridge undergraduate law degree that was pursued as often by those going into government, business, and the foreign service as by those wishing to be lawyers. The qualities that make this law program and other professional training relevant forms of career education can be abstracted and applied to the liberal arts curriculum in the colleges (and, perhaps, even to the basic education curriculum in high school). It is clear that the problem-oriented nature of this form of education causes it to be useful as preparation for the top 30 to 40 percent of jobs in the next century. Moreover, it offers a broad intellectual framework over which it is relatively easy to apply successive layers of specialization as these become required. The multiple career changes likely to characterize the future cry out for such a broad base, while they limit the appropriateness of specialization during one's youth.

And, most important, for the majority who will be unable to find jobs that require the full use of their education, the broad base characteristic of legal training will be important for finding challenge, interest, and growth *off* the job. Consequently, for all social classes and occupational interests and abilities, a broad, liberal training *rooted in practical real-world problems* may be a requisite for survival and satisfaction in the future. In a job environment dominated by change, these will be marketable skills: the ability to understand one's relationship to one's environment, to control the elements in one's life, to understand one's self, to be sensitive to others and to nature, to be able to form one's values in an ethical perspective, to be able to synthesize and analyze issues and problems, to be adaptable, flexible, and curious, to be able to communicate and to lead. All we know for certain about the future is that it will be turbulent and filled with unpredictable alterations. Historically, the people most able to adapt to the vicissitudes of social life have been the liberally educated, for whom learning has always been a way of life. The person who has learned how to learn can always pick up a skill that has become essential. The person best able to cope with the new is the one who has the broadest background and is thus the most flexible. I see no reason to believe that these characteristics will be any less necessary as the speed of change accelerates in the future.

There is evidence that such a background is already *useful* on the job. A recent study (Bisconti and Solmon, 1976) indicates that employed college graduates find math, science, literature, language, history, and the social sciences applicable to their work. Ironically, these subjects don't sound as useful in the middle of a recession as welding, accounting, or aircraft design, but the academic skills apparently give the young graduates greater access to more job options and give them more flexibility in their careers.

But is there going to be demand for such liberally educated people who are oriented toward practical problem solving? Let's look at what Charles Bowen, IBM's program director for education development, has to say about what his company is looking for in prospective employees: "The main thing we want is the ability to understand and solve problems. And I suspect that involves a broader interdisciplinary education of the people we hire, recognizing that as change accelerates, we're going to have to do more job training within industry. . . . There is also much more for the universities to do in education, as opposed to training. So I would say that we would probably expect a broadly educated individual rather than a narrowly trained specialist." Although IBM is probably the prototype of the employer of the future, many educators seem to be responding to a different set of signals sent out by less sophisticated employers. For example, much has been made of a recent poll of employers conducted by the College Placement Council (1975) that shows liberal arts students at a disadvantage on the current job market. The poll, unfortunately, in no way controls for the temporary effects of the recession. Making an assessment of a town's climate in the midst of a hurricane is a questionable sampling procedure, but the Council nevertheless did find that many employers consider liberal arts graduates unattractive as new hires.

These findings might be interpreted in the following light. First, conditions in the world of work are changing, as Bowen indicates, and we should not view the current opinions of employers in a buyers' market as predictive of future attitudes. Second, other polls show that employers who hire specialists often complain that these young people can't read, write, spell, deal with people or solve problems independently (Gallagher, 1973). And third, almost all the employers surveyed by the Council said they *would* hire liberal arts students if only the applicants had some practical or experiential activity on their record, such as a couple of business-related courses (including economics), or a co-op or work-study experience. Thus, employers may not be saying that they favor specialization, but that liberal education should be more practical and experiential. If they can find a broadly educated person who also has some real-world experience, they will provide any needed specialized training.

A Work-Relevant Curriculum for the Future

If Bowen is right, and there is little reason to doubt his forecast, education would be more "relevant" for work if it tried to be less self-consciously relevant. In effect, it should not be consciously or pointedly vocational. Instead, in the early years, it should foster self-confidence, curiosity, and the love of learning, qualities that form the basis for growth throughout life. The basic career competences of reading, writing, and computation should be stressed and integrated with practical applications of such knowledge. But even at the high school level, there should be no specific skills training, other than for such basics as typing, carpentry, auto mechanics, and administration that could be used on or off the job by all students—male and female, black and white, college-oriented and work-oriented. Even four-year colleges might turn their backs on undergraduate technical degrees in engineering, business, and teaching. In that situation specific skills and professional abilities would be acquired on the job, in graduate education, or in continuing education in community colleges.

Governor Brown of California has struck a responsive chord with the electorate by calling for a return to concentration on the three R's. His proposals, many of which are justifiably criticized by educators, have widespread *public* support because of the many recent failures of the schools to equip youth for work and life in postindustrial society. (The most famous of such failures was the celebrated Peter Doe case, in which a white, middle-class high school graduate sued the City of San Francisco because his inability to read at a sixth-grade level left him virtually unemployable.) Peter Doe is not alone: reportedly, 40 percent of the applicants for jobs with Pacific Tel & Tel—one of California's largest employers—cannot read or write at the eighth-grade level. At the same time, the trend in San Francisco and other California cities is away from basics and toward the new vocationalism. When asked to explain this apparent contradiction, many candid educators own up to the fact they know how to teach Johnny how to work a lathe, but not how to read. With the failures of basic education manifested in embarrassingly low reading and college-entrance test scores, the philosophy seems to have become "if we can't teach Johnny how to read, let's not try."

Across the nation, many traditional school subjects have been dropped as requirements in high school and college. The list includes languages, advanced English grammar, the classics, mathematics, and some science courses. These requirements were dropped because (a) students did not like the courses and (b) students' performance in these was not high. In dropping the courses, educators said they were "irrelevant," but perhaps these subjects were not so much irrelevant as unpopular because they were taught poorly or were highly symbolic of the authoritarian nature of schools. Would these courses seem irrelevant is they were taught in an experiential context, in a way that stressed individual performance over competitive grading, in an atmosphere of joy rather than coercion, and in an atmosphere of love of learning rather than learning for better jobs? Have we perhaps mistaken problems of irrelevance of form for irrelevance of content?

Thomas Powers (in press), an innovative vocational educator at Pennsylvania State University, has described how such subjects as English, math, and economics can be taught to vocationally oriented high school students whom most educators would write off as unteachable. The secret is imaginative teaching along the experiential lines suggested by Dewey and Whitehead. Powers visited a program in "food education and service training" (with the lovely acronym FEAST) in which students learned English painlessly by listening to tapes of radio commercials for restaurants. The students identified the "strong" verbs, adjectives, and adverbs in a MacDonald's commercial. Later, they had a writing assignment in which they wrote their own commercials, menus, and other restaurant-related documents. In math class the students converted recipes from small to large quantities, computed the inventory in the school lunch room, and calculated a payroll. Significantly, they also grasped the underlying theory behind their math and English lessons. In this way, what they learned was useful even if they never worked in a restaurant.

But what they learned is not as important as how they learned, for the process belies the easy assumption that the disadvantaged will not and cannot learn abstract skills. Powers relates an interesting incident in this regard:

> I turned up in an English class and, by prior assignment, was to visit with the instructor. She gave the students an assignment that would keep them busy for a few minutes and then proceeded to begin to talk with me—but that proved impossible. The students were very polite and courteous both to me and the instructor but they kept interrupting us with questions. The questions all related to the work and at first I thought this

stream of interruptions would cease in a moment or two. But it didn't and gradually after ten minutes both the instructor and I began to smile because we realized that what the students were saying was simply that I . . . was not going to be allowed to take *their* teacher away from them. The class was theirs. The teacher was theirs. And I could jolly well get my information some other way. We finally just gave up trying to talk and I stood and observed with great interest a class in high school English composed of students, all of whom had been relatively poor students at the point of admission . . . [as they] pursued the English language earnestly through the medium of food service commercials. . . . how many English classes are there in the United States that couldn't be given some busy work to relieve the teacher for a few minutes to visit with an outsider? How many English classes are there in America's high schools who would not *welcome* an opportunity to goof off for a few minutes and get rid of their teacher? [pp. 24–25].

Critics often assert that broadly based education is fine for bright and motivated youth, but that it is entirely impractical for the bitter, sullen, and frustrated young people from the central cities. I would argue that these unfortunate young people are not unemployable because they lack specific technical skills. They are unemployable (controlling for the recession, of course) because they lack the base on which such skills can be developed. Employers know, if educators don't, that the particular abilities needed on most jobs can be gained in less than two weeks. Thus, to subject a disadvantaged youth to four years of vocational training to learn a skill that can be acquired on the job in a short time is not only to admit the failure of the schools, it is to deny him the opportunity to have four years of education.

There is much more to be done for disadvantaged students than giving up and training them for dead-end occupations that the more privileged in society would never dream of touching. For example, new methods such as mastery learning have been shown to be quite effective in lowering the percentage of learning failures. Mastery learning can be understood as a variation on the scouting merit-badge system in which the first thing the student is shown is the final exam (Hoffman, 1975). In effect, the student is told at the outset of each learning module what he or she will have to know at the end of it. Whether it takes the student two minutes or two months to pass each module is irrelevant—the merit badge or performance certification carries the same value regardless of how long it took the student to earn it. Using this method, students can be certified and recertified as meeting various levels of performance with each major hurdle cleared in key subject areas. There could be dozens of levels of performance for each subject, and each individual could progress from level to level at his or her own pace. A student who left or dropped out of school could take a certificate of his level of competence in half a dozen or more relevant subjects (for example, typing level 70, spelling level 62, math level 48). At any time during his life, the student could return to school for instruction or testing in order to upgrade his certificate.

Since the level of performance is based on competence (and *not* on class standing, completion of units, or any of the other current measures unrelated to performance), the individual need only demonstrate skill or understanding in the area of knowledge, no matter where the student attained the level of competence or mastery (in school, on the job, or during leisure time).

Eventually, almost all will experience the pleasure of successfully learning through this method. Failure is all but eliminated; at worst it is a temporary experience. Students are thus motivated through their own accomplishments, and the problem of the unwilling learner disappears. The system transforms students from competitors to teammates (the brilliant student is no longer seen as a ratebuster; the slow student is no longer seen as a dunce). Evidence also shows that the role of the teacher is transformed from that of an authoritarian to an authority and the relative role of the students changes from dependents to independents (Block, 1973). Significantly, the attitudes and behavior that mastery learning generates are those most compatible with what is required in redesigned workplaces where teamwork and worker participation in decision making are the norm. Mastery learning and the related performance-based certification are thus strong alternative responses to the pressures for vocationalism because they directly address the problems of meaningless credentials, class biases in learning, competitive grading, sanctions against dropping out, barriers to continuing education, lack of credit for noninstitutional learning, and lack of credit for technical or applied learning.

Other currently available education reforms are also compatible with the future trend toward human resources development, including work-study, cooperative education, work-based instruction, and flexible modular scheduling. In particular, there is considerable justification for a one- or two-year interregnum between high school and college in which students are exposed to the only form of career education that we know works—a job (Adler, 1971). This policy would not only provide middle-class students with hard data to help them decide what type of education would be relevant for the career they choose, it would also help resolve the problem of what to do with dull students. Presently, the choices are (a) send them on to colleges with open admissions, where they most often fail; (b) send them to vocational schools where their life chances are diminished; or (c) hold them back in high schools they detest while trying to teach them to read against their will. It might be better, at least marginally, to let them work for a period of time in the hopes that at least some of them will see the advantages of education and return to formal schooling as willing learners, seeing the true relationships between education, work, and life.

Obviously, current economic conditions and the structure of the labor market obviate providing jobs for all eighteen through twenty year olds. Some kind of program of national service for youth, perhaps coupled with a sabbatical program for middle-aged workers that would open up job slots for teenagers, is probably in order. Indeed, once the door is opened to the notion of public service jobs for youth, several radical proposals might be entertained. For example, since the time of the French Revolution, it has been suggested that justice would be served if society were to rotate the worst jobs so that no one is condemned to a life of drudgery on a single task. (Necessity is already beginning to bring this about. In the Detroit auto industry, where absenteeism and turnover are high, unions and management have found that college students will gladly work a day or two a week on the assembly line. They do so because of the attraction of high pay, and because, unlike regular workers who are playing hooky on Mondays and Fridays, students do not feel trapped in their jobs; they know they will not be there for the rest of their lives. They are not forced to adopt what for them would be the damaging identity of an assembly line worker—they remain "students.") In relation to public service jobs for youth, one might ask what greater public service a young person could perform than to liberate a less fortunate soul from a dehumanizing task? After graduation from high school, young citizens could spend a year or two doing the dirty, but necessary, tasks of civilization.

Conclusions

In summary, there is no one best system of education. Only one characterized by a wide variety of opportunity and choice can meet the divergent needs of American citizens and the exigencies of an unpredictable future environment. This is not to conclude on a note of educational relativism—some forms of education are clearly more appropriate than others to the future of work.

A prime concern for education must be to prepare young people for a changing and uncertain future, and whatever policies educators choose to adopt should be compatible with this end. Apparently, the new vocationalism is inappropriate to this task. The consequence of pursuing an educational policy that is basically a response to ephemeral economic conditions would be to cripple the long-term ability of our citizenry and nation to cope with a strange new world. The new vocationalism simply narrows the focus of education and, in so doing, eliminates too many options.

Unfortunately, traditional liberal programs are also inappropriate to the needs of many students. The enormous numbers of students who are not interested in careers in teaching, the clergy or the professions are often not adequately served by the liberal curriculum. Consequently, forms of education that seek to fuse the best of liberal and technical education seem most appropriate to the future of work.

We have now moved solidly into the area of normative forecasting. Although "what should be" is dangerous territory, it is also exciting. For example, the concepts of fusion developed here can be applied to the workplace, as the next chapter will show. Indeed, the prospects for developing human resources by blurring the distinctions between work and learning are not only intellectually exciting, but real and readily realizable.

8

Integrating Work and Learning

There is a conspicuous path I have chosen not to take in this analysis of working and learning—the route to a "leisure society." It is worth a slight detour to explain why I have not pursued this option for the development of human resources. There is, after all, ample historical precedent, beginning with Aristotle's *Politics,* for arguing that machines should labor while humans find fulfillment in creative leisure. According to this view, the most significant time of our lives should be spent in the arts, sciences, politics, education, handcrafts, or whatever nonlaboring activities a human chooses that lead to growth—that is, ones that are not mere idling or recreation (Adler, 1970). Such activities might fully and readily provide such social and psychological benefits usually associated with work as the creation of self-esteem, identity, a sense of mastery, and the feeling that one is doing something of value for others. Particularly, since it is clear that not all jobs can be made into good jobs and that traditional full employment is a devilishly elusive goal, it would seem sensible to design ways in which people could achieve their developmental needs off the job.

I have consciously avoided exploring such an alternative for America not because it is unattractive (personally, I find it quite desirable) but because it runs counter to several powerful and unavoidable trends in modern society. Because of three major social impediments, I simply cannot imagine a plausible scenario in which America can get to a leisure society from where we are today.

The first obstacle is that the need to work is such an integral facet of industrial society that it seems unreasonable to assume that humans can be resocialized (even in the span of a generation) to view work as an insignificant or supplementary activity. It is easier to argue that leisure *could* perform the social and psychological functions of work than it is to suggest policies that *would* overcome two thousand years of history in which work has been the only truly legitimate adult activity. Somehow, to say "but it shouldn't be so" seems a pale response in face of the overwhelming importance of work in every country from China to Saudi Arabia (to bracket the ideological spectrum of nation states). Moreover, in terms of an individual's emotional needs, it is harder to design rewarding leisure activities than it is to design rewarding work activities (as anyone who has ever been bored on a Sunday afternoon can attest).

The second barrier is the resource limits of the planet. Even if it were possible for machines to accomplish all the labor needed by civilization (which it isn't, given current technologies or even those likely to be developed in the next quarter century), there is reason to believe that such an automated economy would generate adverse environmental side-effects.

The third impediment is normative: there is simply too much work that needs to be done (including the rebuilding of our cities, providing food for the world, and reducing poverty at home and abroad) to justify the enormous capital investments needed to turn America into a leisure society.

Instead, it seems far more practical, plausible, and justifiable to forecast an alternative future in which work remains the central human activity. Work should certainly be redefined to include some activities currently not included in the definition (such as child care) and redesigned to make it as pleasurable as leisure wherever this is possible—but for most workers there will be no doubt that they are *working*.

While not as tantalizing as leisure, alternative working futures could nevertheless have many advantages over the current way productive activities are organized. By keeping work as the central activity of society, it is possible to create policies to achieve the following kinds of goals: the fullest development of human resources, the careful use of natural resources, a clean and healthy environment, safe and high quality goods, economic efficiency, individual liberty, and full participation in democratic decision-making processes. For simplicity, I call such a future state the Quality Society. As I illustrate in the remaining chapters, it is a complex and effort-requiring response to the crescive turbulence of the future and to the contradictory needs and desires of Americans.

The Quality Society is not some ideal or utopian state that should be imposed on society. Rather, it is a framework for redirecting the multiple and abstract goals most frequently given allegiance in our democratic nation. Achieving these goals will require a new perspective on such issues as the nature of capitalism and the choice of technologies, as I argue in chapters Nine and Ten. It will also require considerable recasting of the relative functions of schools and workplaces, a task that will be a long-term challenge to educators and employers. Fortunately, there is some evidence of existing forces in society that are already blurring many anachronistic distinctions between education and work.

A few years ago Marshall McLuhan, the controversial media sage, wrote that the future of work will consist of "learning a living." Although it is a common failing of seers to predict not what they think *will* happen but what they think *should* happen, there is some selected evidence that McLuhan's forecast might turn out to be accurate. For example:

● In Topeka, Kansas, workers at a General Foods plant have a goal of learning every job in the plant and are compensated for learning the new tasks. Morale and productivity at the plant are high as workers become both teachers and learners.

• In Japan, several large corporations have developed continuous learning programs for all jobs and work levels, not for the sake of promotion, but for individual growth and to make employees more aware of their contributions to the overall effort.

• In Eastern Europe, some industrial workers learn the theory behind what they are doing and are helped to study whatever chemistry, physics, engineering, economics, or other job-related subjects they wish to pursue.

• In Norway, more and more workers are designing courses to assist them with their work tasks and to help them become their own managers.

• In California, engineers at an electronics firm, with the help of in-plant tutors, pursue a Stanford University televised course (and get better grades than competitively selected undergraduates taking the course on campus).

Before returning to some of these examples in greater detail, let us examine a principle of great importance that undergirds them all: *most workers have an innate desire to learn and grow.* In many cases, this generalization extends even to blue-collar and disadvantaged workers who have been turned off by formal institutions of learning. There is, apparently, a large and untapped reservoir of desire for learning among adults. For example, in a Canadian study of sixty-six adults, all but one person had recently initiated one or more do-it-yourself "learning projects" (Marien, 1971a, p. 39). These adults are similar to many workers in the United States who prefer to learn in settings other than classrooms, where competition is viewed as threatening and lessons are often too abstract. Indeed, the Canadian study found that less than 1 percent of the learning projects had been undertaken for formal educational credit. Significantly, evidence from the examples listed above (and from other cases with similar characteristics) indicates that adults feel that learning *on the job* is a particularly rewarding and natural activity. Apparently, being able to satisfy the desire

to grow and to learn on the job enhances worker self-esteem, satisfaction, loyalty, motivation, and, occasionally, productivity.

Who Wants To Learn on the Job?

G.B. Shaw once said that the only time his education was inter-
rupted was when he was in school. Many adults would probably
concur, at least to the extent that they feel they now learn more
working than they ever did in the classroom. Indeed, these com-
monplaces are borne out and expanded on by data indicating not
only that people learn while working but that learning is one of
the prime sources of satisfaction found on jobs. For instance, in
the recent *Survey of Working Conditions* (Survey Research Center,
1971), white-collar workers rated two items related to learning as
the most important factors of a job. This cross-section of American
workers indicated that the first priority was a job that was interesting; second priority was opportunity to develop special abilities.
However, when the data were disaggregated, the survey showed
that less-affluent and less-educated workers ranked these items
somewhat lower than did more-affluent and higher-educated
workers.

Although the trends in society toward greater affluence and
higher levels of education indicate that learning on the job is likely
to become even more important in the future, it is nevertheless
important to analyze why some people seem to desire learning
more than others. A psychological explanation of this phenomenon is that there is a "hierarchy of needs," and only after an individual's lower-level needs (such as income and security) are
satisfied does he or she have the luxury to fulfill higher-level needs,
such as self-actualization. A sociological explanation can also be
offered: the desire to learn is a product of the workers' socialization on the job and in schools. Thus, people in bad jobs, particularly if they are from disadvantaged social classes, come to believe
that they are incapable of learning. Moreover, having failed to
learn in school, these workers come to anticipate future failure
on the job. Many such workers say they are satisfied with dull jobs,
and this attitude carries over to their off-the-job activities: workers
in dull jobs seldom compensate for them with rewarding leisure

activities. Apparently, the same factors that make workers fear challenge on the job also make them wary of involvement in community activities, continuing education, or any other kind of creative leisure. The uncharitable explanation for this behavior is that dull people choose dull jobs and spend their free time sitting quite contentedly in front of the television (Strauss, 1974). Alternatively, there is something in the educational experience of these workers that has affected their work attitudes, or there is something in their life experience that affects their leisure-time behavior, or both.

There is evidence that this sociological explanation is valid. According to Kohn (1969), the educational, family, and work experiences of the disadvantaged and working classes do often destroy the confidence of the individual that he or she can succeed in middle-class activities, such as continuing education or at jobs that lead to growth. Significantly, D.C. McClelland has developed a short training course that builds the self-confidence of workers. A remarkable number of previously timid and passive workers become highly motivated to succeed after taking the course. Moreover, experiments with workers who said they were satisfied with dull, repetitive jobs show that the same workers refused to go back to the old routine work after their jobs were redesigned to include challenging experiences (Davis and Trist, 1974).

What the evidence indicates, then, is that work can often be turned into a satisfying learning experience. However, for many workers, particularly those in low-level or blue-collar jobs, work is often designed in such a way as to prevent learning and growth. Thus, workers who have already been conditioned to failure in the schools have this experience reinforced in the workplace. Just as education was a chore that these workers had to endure in order to gain a credential to get a job, work becomes a chore that they have to endure to pay the bills. This system leads to wasting the talents and potential contributions to society of millions of workers. That many of these people indeed have something to contribute—and would want to learn if given the chance—is supported by the evidence from job-redesign and training experiments presented below. Apparently, most blue-collar workers can come to find rewards in learning, can succeed in challenging work, and can participate successfully in leisure activities that were once the preserve of the middle class.

Irving Kristol (1973) and others argue that such a line of reasoning is elitist—that college professors are trying to get blue-collar workers to share their own preferences for interesting jobs, fulfilling leisure, and continuing learning. Kristol believes that blue-collar workers do not share the values or interests of the upper-middle class and are quite content with jobs that liberal professors find dull, with recreation that the professors find stulti-fying, and with lives that have no growth or developmental paths. Although the desire for a vegetable existence may exist in a small number of workers, the evidence reviewed here and in *Work in America* indicates that this number is, in fact, very small. Indeed, that the figure is as large as it is results in many ways from the Kristolized attitudes of managers and economists who assume that people who dress differently, look differently, are of different color, sex, or social class from themselves have *lower*-order human wants, needs, and expectations. One might well ask who is being elitist, Kristol or the humanists? The conservative critics fail to see that in many cases (not all) the education and work systems func-tion to lower the aspirations of workers by denying them the op-portunities of the more privileged classes.

Models of Work as Learning

That learning is a necessary component of good jobs has been recognized by management theorists for some time. Indeed, the ascendent management philosophy of the day, organizational development, is predicated on the assumption that training tech-niques can be employed in such a way that individual growth and organizational growth can occur simultaneously and compatibly. In practice, unfortunately, the processes of organizational develop-ment have been applied mainly to managers. A less well-accepted offshoot of organizational development, called socio-technical systems, has applied some training techniques to lower-level jobs with success in the United States (for example, at General Foods and Procter and Gamble) and in Europe (at Volvo and Fiat, for instance). In these experiments, learning becomes a major part of the blue-collar worker's labors. Thomas Green goes a step further and argues that jobs should be designed as mastery learning experiences. Employers should "attend to the hidden curriculum of the job structure itself in an effort to see that there are no jobs that have the character of a total mastery setting leading to no subsequent lesson. This would mean, of course, that the structure of employment institutions would then have to be examined in the light of their *educational* potential as a setting for human learning and development" (1975, p. 215).

Unfortunately, many of even the best-designed blue-collar and white-collar jobs offer few "subsequent lessons" after the initial, short period in which the job is learned. For example, within a few weeks, one can learn all there is to know about making a light bulb, including how to repair the machines that do most of the work. In cases such as this, the opportunity for human growth is severely limited by the lack of complexity of the job. For this reason, socio-technical experts advocate rotating jobs so that eventually every worker has learned how to do everyone's job in the plant, office, or company.

This system differs from the traditional practice of worker development in America, whose primary purpose has been promotion: one learns the boss's job in order to one day take his or her place. As a result, training does not develop the whole person; rather, it channels the person to meet the technical requisites of the next job.

Peter Drucker has contrasted this system with the Japanese practice of "continuous learning." In many Japanese industries, every worker attends a scheduled weekly training session designed to foster individual growth and community spirit among the workers, not to teach a particular skill. According to Drucker (who has been known to embellish), the president of a corporation might attend a session in welding taught by the workers. Drucker contrasts the purpose of learning in Japanese industry (the "Zen approach") with the Western and Chinese "Confucian approach":

> The Confucian concept, which the West shares, assumes that the purpose of learning is to qualify oneself for a new, different and bigger job. The nature of

learning is expressed in a learning curve. Within a certain period of time this student reaches a plateau of proficiency, where he then stays forever.

The Japanese concept may be called the "Zen approach." The purpose of learning is self-improvement. It qualifies a man to do his present task with continually wider vision, continually increasing competence, and continually rising demands on himself. While there is a learning curve, there is no fixed and final plateau. Continued learning leads to a break-out, that is, to a new learning curve, which peaks at a new and higher plateau, and then to a new break-out [1976, pp. 247–48].

Drucker makes a strong case for the West's adopting a system similar to that which he claims exists in Japan. As he sees it, the current system in the West is "actually a bar to true learning."

There are other models for making work a learning experience. In some plants in Eastern Europe, for instance, managers recognize that the maker of light bulbs will quickly learn everything there is to know about his actual job. Therefore, through a system of continuing learning, the worker is encouraged to learn the theory behind the industrial practice—the physics of light and electricity, the sources and chemistry of tungsten, manganese, neon, or whatever raw materials are used in the light bulbs, and the engineering principles on which the machinery that makes the bulbs is built. In short, there is no limit to how deeply or broadly the worker might pursue knowledge about his work. This system comes close to Dewey's ideal that each worker should be given the tools to find all that is interesting and ennobling about his work.

The record of American employers in organizing jobs to encourage human growth is mixed, as a pair of examples from the federal bureaucracy illustrates. Example One: in 1975, I ordered several pamphlets from the Government Printing Office, which I received a month or so later (along with a marvelous book about Tanzania that I had not ordered). On the receipt that accompanied the publications there were marks made by three different rubber stamps: "Picked by PB-7," "Worked by PB-24," and "Checked by PB-46." (I have changed the numbers to protect the innocent!)

Such fractionation of what is logically a single task is at the heart of much of the underemployment among lower-level workers.

Example Two: the Social Security Administration (which was once managed along the anachronistic lines still prevalent in the GPO) is now developing and better utilizing its human resources by eliminating assembly-line paper work and assigning a single caseworker to handle an entire claim or complaint. Although the changes at the SSA have not been radical, complex, or even terribly imaginative, they are important because the agency has compiled an impressive record of productivity and efficiency *without* having to significantly automate its processes. This method presents an alternative to the automated operations of private insurance companies that most observers have felt were necessary to remain efficient. At the SSA, the development of human resources has led to greater efficiency and more interesting jobs.

The most successful efforts at human resources development in the United States have entailed total job redesigns of the kind described in Chapter Five. Unlike the simple job enrichment at the SSA which can be seen as a case of managers replacing an inefficient, rationalized job system with another more efficient but nonetheless rationalized process—the total redesigns are characterized by openness, flexibility, worker participation, and a significant increase in the opportunity to learn and to grow.

In the Topeka General Foods plant I mentioned earlier, for example, almost all workers, including those who have minimal education, know how to repair the plant's complex, transistorized computer-monitor with its thousands of circuits and switches. In this plant, learning is clearly the key to job satisfaction. Even more important, this desire to learn has spread beyond work activities. General Foods offers to refund the tuition for any course pursued by any employee in his or her free time. The number of workers in the Topeka plant who take advantage of this offer is three times the average for all other General Foods plants. Apparently, learning on the job has whetted the workers' appetite for more education. It has overcome the sense of educational inadequacy which afflicts so many blue-collar workers. A second positive effect is that employees in the plant participate in community and civic activities at rates high for blue-collar workers (Walton, 1974).

In the Bolivar, Tennessee, car-accessory plant (described in Chapter Five) one of the major benefits of the total change of the work system has been to increase the opportunities for workers to learn. Redesigned jobs have led to increased participation in decision making, problem solving and self-management for hundreds of workers who are semiliterate or who have had only a few years of education in rural schools. The sharing of productivity increases in the plant allows workers to quit their jobs early in the day in order to take courses in a company-sponsored "college." At first, the "faculty" of the college was composed of workers and managers from the plant who had skills they were willing to teach to fellow employees. Now, the school is so successful that it is becoming a rather special kind of community college, open to the family and friends of the workers. Unlike those in the Topeka plant, the jobs at Bolivar cannot all be turned into learning experiences, but learning can still occur in the sheltered, work-related environment of the company college.

Developing the Human Resource

If employers are to attract, motivate, and retain workers in the future, they will probably find it necessary to create conditions in which educated workers can realize their desire to learn on the job. The central task of management will be to develop human resources with the same energy with which it has developed natural resources and capital goods. There are many policies and programs that would help managers realize these goals, but these efforts are often undercut by traditional work-force forecasting, planning, and training concepts that are incompatible with meeting the emerging needs of workers and the changing realities of the labor market.

As a first step toward more fully developing human resources, the nation will have to abandon its goal of accurate forecasting. Because it will be increasingly difficult to predict labor-force demand in the future, and nearly impossible to train workers for the nebulous generalist and service careers likely to dominate in the future, a new concept of work-force planning may be called for.

Instead of trying to predict demand, train workers for specific tasks, and match them to jobs (an effort that, at any rate, would require authoritarian measures in order to do much more than what America is already accomplishing in these areas), we can create a labor market that is fluid, flexible, and diverse, one characterized by change, greater freedom of choice, and a heavy accent on providing workers with the opportunity to achieve their own growth and learning needs—as *they* define them and at their own pace. Significantly, this freedom could exist within the existing corporate organizational framework. In short, the making of plans and policies on employment and training might shift from the national level to the more manageable and pluralistic level of individuals and firms.

In his forecast of the future of work-force planning in large corporations, management consultant James Walker (1974) sees organizational structure, job design, the work week, compensation schedules, and almost every other facet of management becoming more flexible. Already, more and more workers are being given the responsibility and resources for planning and evaluating their own career development. For example, in place of a fixed employment and training plan, Walker writes that some companies are experimenting with a free, internal job market in which openings are posted, informing workers of the skills, training, and experience needed for the jobs.

Companies are taking the following kinds of other actions to enhance career and job flexibility and to develop human resources:

● increasing individualized career planning and development, with an emphasis on continuous training for all workers.

● introducing flexible work schedules which permit time off for reschooling, child care, and other activities.

● facilitating sabbaticals, including exchanges of employees among government agencies, industries, and schools.

● providing lateral transfers and temporary project assignments to develop and stimulate workers when traditional career paths up the hierarchy are blocked.

● establishing company schools to cater to the education and training needs of employees.

Consequences for the Schools

Simply stated, there are signs that much of the burden for social change will be placed on the shoulders of employers as society relies less and less on the schools as agents for the reformation of society. The implication of this nascent shift is a radically altered role for the schools in preparing youth for work. This transfer might occur quite smoothly, because the functions of schools are not fixed by any set of natural laws. In any time, place, or culture, societies can place quite different demands on schools (within the broad framework, of course, of socializing the young and instilling some of the inherited wisdom of the race).

In fact, in the United States the tasks assigned to the schools have grown enormously over the past two centuries. Although the family once had the prime responsibility for the social welfare of the young, since the American Revolution one can trace a slow but persistent encroachment on this function by other institutions. Starting with Horace Mann's attempts to use education as the means to remake America into a classless society, reformers have increasingly looked to the schools to achieve all sorts and kinds of social change. By the late 1960s, schools and colleges were broadly charged with the following kinds of social functions: achieving social equality; integrating the races; eliminating sexism; cooling off the expectations of the lower classes; baby-sitting and other custodial activities; warehousing youth to keep them off the labor market; increasing the gross national product through upgrading the work force; training youth for jobs; sorting, certifying, and selecting talent; catching up with the Russians in science and technology; recruiting and training youth for the military; providing hot lunches, health care, and counseling and instruction about sex, drugs, and driving.

The schools have not yet, to my knowledge, been used as centers for the eradication of those quintessential American scourges—halitosis, dandruff, and tired blood—but the odds would favor it if present trends were to continue. In short, society has attempted to utilize the schools as levers to correct nearly every evil known to humankind. As a consequence, they have corrected very few. The recent criticisms of the schools by Jencks, Coleman, and others merely document what most Americans have suspected: no single institution—not even one as important as the schools—is able to fully compensate for the failures of the society, economy, polity, community, and family. More important, the schools have never really been on the cutting edge of change in America; they have traditionally served as handmaidens for the economy, military, agriculture, or science.

Much of the current disillusionment with the performance of the schools, then, is misplaced. Nevertheless, voters, elected representatives, and government administrators are likely to continue to balk at requests from the schools for greater financial support. In their eyes, the schools have "failed." To the school official worrying about the next year's budget, this situation constitutes a crisis. In the long run, however, this contraction of support may be salutary for the schools, for there is nothing more astringent for an institution than a little lowering of expectations. When society no longer looks to the schools to serve as universal ameliorators, the schools will find themselves rid of a great deal of excess baggage they have been forced to pack around.

Employers' Shoulders Must Be Broad

Still, transferring so much responsibility for developing human resources onto the shoulders of employers has many potential pitfalls, not the least of which is the understandable reluctance of employers to assume any additional social burdens. And there is a real risk of exploitation of workers—historically, it cannot be claimed that most employers have placed the well-being of workers very high on their scale of values. However, these problems are not insurmountable. Society has had to monitor employer performance in almost all areas of job-related benefits, including pension plans and health insurance, and thus the monitoring of employers' handling of human resource development should not present a new order of problem. Moreover, this is clearly an area where labor unions could effectively use their considerable clout to protect their members. And, one hopes, the changing demands placed on managers by the young workers they must motivate and retain will lead to a shift in employer attitudes in the long run, making human resources development as natural a task for managers as planning, coordination, and control are today.

Most clearly, this shift implies a greater role for on-the-job training than for vocational schooling. Training employees at the workplace has several fairly obvious advantages: it is a long-range employer investment rather than a temporary measure at public expense; trainees are paid while they learn; there is less emphasis on educational credentials; problems of forecasting do not arise because employers know their needs and can meet them quickly; the skills developed are really put to use by employees; and workers are positively motivated to learn.

Unfortunately, most such training programs do not lead to the fullest development of human resources because they are characterized by one or more of the following shortcomings:

● Uneven distribution of training opportunities. Managers and professionals benefit from most of the training; blue-collar workers may scarcely participate.

● Lack of quality programing.

● Narrow training—instruction may be focused only on specific tasks; there may be no teaching of theory or adaptable skills, or human growth may not be a goal of the program.

● Untransferability of skills learned—there may be no academic credit offered. Thus, training tends to tie workers to current employers.

● Lack of employer knowledge about education. There are shortages of qualified instructors, there is often an inability to teach theory, and there are problems in coping with differences in learning motivation based on class, sex, race, or age.

A small but increasing number of employers are recognizing these shortcomings and establishing innovative training programs to more fully develop their human resources. IBM, for example, has published a "Personal Growth and Vitality Inventory," which is designed to help employees assess their own needs and to develop themselves and their careers, often through utilizing the resources of one of the company's 275 education centers. Kimberly-Clark offers employees two weeks of annual leave with pay to go to school and up to one year of educational leave with pay for work-related study; it has also established "educational savings accounts" that can produce as much as eight thousand dollars in fifteen years for schooling for employees and their families. The RAND and Arthur D. Little corporations are accredited to grant doctorates, providing the instruction themselves. General Motors Institute offers a bachelor's degree in engineering or industrial administration for a five-year program in which six-week work and study programs are alternated. The 3M Company offers college-level courses in math and science and a variety of levels of instruction in many other subjects. Xerox Corporation recently opened its International Center for Training and Management Development, a seventy-five-million-dollar "university" featuring innovative educational techniques. RCA makes videotapes available to workers for use on their own time.

Credentials and Meritocracy

Increasing industry's training role is likely to compound the already Byzantine system of credentialing workers and learners. America is currently without a fair and rational system for legitimating hierarchical differences in the labor market. Our current credentialing system is corrupt, illogical, anachronistic, and at the core of the worst disjunctions between education and work. And the recent invalidation of I.Q. and other tests, the inflation of grades, the advent of open admissions and affirmative action, the move toward broader and more far-reaching professional certification and occupational licensing, and the unjustifiable credential requirements placed on every job from boxing groceries to practicing medicine have all conspired to undercut the nation's progress toward creating a legitimate meritocracy. A meritocracy will only flourish where competition is seen to be fair, where credentials are perceived to be accurate representations of performance and attainment, where standards are viewed as just and nondiscriminatory, and where the criteria of excellence are seen as equitable bases for distributing jobs, status, and the other valued resources and rewards of society.

Since there is no likely future in which credentials will cease to exist, the question is whether it is the school, the employer, or a combination of both agencies that is to be charged with training and credentialing. Even if the courts continue to rule against the improper use of credential requirements for job applicants and for promotion (as they have in *Griggs* v. *Duke Power Company* and *Buckner* v. *Goodyear Tire and Rubber Company*), some kinds of licensing and credentialing will persist. Thus, the problem is to create a credentials system that does not subvert the processes of learning and growth on the job. All that can be hoped for in this regard is to create a system that is fair; that is, one that allows for equal access, easy upgrading, and credit for experience, however gained. The basic framework for such a system may exist in competency-based credentials, which were discussed in the last chapter. The task is to join this kind of school reform with the workplace reforms designed to make jobs into learning experiences.

For such a marriage to occur, there would have to be broad acceptance of new criteria for what constitutes an educated person. Stephen Bailey argues that a person is not necessarily educated because he or she has served a twelve- or sixteen-year sentence in an educational institution; more precisely, the educated person "knows how his field of specialization relates to other areas and divisions of human knowledge and experience" (1973, p. 230). To Bailey, the educated person is one who manifests that he has undergone a process of personal growth and shows excellence in his chosen field. Bailey makes a strong case for recognition of such excellence achieved on the job: "In the way of illustration, a master plumber who had understood physical theories of water pressure, levers, and valves; who had extended his interest in pipes to include the physical and musical principles underlying the trombone; or who had traced water in the faucet back to ecological issues of water conservation should be recognized and academically credentialed as "an educated person," whether or not he had met formal distribution requirements in some college catalog" (p. 230).

A New Role for the Schools

A difficulty that arises in the integration of Bailey's proposal with on-the-job training is that few employers are competent to teach the theoretical information that underlies work, and even fewer are in the position to examine or meaningfully credential their workers. Some workers will overcome this problem by attending classes at local schools or colleges and by convincing school authorities of their competence. But there are real limitations to the amounts of such self-initiated activity that we can, or should, expect. First of all, only 4 percent of those involved in formal adult education have less than a high school diploma; blue-collar workers simply are uncomfortable in middle-class educational institutions. Second, why should we expect workers to pursue rigid, formal, school-based educations just when nontraditional approaches are being advocated for young middle-class students?

That workers want their learning to be work-based should be viewed not as an obstacle to offering them academic credit but as an opportunity for the true integration of work and learning. Schools could take the initiative and approach employers with programs for granting workers academic credit for what they learned on the job. Using flexible performance certification or competency-based systems, the educational institution would grant credit for learning that occurred on the job, in class, or wherever. The hallmark of such a system would be that it facilitated the continuous upgrading of workers' credentials.

Educators would work with employers to improve the quality of on-the-job training. They would help to apply the principles of mastery learning to take workers through successively more complex stages of information about their work. Educators could offer theoretical instruction on the job, and they could develop supporting courses in the classroom, perhaps team-taught with supervisors from the company. In addition, educators could serve as expert consultants—developing sound curricula, helping to overcome the learning problems of older and disadvantaged workers, and, most singularly, offering a system of recognition and transferable credits for what workers learn.

Schools and universities, currently searching for new clientele, would benefit from an arrangement that gave them access to adult workers. Employers would provide equipment and facilities and give employees some time off for educational purposes. They would pay for tuition and would offer their own staffs as teachers on the job and off. (Although this sounds a bit utopian, the 3M Company has instituted a remarkably similar experiment.) However, some employers, particularly small ones, would probably contend that the return from such a system did not warrant the expense. In response, one can only argue that job-redesign experiments in which learning has been the goal have led to decreases in absenteeism, turnover, and job dissatisfaction. Moreover, several recent studies show that employers feel their rate of return on the twenty billion dollars or so they spend annually on training is low, and many employers look to improving school-employer relations as a step in increasing this return. Also, employers have seen the value of their own executive development programs and, hence, may be open to finding out whether such benefits will accrue from similar programs for middle- and lower-level workers. Finally, the chronic problems of underemployment may come to force employers to stress learning on the job.

There is a crucial distinction between what I propose here and the current trend among some small liberal arts colleges toward turning themselves into vocational training centers for industry in order to avert bankruptcy. According to the *Wall Street Journal*, Lambuth College in Tennessee, for example, has become a center for training future Holiday Inn employees. Its chairman of philosophy and religion objects to this development, arguing against the notion that "education's prime purpose is to teach young people how to earn a living." However, Lambuth's president has a different philosophy. He says that "we're all economic creatures, no matter how idealistic we like to be." But if Dewey's principles were to be followed, the integration of work and learning would not lead to schools' becoming the handmaiden of industry; rather, this marriage could lead to a healthy reform and revitalization of both institutions. If such were the case, then trade-union opposition to human resources development activities might also be overcome. The need for this is great—not only to ensure the protection of workers, but to free the one to two billion dollars designated for worker education that is currently sitting unused in union trust funds. Exactly how much money is available or why it is unused is unknown, yet one may speculate that it is untapped because: (a) some workers are unaware of its availability; (b) it may only be used in traditional educational institutions that are threatening or inconvenient for workers, or (c) the educational programs that are open to workers seem irrelevant to their interests or needs. Overcoming these problems offers unions the opportunity to realize the Dewey-like vision that Samuel Gompers offered to the National Education Association in 1916: "education should provide so wide an understanding of the relation of one's work to society that no vocation could become a rut and no worker could be shut off from a full and rich life in his work itself" (quoted in Herman, 1974, p. 67).

What is most evident is that workers would benefit from a change in the current education-work system. Although such reforms alone cannot meet the problems of underemployment, they nevertheless can do some things to remove the growing contradictions between expectations and realities in industrial society. In order to increase the opportunities for individual growth, increase social justice and social productivity, ways need to be found to provide greater complementarity between the learning and work aspects of life.

Most important, these workplace changes would complement a broader dismantling of the outdated, mechanistic life path that has developed for workers in industrial society—the canonical path in which education is synonymous with youth, work with adulthood, and retirement with old age, the pattern that segments life into age traps and segregates generations into age ghettos. With the development of human resources as the society's central goal, education, work, and leisure could be experienced as continuing strands running throughout each person's life, each to be stressed by the individual at the appropriate stage in his or her career.

What is keeping American unions and employers from acting on this opportunity? The obstacle, we are often told, is that such reforms are incompatible with our capitalist system. The next chapter is a critical analysis of this widely shared contention.

9

Capitalism:
The Problem
or the Solution?

Two widely divergent paths are currently being advocated as leading to solutions to the problems of work in America. Much that is attractive can be found down both paths; unfortunately, each is also beset with serious obstacles that seem to make the route unsatisfactory.

The Left Path

E.F. Schumacher, Barry Commoner, Michael Harrington, and John Kenneth Galbraith have come to the conclusion that human and natural resources will never be properly utilized in a capitalistic economy. The record of free-market economics leads these critics to decide that only some form of socialism (that is, the state ownership or control of the major means of production) offers hope for improving the quality of life of the employed, unemployed, and underemployed.

In some respects, the record *is* clear: in the Marxist states there is little or no unemployment. The hitch, of course, is that in Russia and China one has practically no choice about where one will work; moreover, if one chooses not to work, one in effect also chooses not to eat. Marxist states are not welfare states; with few exceptions, the provision of food, clothing, shelter, and health care is contingent on a work effort. This streak of inhumanity added to the loss of freedom and efficiency inherent in centralized planning, is enough to dissuade most Western critics from adopting the classical Marxist model.

Consequently, in Western Europe, the goal has been to create "socialism with a human face." In England and Italy, where the nationalization of industry has gone farthest, unemployment rates have, indeed, been lower than they have been in the United States. However, it is not true as a rule, or even as a generalization, that *more* socialism correlates with *lower* rates of unemployment in the Western democracies. For example, Germany, Switzerland, and Sweden, whose economies are more market-oriented than those in Italy and England, are having lower rates of unemployment during the mid-1970s recession. Thus, government ownership of the means of production is not all that determines a democracy's ability to cope with unemployment. Other variables such as culture, national will, the relationship between management and unions, the availability of capital, and sound economic stewardship in the national parliaments are more important.

Underemployment, too, does not seem to be amenable to simple Marxist solutions. Even the most final of all "solutions," the complete nationalization of industry and the abandonment of a free labor market, does not seem to solve the problem. A glimpse into the Soviet method for dealing with manpower planning is provided by the following item from the *National On-Campus Report* (July, 1973):

> All of this year's 40,000 college graduates in the Soviet Union will get jobs in their specialties, the Deputy Minister of Higher Education of the U.S.S.R. recently reported. And what's more, the students won't be hassled with interviews, resumes, tired feet, or decisions

because personal appointment of the young specialists
to their jobs is taken care of by each educational institution's commission. What if the student doesn't like the
commission's choice? Oh well, that hardly ever happens,
says the Deputy Minister. But if a student can give
weighty reasons for his dissatisfaction, the commission
may reevaluate the decision. Illness or parental dis-
ability are considered valid reasons for a graduate
opting for a job outside his specialty.

Not only is this "solution" to the problems of underemployment unacceptable to Western liberals, it isn't any more effective
than our sloppy methods based on individual freedom of choice.
Job dissatisfaction, low productivity, and class inequalities seem
to be as rampant from the Danube to the Volga as they are in the
Western democracies. It is clear that underemployment falls in
the same category of problems as pollution and alienation, which
are endemic to advanced nations (be they socialist, capitalist, or
some mutant) and are a part of the price paid for materialism and
a relatively high standard of living. Therefore, I conclude that—
short of following in the path of China or Tanzania by severely
limiting education, restricting more than 80 percent of our population to agricultural pursuits, and switching to the production
of steel in backyard furnaces—socialism is no answer to the problems of underemployment.

In fact, managers of state-owned firms seem even *less* concerned with the quality of the lives of their workers than do managers in private companies. In Europe, for example, privately
held Fiat, Volvo, and Saab are light years ahead of such state-
owned auto makers as Renault and British Leyland Motor Cars
in experiments to humanize working conditions. (And if a clean
environment is your goal, don't depend on state managers to
achieve it: Marshall Goldman (1973) has shown how growth-
oriented Soviet managers are even more insensitive to the problems of pollution than their capitalist counterparts.)

The Right Path

In America, most economists would argue that the problems of
unemployment could be greatly alleviated if there were freer play

in the market. There is no doubt that reducing the government's role would lead to a more "rational" allocation of resources and that the resultant increase in competition would spur the economy, thus creating more jobs. However, it is a bit unrealistic to advocate an Adam Smith model for the U.S. economy: about a third of the G.N.P. is generated by government activities, and there is no practical prospect of a withering role for federal, state, and local governments. At a certain age, one must quit believing in the tooth fairy.

Underemployment is a trickier problem, but many excellent and progressive economists are bullish about the market's solving it. Howard Bowen, for example, believes the market will adjust to the greater supply of educated workers, forcing employers to redesign some jobs, automate others, and create new, good ones. He even predicts that a large supply of highly educated workers will break the invidious connection of educational credentials and job status. Unlike most critics, he sees few problems arising from truck drivers' having Ph.D.s:

> A future society in which everyone is educated to the limit of his abilities and interests, in which the connection between education and jobs is recognized as the loose and flexible one it really is, in which there will be relatively few menial jobs, in which the range of compensation between white-collar and blue-collar jobs will be greatly narrowed, and in which blue-collar work will gain increasing respect as well as compensation—such a society is to be viewed with favor [1973, p. 11].

This is a most attractive future. In fact, if one looks hard enough, one can find some evidence that the labor market is adjusting itself to cope with underemployment in the way Bowen posits. Unhappily, at the rate it is adjusting, it would probably take several decades before it could meet the needs and desires of most workers—a fact that offers scant comfort for recent college graduates. An alternative future is one in which the attitudes and expectations of workers will change to meet the requirements of the labor market. For example, a recent newspaper article (Harris, 1976) tells of a twenty-nine-year-old college graduate who has taken a job as an "elevator mechanic helper" although his degree is in psychology. When asked if he is happy repairing elevators, he replied: "Sure. I'm satisfied. I always felt psychology was more of a subject I wanted to study for self-improvement." This remarkable young man plans to continue taking courses in psychology as well as courses directly related to his job. The reason why he is remarkable, of course, is that he is so unlike others of his generation. How long would it take before his attitude about the purpose of education came to be the dominant attitude of society? The time needed to change either jobs or attitudes is thus a limitation to the otherwise desirable free-market future that Bowen describes.

There are several other major shortcomings and untoward second-order consequences to the policy of "giving the market a chance to work" on the problems of unemployment and underemployment:

● It was the market that created such problems as underemployment, chronic pockets of unemployment, and dissatisfying jobs. Thus, it would be naive to expect the market to turn around and solve these without some guidance.

● The market does not automatically internalize the total social costs of a product, such as the cost of air pollution or the poor health of dissatisfied workers. Thus, there are some inefficiencies in even a free market.

● Left alone, the market tends to eliminate competition (creating oligopolies and monopolies) and fails to provide adequately for public goods and services (clean air, parks, hospitals, museums). Thus, although the market is exceptionally efficient in the short term, it does not always efficiently allocate goods and services in a way that will produce the maximum long-term benefits for the society.

● The market satisfies those needs that are based on purchasing power. The distribution of goods and services is "just," then, only insofar as the distribution of incomes is just.

• The labor market probably does not behave like the classical market for eggs, coal, or television sets. Indeed, there may be certain humane objections to allowing the full consequences of a labor market to be played out in the way that it is efficient to, say, let unproductive firms fold and products go off the market.

These inefficiencies and negative secondary results make it difficult to advocate a totally free-market solution to the employment problems of the society. And since socialistic policies entail certain losses of efficiency, standards of quality, and freedom (and even compound some of the worst problems of the economy, such as the creation of monopoly and noninternalized costs), it also seems inappropriate to advocate socialism as the best way to develop human resources.

Nevertheless, this dilemma-in-the-making can be overcome by applying a liberal imagination. The challenge is to find policies that will respond to the market-induced problems of work without resorting to the inefficient and freedom-threatening nationalization of industry. What is needed is a just alternative to socialism.

Such an alternative might take many forms. Since society is unlikely to invent an entirely new way to organize work and to allocate goods and resources, any future system would be eclectic. In some respects it would draw on capitalistic concepts, and in other respects it would require a forceful government role. Although this system might appear somewhat similar to the system already in effect, it differs in that market mechanisms would be consciously used as tools to achieve specific, democratically chosen goals (such as the development of human resources). Currently, there are no goals for the society, and we allow the market to determine where we will go as a nation. As Daniel Bell (1971) points out, we thus confuse means (the market) for ends (consciously chosen goals). The consequence is a national sense of floundering and drift and often even arriving at a goal we would never have consciously set.

On the one hand, market competition is appropriate to the future of work in several ways: it eliminates the need for Soviet-style central planning and it offers more conditions of work and greater freedom to choose among these. Choice, freedom, diversity, and flexibility—the hallmarks of market systems—stimulate the innovation and experimentation needed to break down the current monolithic structure of life paths and the rigidity of job structures. History shows that satisfaction with life and work cannot be mandated. This is why current efforts to legislate the proposals made in *Work in America* (Solomon, 1975) not only are doomed to failure, but are likely to create a negative reaction among business and labor leaders—a reaction that will actually forestall reform.

On the other hand, government does have a role in meeting the problems of American workers. While the market will ensure freedom and efficiency, the government must act to provide greater equality and justice. Some kind of democratic, national indicative planning (without the powers of allocation and price setting) is needed to achieve the necessary goal setting for the society. And the means must be found to increase the accountability of managers of giant corporations to the needs of their employees and of society in general.

In some ways, the major stumbling block to developing liberal human resource policies is the values and norms of the managers who run the nation's largest and most powerful private and public institutions. For a variety of reasons, spelled out in Chapter Four, the prevailing managerial culture in America is wary of the innovation, experimentation, flexibility, and risk taking required to achieve a Quality Society. Moreover, the managers of the one thousand largest corporations in the United States are often capable of working their will against the interests of the majority of Americans, as well as against the interests of their workers and shareholders. At issue, then, is not greedy capitalists but security-conscious bureaucrats who manage the major corporations in the United States.

Capitalists and the American *Apparatchik*

Newspapers across the nation recently ran dramatic and foreboding stories concerning public attitudes toward the American economic system. The following headline from the *Los Angeles Times* was typical: "Distrust of Capitalism Found in U.S." (August

31, 1975, p. 5). The article under those words dealt with an opinion poll conducted by Peter Hart, the findings of which belied the glib and portentous tone of the headline writer. According to Hart's poll, Americans are indeed upset with many of the economic policies of big government and the practices of big business that, together, have led to high unemployment and chronic inflation. But in the midst of a recession, these are hardly startling findings. In fact, Hart's poll would have been noteworthy in this regard only had he found otherwise.

Hart's poll is significant, nonetheless, because of his counter-intuitive finding that Americans actually do *not* distrust capitalism (a finding which must have upset the radical People's Bicentennial Commission that sponsored the poll). Assuming that Hart's poll is accurate, what is unexpected and important is that overwhelming numbers of Americans seem to favor more capitalism rather than less. What Americans appear to distrust is the giant U.S. and multinational corporations that wield enormous economic, social, and political power. The problem Americans have with these institutions is not that they are capitalistic but that they lack accountability. Peter Drucker has written that corporations should be accountable to their owners and to the societies in which they operate and responsible for the well-being of their workers. Apparently, what irks the majority of Americans is that many corporations find it possible to shirk their responsibilities to all three of these constituencies.

The managers of such corporate giants as GM, Mobil Oil, and I.T. and T., for example, are not easily held accountable by the owners of the firms. The simple reason is that no one individual or readily identifiable group of people "owns" a company like GM—the majority of its shares are held by other institutions. There is not even an independent board of directors to monitor the behavior of the firm, because the majority of the board members at GM and many other large companies are not outside shareholders but managers of the firm. If this situation were not enough to send shivers down the spine of a disciple of Adam Smith, another element would be: many of the most powerful corporate leviathans are not even held in check by the competitive forces of a free market—the auto and computer industries, to name only a significant pair, are oligopolistic.

Nor is society fully able to hold the giants accountable to its needs and wishes through governmental laws and regulations. Because of the political clout that results from their economic power, large corporations can often lobby, evade, or, as we have seen recently, bribe their way around governmental checks and balances. And if their backs are to the wall, such companies can simply pack up and move their operations to more compatible shores. (The president of Mobil recently threatened the Congress that he would move his firm out of the United States if they dared to buck his wishes on a key piece of legislation.) And in the area that affects Americans most directly—the safety, mental health, and physical health of workers—few large corporations demonstrate great concern, let alone concern for developing and utilizing their skills and ideas. Consequently, demands for more worker participation and an improved quality of working life have greatly increased in the United States and in Europe. In short, the distrust of the system is directed at the large corporations, whose *managers* are often unaccountable to owners, to a competitive marketplace, to governments, or to workers.

Nevertheless, according to Hart, 81 percent of Americans see great danger in transfering the control of these corporations into the hands of the government. The public, though disillusioned with the status quo, seems to understand that such a "reform" would not increase corporate accountability. In the Soviet Union, for example, it is not the people but a managerial party elite who control the wealth of the nation. In the Soviet system, property rights (more important than actual ownership) inhere in the state. In effect, under "state capitalism," economic power is controlled by the *apparatchik,* who, in turn, hold the preponderance of political power. Two decades ago, in the important but overlooked book *The Capitalist Manifesto,* Mortimer Adler defined the issue in this way: in all societies the formula for holding political power is the same—those who control the nation's wealth also control its politics. The problem with this equation, of course, is that those without political power are usually denied their full share of liberty, equality, and legal justice. To create a just system in which liberty is guaranteed and equality nurtured, it is therefore necessary to have a low concentration of political power. Socialism can never be such a system because wealth, and thus political power, is concentrated in the hands of the state, and party bureaucrats and state managers become a powerful force accountable to no one. Indeed, following Adler's line of reasoning, the prime reason why the United States is a more just society than the Soviet Union is that political and economic power is more widely dispersed in this country.

What is alarming to a growing number of Americans, however, is that the managers of giant corporations in this country are beginning to become a kind of American *apparatchik*. The system of growing unaccountability of large enterprises might even be evolving into what could be called corporate socialism. John Kenneth Galbraith and other socialists hail this trend, realizing as they do that the concentration of wealth and power facilitates the ultimate nationalization of industry.

In a recent article, Galbraith (1975) called for the stepped-up training of public managers to prepare for the day when they will run the productive enterprises in the American economy. Such preparations are probably unnecessary; if European experience is any guide, managers are only too happy to stay on and work in recently nationalized firms. To the professional manager, ownership appears to be irrelevant. State-owned enterprises and large publicly held corporations often even share the same goals and managerial culture; both place growth above profits, and managerial security above innovation and entrepreneurial activity.

According to the Hart poll, Americans wish to reverse this trend by administering a strong dose of capitalism to the economic system. Something like 66 percent of those polled favor employees' owning most of the stock of the companies for which they work. There seems to be a rather widespread feeling that accountability and responsible behavior are more likely in firms owned by workers than in those in which owners are mere speculators who take no interest in the management of "their" firms. Moreover, Americans seem to feel that capitalism is the most just system in terms of providing liberty, equality, and access to property. By logical extension, they seem to be saying that if capitalism is a just system, then justice would be served by broadening the base of capitalism.

In addition, Adler argues that broadening the base of capitalism is the only way to pursue equality and liberty simultaneously. Under all other possible systems, these central goals of a society are antithetical.

This dispersion of ownership is something quite different from what Drucker writes about in *The Unseen Revolution: How Pension Fund Socialism Came to America*. Drucker misses the mark in several key respects. He claims that because pension funds own 25 percent of the stock in American industry, this country is on its way to being the first truly "socialist nation." Hardly. First of all, Drucker's definition of socialism is inaccurate. Socialism is ownership of the means of production by the state, not by the workers, as he claims. Second, the kind of stock-market ownership to which he refers is basically meaningless. That is, no one any longer thinks of the shareholders in major corporations as the "owners" of the firm—they are mere investors or speculators. To claim, then, that the members of the United Auto Workers whose pension funds are invested in, say, Mobil Oil stock are the owners of Mobil is as ridiculous as to claim that the depositors in a mutual savings and loan institution are its owners. The rights of ownership are held by the professional managers who control these firms. Control is what is important, and the managers have shown that control can be achieved without stock ownership. Moreover, the pension funds are usually invested in companies other than those in which the workers are employed. Logically, then, workers cannot think of themselves as owners of their firms or as managers of their own fates. If the goal is to allow workers the right of self-management so they can participate in decisions that affect their own future, then pension-fund ownership is of no more value to a worker than state ownership. Thus, only in the sense that workers have no control over the firms in which they work is there any parallel to socialism in what Drucker describes.

If I read the Hart poll and the recent demands for increased worker participation accurately, our citizens are not simply saying that they want to "own a share of America" (as an ill-fated program of the New York Stock Exchange once promised), but that they want to share both the ownership and the management of the companies in which they work.

Universal Capitalism

The recent purchases of several firms by employees indicates that this desire is real, not just the product of the idle imaginations of professors. As such, it deserves to be recognized and evaluated by public and corporate decision makers. In point of fact, the Employment Retirement Income Security Act of 1974 and the Tax Reduction Act of 1975 give considerable incentive to the movement that is coming to be known as "universal capitalism." Although this system is by no means the only just alternative to socialism, or necessarily the most desirable one, its increasing popularity commands our attention:

● In northern Vermont, 180 asbestos miners bought their mine from the G.A.F. Corporation when the company decided to close the plant rather than spend a million dollars for pollution control equipment. The workers purchased the mine in 1975 for two and a half million dollars and, thanks in part to their greater productivity and a booming asbestos market, were soon running the mine in the black.

● In 1975, forty one employees in a knitting mill in Saratoga, New York, purchased their plant from its parent firm for less than a million dollars. Their goal was to rehire another seventy workers who had been laid off when the firm's original owners started cutting back production in the mill.

● In South Bend, Indiana, four hundred forty employees in a lathe company bought their plant for ten million dollars. In the first year of employee-ownership, productivity increased by twenty percent and profits by ten percent.

● In Washington, D.C., after innumerable legal hassles, three hundred employees of International Group Plans, an insurance company, now own half of the company and occupy half of the seats on the board of directors.

But worker ownership is not new in the U.S. It has been a fairly common response to the threat of unemployment that often accompanies the announcement of the closing of an unprofitable firm. For example, during the Depression the employees of a couple dozen small plywood mills in Oregon bought out the owners when it was announced that the mills would be closed. Thirteen of these firms are still in business as cooperatives. There is nothing "leftist" or socialistic about cooperatives. The conservative magazine *U.S. News and World Report* is owned entirely by its employees. Worker capitalism is a more attractive option than socialism, for several social, political, and economic reasons, some of which are illustrated in the following tale of two cities.

In New York City, it was commonly accepted that garbagemen had bad and dirty jobs. Service was miserable, and the cost of collection was high. In an attempt to meet this problem, the city raised the salaries of garbagemen to nearly $13,000 per annum. But service remains miserable, the cost of collection is higher, garbagemen are thought by their neighbors to have such poor jobs that they have to be bought off—and an inflationary spiral of wage hikes among other city employees has been launched. In San Francisco, on the other hand, it is commonly accepted that garbagemen have good jobs. Service is excellent (one management consultant from New York has said, "In San Francisco, the garbagemen *run* from trash can to trash can"), the cost of collection is low, and garbagemen are thought of by their neighbors as businessmen. Unlike those in New York, San Francisco garbagemen are owners in a collective enterprise, sharing in profits, in all duties (including fee collection), and in decision making.

Universal capitalism is particularly attractive *if* we hold that (a) workers have widely diverse wants and needs, (b) no one party can or should dictate to the heterogenous work force what "satisfying work conditions" are or should be, and (c) workers themselves should decide when, how, and with whom they will work. If these are the conclusions of society, then putting the power to make such decisions clearly in the hands of workers/owners makes sense.

Countries as diverse in their political orientation as Peru, Iran, Sweden, and Yugoslavia have all made worker ownership a keystone of their future political policies. In America, however, many managers are outraged by the thought of workers acting as capitalists. Managers feel that they stand to lose a great deal of power if the trend continues (workers in some firms, for example, reportedly have found that they can achieve significant savings by eliminating levels of managers—a lesson not unnoticed by managers in other firms). Even some socialist intellectuals are alarmed by the prospect of greater democratic participation in the owning and running of productive enterprises. These individuals have repeatedly experienced rejection by workers who "don't know what is good for them" (witness the McGovern campaign). Politicians, bankers, and government bureaucrats also seem wary of the potential consequences of universal capitalism. The idea has support, it would seem, "only" from two-thirds of the American public.

This apparently broad base of support does not suggest, however, that universal capitalism is an idea whose time has come. In practice, like many other noble ideas, this one has often not worked very well. In Great Britain, for example, worker-ownership in the motorcycle industry was a multimillion-dollar fiasco. Part of the failure of the company was because it was already in such a shambles when it was turned into a cooperative that there was no way to save it. Nevertheless, it is clear that worker-ownership is no panacea for mismanagement. In the United States, most companies that have been purchased by workers also have disappointing records, particularly in enhancing worker participation in decision making and in improving working conditions—areas in which, one presumes, the workers/owners would most clearly see their self-interests to lie. What has often happened is that the prerogatives of management have not passed to the workers upon their assuming ownership. For example, when one older plant in the South was willed to the employees on the death of its owner, the transfer of ownership had little to recommend it. The firm has been so marginal economically that the workers have been virtual prisoners of their creditors (who feel that "dumb" workers can't run a plant).

In companies purchased under Louis Kelso's Employee Stock Ownership Plan, real control of firms has usually remained in the hands of professional managers or former owners. The Kelso Plan received a tremendous boost with the passage of the Tax Reduction Act of 1975. Under the provisions of this Act, corporations that form Employee Stock Ownership Plans (ESOPs) are entitled to larger investment tax credits than companies without such plans. ESOPs often involve complicated tax-sheltered trusts formed by employees for purposes of borrowing money for capital improvements in their firms. For example, the trust borrows a million dollars from a bank to enable the company to build a new plant. In exchange for the million, the company issues a like amount of stock in the name of the trust, which is then used as collateral for the loan. Once the loan is paid off, the employee trust has the stock free and clear. The transfer of stock gives the former owners a nice tax break and cheap access to capital, and the employees receive a rather decent pension plan, but real control does not go to the workers.

Thus, the expansion of universal capitalism is currently blocked by the absence of a financing mechanism that would facilitate the widespread purchasing of healthy firms by employees in a way that is equitable to both workers and former owners, and that leads to worker control. Other difficult issues, such as whether and when workers/owners should be able to sell their shares, are still open to considerable debate. Thus, the promise of universal capitalism to create a just society is still only a promise. Ironically, some large corporations have so far done more for their workers than workers have done for themselves in employee-owned firms.

Several explanations may be given for the failures of employee-owned firms. It may well be that universal capitalism is simply too new an idea and that workers do not yet have the experience or self-confidence needed to create a better workplace and life for themselves. Moreover, the examples cited above indicate that managers may have either actively or unwittingly sabotaged the efforts of workers. Then again, perhaps universal capitalism is merely a utopian dream, and other alternatives to socialism offer greater possibilities for justice, equality, liberty, and a higher quality of life for Americans. Certainly, the behavior of some large corporations, such as Xerox, Levi Strauss, and Atlantic-Richfield, suggests that a world of corporate giants may not be inimical to the creation of a more just form of capitalism. These examples raise the hope that accountability can be achieved in a system in which ownership is separate from management. At the least, we should explore how America might make the corporate world in general more like the best aspects of these often socially responsible firms.

If worker capitalism is not the best alternative to socialism, we need to identify other possible futures and to develop realistic policies for fulfilling the best of these. The choice of which option to pursue will, of course, be made by the American people. In this context, Hart's poll tells us two things of great importance: first, Americans favor some form of capitalism over the socialistic alternatives; second, Americans are impatient with the status quo and are demanding significant experimentation with and reform of the system. Of course, the argument for developing more humanistic, responsible, and innovative forms of capitalism should not rest on evidence as flimsy as a single opinion poll. Those who believe in the intrinsic value of market mechanisms and decentralized planning and decision making should favor reform simply because it is just.

The next chapter reviews some other liberal means for creating a Quality Society, a society whose goods, services, and environmental standards are excellent and whose human resources are highly valued and more fully developed.

10

Technology:
Or, Who Wants
To Be a Buddhist?

Most of us are willing candidates for seduction. We secretly wait for a beguiling dark stranger to come along and sweep us off our feet. Seduction is attractive because it comes suddenly, unexpectedly, and without our encouragement, thus absolving us of responsibility and potential guilt. Whether the seducer is a lover, a charismatic political leader, a new religion, or a political idea, the effect is the same—suspension of our normal cynicism that acts as a guard against precipitous behavior.

Schumacher's *Small Is Beautiful: Economics as if People Mattered* (1973) is a thoroughly seductive text, if ever there was one. It arrived on our shores unannounced and, in a romantic fashion, swiftly allured and captivated the hearts and minds of a generation thought to be too cynical and jaded to succumb to the blandishments of a simple and dramatic idea. Schumacher summarizes this idea in a nutshell: "I have no doubt that it is possible to give a new direction to technological development, a direction that shall lead us back to the real needs of man, and that also means: *to the actual size of man.* Man is small, and therefore, small is beautiful" (p. 159). Schumacher provides a blueprint for a society shorn of the myths and conceits of modern economics. With brilliance, wit, and imaginative insights he literally shatters a century's worth of economic theorizing. With graceful and elegant prose he paints an alluring picture of a new society freed from the self-destructive demands of the Bitch Goddess Growth, a society in which technology is in harmony with nature, and in which there is quasi-religious dedication to the principles of "peace and permanence":

> It is easy to see that the effort needed to sustain a way of life which seeks to attain the optimal pattern of consumption is likely to be much smaller than the effort needed to sustain a drive for maximum consumption. We need not be surprised, therefore, that the pressure and strain of living is very much less in, say, Burma than it is in the United States, in spite of the fact that the amount of labor-saving machinery used in the former country is only a minute fraction of the amount used in the latter.
>
> Simplicity and nonviolence are obviously closely related. The optimal pattern of consumption, producing a high degree of human satisfaction by means of a relatively low rate of consumption, allows people to live without great pressure and strain and to fulfill the primary injunction of Buddhist teaching: "Cease to do evil; try to do good" [p. 58].

Such a vision overwhelms us. Even the governor of our most populous state has given himself over to the enticements of Schumacher's Buddhist economics. But strange things often happen after "zipless" debauchments. In the light of morning we awake to find that the dark stranger with whom we have shared our bed is an afflicted harridan, gone in the teeth. Paul Theroux's description of his travels in Burma throws cold water on Schumacher's idealized portrait of lotus land:

Pariah dogs leap from nowhere to snarl over the leavings.

"Why don't they shoot those dogs?" I asked a man at Toungoo.

"Burmese think it is wrong to kill animals."

"Why not feed them then?"

He was silent. I was questioning one of the cardinal precepts of Buddhism, the principle of neglect. Because no animals are killed all animals look as if they are starving to death, and so the rats, which are numerous in Burma, co-exist with the dogs, which have eliminated cats from the country. The Burmese—removing their shoes and socks for sacred temple floors where they will spit and flick cigar ashes—see no contradiction. How could they? Burma is a socialist country with a notorious bureaucracy. But it is a bureaucracy that is Buddhist in nature, for not only is it necessary to be a Buddhist in order to tolerate it, but the Burmese bureaucratic delays are a consistent encouragement to a kind of traditional piety—the commissar and the monk meeting as equals on the common ground of indolent and smiling unhelpfulness. Nothing happens in Burma, but then nothing is expected to happen [Theroux, 1975, p. 184].

Of course, it is not Burma that Schumacher advocates as a model for the world. But could a nation avoid ending up like Burma if it followed Schumacher's precepts? Jolted back to reality by Theroux's stark image, I returned to *Small Is Beautiful* for a clarification of what Schumacher is proposing. I ended up even more confused. He writes that he is offering an alternative to socialism; yet he rejects the market and private ownership of the major means of production. He writes that we should find more appropriate technologies; yet, he advocates only small-scale technologies that often seem inappropriate to the social needs of advanced nations. He writes that he is dedicated to freedom; yet, there is no place for any set of values other than his own in the land of peace and permanence. He writes that his philosophy is appropriate to all stages of economic development; yet, what he advocates seems only a valid prescription for the underdeveloped world.

What sense can be made out of these real or apparent contradictions? What is there that is important and enduring in *Small Is Beautiful,* and what is misleading and faddish? There is value in sorting all of this out, I believe, because Schumacher has had the audacity to break with conventional economic wisdom. He has freed us from the economic constraints and myths that have hampered our ability to develop a meaningful philosophy of human resources. Ironically, before we can develop this philosophy we must first free ourselves now from some aspects of Schumacher's Buddhist economics.

Many Americans have been so carried away with Buddhist economics that they overlook the fact that it is an appropriate philosophy only for the underdeveloped world. Although we share Schumacher's goals of clean environment, the conservation of energy and natural resources, and a human-oriented, full-employment economy freed from undisciplined growth, we must be careful to recognize that the processes by which he intends to achieve these goals would be impractical, probably downright dangerous, if applied to America. Buddhist economics would lead the United States from its current smoggy, hectic, often alienating condition into an impoverished, unproductive, bureaucratic, and authoritarian one.

For as surely as the Judeo-Christian culture is at the root of the social and material progress of Western Europe and America, Buddhist ethics and principles are at the root of the neglect and poverty found in all Buddhist countries. Changing technology, as Schumacher advocates, will not change culture. And changing culture to accept new technologies is much more difficult than Schumacher posits. Perhaps the most naive assumption in the Schumacher book is that meaningful change will come about when "wisdom" is achieved—that is, when society accepts the primacy of Schumacher's values of "peace and permanence." Pluralistic societies simply do not alter their values in any way that even approximates unanimity—nor should they if freedom and democracy are valued. Thus, if Schumacher is not advocating a totalitarian, enforced change of values and priorities, he must anticipate that the change will result from educational efforts. But altering the attitudes and values of Western man would be the hardest

thing in the world to achieve. Since no one ever got rid of sin by
bemoaning its existence, Schumacher is advocating a process of
change that may take thousands of years—and the urgency of the
problems he identifies would indicate that we can't afford to wait
that long for envy and greed to pass from the Western character.

An even more misguided aspect of his argument is found
in the general assertion that "small is beautiful." As stated, it is
simply wrong in the American context. Small is not *always* more
desirable than big. The "big, bad guys" at IBM, Sears, Xerox, and
Polaroid, for example, are the industrial leaders in protecting
consumers, fighting pollution, hiring minorities, and providing
their workers with interesting jobs, meaningful training opportunities, security, good pensions, and safe and healthy work environments. The small- and middle-size employers—the "alpha"
foundries and "beta" chemical works that compose the majority
of American industry—are the ones primarily responsible for
unsafe products, pollution, and providing workers with low salaries, long hours, and harsh and arbitrary discipline. Not even a
Buddhist would choose working for the Mom and Pop Iron Works
if he could work for U.S. Steel instead. No doubt corporate size
is a major problem in the United States. The giant corporations
wield—and often misuse—enormous political, social, and economic power. But this doesn't always make big ugly, or small beautiful. Such conclusions are much too simple. Earlier I criticized
the contemporary disciples of Adam Smith for their unrealistic
longing for an anachronistic world composed of cottage industries.
Ironically, Schumacher seems also to hanker for an eighteenth-
century economic order. If this attitude is unrealistic on the part of
capitalists, it must be equally unrealistic on the part of Buddhists.

There is one important way in which Schumacher's philosophy
differs from Smith's: Schumacher advocates the partial nationalization of the major means of production as the way to promote
sensible growth and sane technologies and to achieve full employment in meaningful jobs: "I postulate that the public hand should
receive one half of the distributed profits of large-scale enterprise,
and that it should obtain this share not by means of profit taxes
but by means of a 50 percent ownership of the equity of such enterprises" (p. 285). This aspect of Schumacher's philosophy is

seldom mentioned by those Americans to whom he has become a kind of guru. Admittedly, his discussion of socialism comes late in *Small Is Beautiful;* therefore, on the chance that some people may have missed this essential aspect of Schumacher's philosophy because they have not finished the book, consider the following: "In large-scale enterprise, private ownership is a fiction for the purpose of enabling functionless owners to live parasitically on the labor of others. It is not only unjust but also an irrational element which distorts all relationships within the enterprise" (p. 267).

Schumacher is a humane and intelligent man. He does not favor the nationalization of industry along the lines of that undertaken in the Soviet Union, or even in Great Britain. He wishes to avoid centrally planned, nondemocratic, and growth-oriented forms of socialism as much as he wishes to avoid the materialistic, nondemocratic, and growth-oriented forms of corporate capitalism. He seems to favor the Yugoslavian model in which ownership and control of productive enterprise is in the hands of representatives of the community in which they are located. Thus, instead of a capitalistic board of director-owners, or a communistic state planning council, the governing body of a firm should be a "social council" formed "without political electioneering," and composed of the following. "One-quarter of council members to be nominated by local trade unions; one-quarter by the local employer's organizations; one-quarter by local professional associations; and one-quarter to be drawn from local residents in a manner similar to that employed for the selection of persons for jury service" (p. 289).

Significantly, the rights of ownership held by this "public hand" would "normally remain dormant" (p. 288). In effect, the firms would be run by their managers—pretty much as they are today in large American firms and in Soviet enterprises. Although Schumacher does not recognize the fact, the major criticism of the Yugoslavian system is that control of firms in that country has remained in the hands of managers and not in the hands of workers or local community representatives. Moreover, the Yugoslavs have not had great economic success with their system. While more successful than state-owned enterprises in Eastern Europe, Yugoslavian firms lag far behind Western enterprises on almost all

commonly accepted measures of industrial efficiency. Also, the social performance of the Yugoslavian system is not terribly impressive. The country has neither a clean environment nor anything
approaching a full-employment economy. Finally, the political
record is a disaster: The system of industrial governance complements the centralized, authoritarian political structure of which it
is a part.

For some reason, Schumacher refuses to accept that there is
an inescapable relationship between a nation's economic and political systems. Apparently, he feels that it is possible to have, say,
centralized economic planning *and* political freedom. He conveniently ignores the historical and empirical evidence: no country
in the world with central planning and collectivized ownership
offers political freedom. It is clear that a free-market economy and
private property rights are necessary (but not sufficient) conditions
for political liberty. Because Schumacher fails to come to grips
with this evidence, he is not at all convincing when he explains how
he is going to turn the trick of making socialism democratic, non-
bureaucratic and efficient. Moreover, he specifically rejects the
model of worker capitalism for large-scale enterprises (while,
curiously, he favors it for small firms). And he never considers
achieving a small-scale economy by breaking up corporate giants
through vigorous anti-trust activity.

Politically, what is most alarming is Schumacher's badly stated
opposition to "marginal adjustments" (p. 22). Unfortunately,
democratic societies can only make marginal adjustments. Thus,
it appears that democracy is incompatible with his Buddhist policies. Moreover, if the issue were put to a vote, it is clear that the
American people would overwhelmingly choose the culture and
quality of life of Boston over Burma, of New York over New Delhi,
and even Trenton over Thailand. Of course, Schumacher is not
advocating Burma or Thailand as is, but as he would like to remake
them. (This proviso should be of rather scant reassurance to the
American electorate.)

Nevertheless, for India, Bangladesh, Burma, and for most of
the third world, Buddhist economics are probably appropriate
and desirable. In lands without a democratic heritage, without
commitment to the rights of individuals, and without advanced

economies, there is little doubt that Schumacher's economics would be more suitable than the current aping of the industrial growth policies of the West. And any economy at almost any state of development should probably turn away from the polluting, resource-wasteful, and dehumanizing technologies of the industrial revolution, such as the assembly line. In countries with little or no capital base, it is probably sensible to move toward the simpler tools and methods that Schumacher advocates. But in a postindustrial society such as the United States there is another option, one that Schumacher conspicuously and fatally overlooks. In the developed world, it often makes sense to utilize even higher technologies (such as computers) because these create the wealth and productivity on which great numbers of workers engaged in services and low-technology jobs can be economically supported. Schumacher also fails to recognize that high technologies are often human-intensive as well as being capital-intensive. For example, computers and Xerographic equipment require the labors of an incredibly large number of scientists, engineers, managers, technicians, production workers, operators, sales people, and repair people — people in good, rewarding jobs.

But simply because Schumacher fails to recognize the importance of clean, human-intensive, high technologies does not mean that the United States can afford to ignore his significant insights about the interrelationships of growth, size, technology, economics, and work. Rather, we should make use of these insights by inventing a context for them that is appropriate to the American condition and experience. Since Americans are unwilling to abandon a high standard of living, individual freedom, and democratic processes, Buddhist economics are simply inappropriate for this nation. What we require are practical, liberal policies for developing human resources within the democratic traditions and cultural imperatives of Western society. Thus, it is not a Buddhist Economy, but a Quality Society that is needed in America. Let me take a brief pass at trying to make this translation.

Goals of the Quality Society

Authoritarian societies often pursue single goals; with a fervor bordering on fanaticism, the Soviet Union pursues economic growth, China pursues equality, and Iran pursues industrial development. Contrariwise, democratic, pluralistic societies are characterized by myriad competing goals and by conflicting priorities among these. For example, in the United States proposed public policies are often measured against the following kinds of performance criteria which reflect the prime social, political, and economic goals of the many interest groups and stakeholders in the nation: a low rate of unemployment; a low rate of inflation; a reduction of inequality (defined by some as equality of opportunity, by others as equality of outcomes); a high standard of material affluence; individual liberty; freedom in the market place; high productivity and economic efficiency; conservation of energy and natural resources; a high quality of life (including a clean environment, meaningful work and goods that are safe and durable).

To be politically acceptable to the American publics, major policy changes must have few negative consequences when measured against such subjective, shifting, and conflicting standards. Although Schumacher's Buddhist policies would have positive effects on such elements as the quality of life, conservation, unemployment, and equality, they would have negative effects on inflation, the standard of living, liberty, productivity, and efficiency. Hence, they would be unacceptable to management, unions, and to "middle Americans" in general. But is there anywhere a policy that would permit the fuller development of human resources while at the same time meeting these diverse performance criteria?

In Chapter Eight, I called the condition under which these diverse goals are simultaneously maximized "The Quality Society." Although I doubt that there is any single *policy* to achieve this condition, I nevertheless believe that *processes* are available that would lead to the Quality Society. Following Schumacher, I believe one means would be to move away from the technologies of the industrial revolution that currently dominate American industry. But in order to maximize the goals of freedom, productivity, efficiency, a high standard of living, and low inflation, there would be two significant departures from Buddhist economics: (1) the movement would be to high technologies as well as to low technologies, and (2) the movement would occur as the result of market forces—

that is, there would be no nationalization of industry or central economic planning. (There would be goal setting on a national level using existing political structures and limited indicative planning if we could develop useful methods for doing this.) For reasons I outline below, such conditions would allow a more efficient and appropriate choice of technologies than Buddhist bureaucrats could ever dictate. Thus, the shift to a Quality Society would not be accompanied by the bang of revolution or the bark of command, but by the whirr and whine of marginal substitution and democratic change.

In fact, the change is beginning to take place now, and to be successfully realized, it requires only the helping push of liberal policies to replace some of the anachronistic private practices and public policies developed by economists, engineers, and managers over the past four decades.

Rethinking Some Basic Assumptions

Many of the most basic and cost-sensitive practices of American industry are based on assumptions formulated and promulgated by economists and industrial engineers. Managers have been almost entirely dependent on the calculations of these specialists when choosing, designing, and operating the tools of production in their plants. This dependence is creating a new order of problems for management. For example, in many industries (and for many different reasons), economists and engineers have often viewed energy as a "free" factor of production. Like air and water, energy was viewed as so "cheap" during the 1950s and '60s that it was scarcely necessary to reckon its contribution to the cost of a product. Businessmen followed the advice of the experts and chose energy-intensive technologies whenever possible, just as they had chosen technologies that made ample use of "free" clean air and water. The process was rational by the standards of the economists and engineers and paid off in highly "efficient" and "productive" industrial methods.

Then came the reckoning. During the past decade it was discovered that clean air and water do, indeed, come at a price— often a high one. Today, managers are struggling to raise capital to install costly antipollution equipment. And now, thanks to the cartelization of oil, American managers are finding that energy is not free, either. Many industries have chosen energy-intensive technologies on the assumption that the government would keep the cost of energy low enough that it would not be a major cost concern in the future. Now, in many industries, once-efficient capital goods are becoming increasingly expensive to operate as energy becomes ever more dear.

Another assumption on which many basic industrial practices are based is that technology is fixed. Industrial engineers have often led managers to believe that there is only one way to efficiently produce a given product—the way it is currently being produced. Such technological determinism is fast becoming one of the most uneconomical assumptions of American industry. Now, finally, a few farsighted industries are finding that cars, radios, and other consumer goods can be produced efficiently without using assembly-line methods. Continuous process technologies (in which various substances are mixed and treated mechanically and continually instead of by hand and in batches) have also been redesigned to meet human needs. And, in many construction industries, high technology processes have been introduced to create healthier and safer work environments.

Outmoding of Traditional Production Functions

In the past, the appropriate type and scale of technology could be determined through the optimization of what economists call production functions, which are basically equations used to find the best mix of labor, capital, and natural resources to produce a good. But industrialists will be unable to solely rely on this quantitative method of achieving profit maximization in the future. "The one best way," "optimization," "maximization," and "industrial efficiency" are, as Daniel Bell has written (1971), not the only concepts that will impinge on the industrial decision-making process in the late twentieth century. Already, industrial organizations are finding that society will not permit them to pursue a single goal (profit maximization). As executives of most of the leading firms in America are beginning to recognize, businesses are becoming social institutions with many constituencies and many goals. They are still under pressure from stockholders to use capital efficiently in order to increase productivity and profits, but there are new pressures, too: from conservationists to use processes that are environmentally sound; from the government to use energy efficiently; from consumers to produce safe and durable goods; from unions and society to create jobs; and from workers to provide satisfying jobs.

Thus, the traditional task of choosing the right technologies and the right production mix is more important than ever, while the factors influencing the decisions are concomitantly more complex and the consequences of the options less clear. A new calculus, if it can be called that, is needed to incorporate the new qualitative concerns of the society along with the usual quantitative concerns of management for industrial efficiency.

How would this calculus be applied? Not according to any magic formula, because technological tools and methods differ from industry to industry and from plant to plant. And not with a sudden and mass abandoning of current plants and machines. More likely, there would be a gradual shift as new plants and equipment replaced obsolete capital goods. Within these broad parameters, future executives might have to choose processes near the ends of the technological continuum (see Table 7) and move away from the middle-range technologies that were developed in the latter part of the industrial era.

TABLE 7. New Calculus for Choice:
The Technological Continuum

	Low Technology	Middle Technology	High Technology
	◄———————— Trend ————————►		
1. Energy efficiency	Very high	Low	Medium
2. Capital use efficiency	High	Medium	Very high
3. Productivity	Medium/low	Medium	Very high
4. Quality of goods	High	Low	High
5. Environmental soundness	High	Low	Medium
6. Worker satisfaction	Very high	Low	High
7. Labor intensity	Very high	Medium/low	Medium/high

Source: O'Toole, 1976b, p. 111.

It is clear that middle-level technologies are suited for industrial eras characterized by cheap energy, surplus capital, high consumer demand for cheap, mass-produced goods, little environmental concern, and a poorly educated work force. Since the future appears antithetical to all of these characteristics, industry is likely to select either the high productivity of high technology or the high quality of low technology.

In the auto industry, for example, growing pressures for energy and capital efficiency, productivity, and worker satisfaction will probably lead managers over the next twenty years to produce cars using either fully automated processes (such as an assembly line without semiskilled production workers) or teams of highly skilled manual workers. Which way the industry or company goes will depend on the price of its product, union pressures, and dozens of other factors too numerous to list here. What is important is that industry will usually be unable to stay in the middle of the continuum, and moving either way from the center will require the invention of new technologies.

Low-technology solutions need not entail a return to back-breaking labor. For example, Volvo has shown that new low technologies can be highly productive and labor saving and can require as much engineering genius as high technologies. In their plant at Kalmar, Sweden, they have replaced the assembly line with 250 individual "car carriers"—eighteen-foot-long platforms that deliver cars to twenty-five different assembly teams. Not only is the monotony of the assembly line avoided, the painful necessity of working in the uncomfortable over-the-head position typical of assembly lines has been replaced by the capability of the car carriers to be tipped on their side, thus allowing the worker to perform his tasks at a normal eye-level position.

What is being discovered around the world is that there is *choice* where technology is concerned. Schumacher is developing new labor-intensive, energy-efficient, inexpensive, "intermediate" technologies appropriate for the developing economies. These methods and machines correspond to the low technologies on my technological continuum. The managerial challenge of the future is to find technologies that are environmentally sound, energy-efficient, and satisfying for workers in advanced, industrial nations.

A Future of Economic Substitutions

The technological continuum illustrates not only the alternatives for a given industry but the probable general drift of the American economy as a whole. What is important to understand about the aggregate effects of a departure from middle-range technologies is that (1) the shifts would be gradual; (2) the shifts would go both ways—not just to the high or just to the low end; (3) we do not know which industries would go which way at this time; (4) the shifts would be voluntary responses to market and social pressures; (5) shifts to *low* technology would not necessarily entail abandoning *modern* technology or high productivity.

These changes have antecedents in the contemporary economy. First, the United States is already moving toward a services economy and beginning to rely on foreign nations to provide many mass-produced and some energy-intensive goods. These actions are likely to continue for as long as there is a less-developed world and for as long as some underdeveloped countries have ready access to cheap natural gas and oil. Second, American industries are beginning to adopt the so-called socio-technical philosophy that technologies can be designed to meet social needs. Third, there is some, if not a great deal, of rekindled interest in the production of high-quality goods by craftsmen. Fourth, some mass-produced goods that contribute only to waste or planned obsolescence are being abandoned (beverage cans, for instance). None of these incipient trends constitutes a revolution, and no revolution is being forecast. Rather, the higher costs of energy and resources, when combined with the larger package of new social and economic demands, will encourage the following kinds of substitutions:

● energy for energy—for example, an abundant resource like coal is substituted for a scarce one like natural gas.

● capital for energy—a new, more energy-efficient technology is adapted.

● a product for energy—a dress is made from cotton rather than nylon, for instance.

● processes for energy—for example, windows that open are installed in office buildings.

● labor for energy—a radio is assembled by hand instead of mechanically.

Some of these substitutions, such as capital for energy and energy for energy, find precedents in the traditional assumptions of economists and thus are not controversial. But the substitution of labor for capital runs contrary to the notions of economic progress that have dominated economic and industrial thinking for over a hundred years and thus requires further explication.

Effects of Substitution of Labor

There is an enormous body of literature concerning the relationship of labor and capital in production. The basic conclusion of most economists is that there is an elasticity of substitution between capital and labor (which means, for example, that when the price of labor increases, machines will be substituted for some workers). It has also been discovered that capital and energy are "complements"; that is, an increase in the relative price of energy leads to some substitution of labor for energy-intensive capital goods. Indeed, the United States may already be witnessing some marginal and temporary substitution of labor for capital as a result of rising energy prices (Clark, 1976). Why would the increased cost of energy lead to a substitution of labor for capital? In the past, industry could always assume that energy would be abundant and cheap. Since it takes energy to produce and to drive machines, and since energy was viewed as almost a free good, as noted above, the cost of capital goods was relatively small compared to the continually soaring costs of labor. Therefore, cheap energy increased the attractiveness of capital over labor. (Capital and energy were also made more competitive with labor through such government policies as permitting tax benefits for capital depreciation and oil and gas depletion.)

Today, the price of energy is *starting* to reflect its real costs (the price of energy is set, in part, by the price of available substitutes), and this price, in turn, is driving up the initial and lifetime costs of machines. Some data are instructive on this point. Between 1920 and 1960, the amount of energy needed to produce each dollar of G.N.P. fell gradually and irregularly. But beginning in the late 1960s, this trend reached a plateau and started creeping upward even before the oil embargo caused its reversal in 1974. Also, there is now a trace of evidence (O'Toole, 1976b) that the ratio of wages to the cost of energy (and to the cost of machinery) will be starting to decrease for the first time since economists began to make accurate estimates of these indicators.

This much is easy. The difficult analysis occurs when one attempts to estimate just *where* the substitution of labor for capital/energy will actually occur, because it will depend on the industry, the type of technology, the form of energy, and the skill level of workers in question. But *in the aggregate,* if energy prices continue to rise, the United States is likely to see a major reordering of the relative weights given to the factors of production. Thus, the historical trend of substituting capital and natural resources for labor will most probably be slowed if not reversed. Industries and nations will have to make better use of the most important, resilient, and least-tapped factor of production—humans.

Will increased substitution of labor for capital mean an unmitigated step backward to a lower standard of living? Clearly, it could bring about a stagnant economy and lead to a cessation of artistic, medical, scientific, and social progress. Ten years ago, this problem would have been threatening. But tomorrow's high energy prices, shortages of capital, environmental problems, and changes in values may obviate the issue. For example, as I have been maintaining throughout this book, the major manpower problem facing America in the next three decades will be underemployment—the underutilization of skills, training, education and other human resources. Moving the economy from the center of the technological spectrum to the two ends not only could create good, meaningful jobs in energy- and capital-saving industries, but could also have a positive effect on national productivity through tapping the latent and growing reserves of human resources. (For a discussion of the effects on inflation of such a shift, see O'Toole, 1976b, pp. 46.) Developing these human resources more fully will be the "technological" challenge of the Quality Society, as the development of better tools and machines was the ultimate source of productivity in industrial society.

New Liberal Policies

Could the Quality Society be achieved solely through market mechanisms? For the reasons outlined in the last chapter, the answer is an emphatic no. Although there is no need for nationalization or central planning, there is clearly a need for government action to encourage the kinds of substitutions needed to achieve the Quality Society. For example, a reordering of the way federal expenditures are made would be a necessary condition for such changes. In choosing whether the United States should invest a billion dollars in "X" or "Y," the Congress should decide on the basis of which alternative uses resources most efficiently, which employs labor most intensively, and which enhances the quality of life the most. The new "foresight provision" recently passed by the House, which calls for an analysis of the potential long-term consequences of public expenditures, is a first step in this direction. Subsequently, the Congress might also need to mandate "employment impact statements" to accompany all important pieces of proposed legislation (building on the precedent of environmental impact statements). The need for such instruments of foresight is demonstrated by recent experience: In 1975 the government chose to spend several billion dollars on a highway program creating about 256,000 jobs instead of on a health program that would have produced roughly 423,000 jobs. In a Quality Society, the consequences of such investments would be known to politicians and to the public, and the investment decision could be made on the basis of somewhat more objective criteria. The opportunities for using public policy in this way are enormous.

This analysis is, of course, incomplete, but there is evidence that a Quality Society is possible in an advanced nation without significantly reducing the standard of living of the people. (For example, the banning of returnable beverage containers that I described in Chapter One is an example of a policy that takes us one small step toward a Quality Society.) Clearly, the restoration of our air, water, and cities could constitute the basis for a multibillion-dollar economy. The end of planned obsolescence could conserve energy and resources *and* create meaningful work and quality goods. Shifts to higher aesthetic standards in architecture and consumer products, to goods that are more durable, and to a greater emphasis on recycling could all contribute to the goals of the Quality Society. And all of these changes are possible in a democratic country with a free-market economy.

Governmental policies that would create the conditions, context, and incentives in which the free play of the market would lead to the Quality Society include the following:

• Policies to keep the price of energy and natural resources high in order to encourage conservation and the substitution of labor for capital (and negative-income-tax policies to offset the effects of such higher prices on the poor).

• Policies designed to internalize the full social costs of industrial pollution, job dissatisfaction, and occupational health and safety.

• Policies designed to bring "human-depreciation" benefits to industry that would match or exceed current capital-depreciation benefits.

• Policies to encourage industries engaged in labor-intensive rehabilitation, recycling, and repair and in the production of durable and aesthetic goods.

Although these policies alone are inadequate to the task of creating a Quality Society, they nevertheless suggest that it is achievable within the existing democratic and economic institutions of the nation. At the least, I believe it is premature to abandon the liberal premises on which our culture, politics, and economy are built in favor of the seductive, mystical promises of Buddhist or any other kind of socialist economics. The United States can create a just alternative to socialism, one in which the development of human resources and the preservation of freedom are complements rather than trade-offs. Certainly this challenge is imposing and risky and requires some degree of blind faith in the possibility of its achievement, but the rewards for success would be uncommonly high.

11 ～✦～✦～✦～✦～✦～✦～✦～✦～✦～✦～

Recapitulation
and Conclusions

The Western world is in the midst of a scientific revolution. For two hundred years, free economies have been guided by the "laws" of economics. But today, the behavior of observed economic phenomena is no longer consistent with the paradigm of the discipline of Adam Smith. As fifteenth-century observers were troubled by the lack of correspondence between the movement of the heavens and Ptolemy's earth-centered model of the universe, many observers today note that full employment, efficiency, freedom, and equality do not emanate from the free play of a growth-oriented economy. Although it is still too early for a new economics to have appeared (indeed, the Copernicus and Kepler of the new economics are nowhere in sight), there is nevertheless a large and growing body of criticism of the established discipline. For example, let us look at one of the most sacred assumptions of the ascendant economic paradigm: that full employment flows as naturally from economic growth as pure water flows from mountain streams.

If one asks an economist how employment and economic growth are related, one receives a straightforward and simple answer. Arthur Okun has even developed a "law" to explain the relationship: for every 1 percent increase in the annual Gross National Product, there is an accompanying one-third of a percent decrease in the rate of unemployment.* If one asks a futurist the same question, the answer will be more complicated, even frustrating for those who are impatient for "the facts". The futurist might respond in the following way. With the possible exception of the relationship between supply and demand, there are no laws governing economics. Unlike those in the natural sciences, the conditions under which economies operate are created by people, not by God. Thus, the relationship between growth and employment depends on the public policies a nation chooses to pursue.

The key to the futurist's perspective on public policy is thus the concept of choice. "But some economic laws are based on historically supportable evidence," the more hard-nosed and practical among us might object; "look at the trade-off between inflation and unemployment. The futurist surely can't deny that it exists." Clearly, there was—and, to some extent, still is—a trade-off between inflation and unemployment. Given the Keynesian policies that have been followed in the United States, Britain, and many other Western countries over the past quarter of a century, there will usually be such a relationship. But pursuing other policies will give other outcomes. For example, job-creation efforts that do not rely on macro-economic stimulation of the economy will probably not lead to inflation.

There are several things wrong with Okun's law and the other "answers" that economists might offer to the question of how economic growth and full employment are related. Often, economic models** leave out too many important considerations, such as the

*More precisely, for each percentage point by which real G.N.P. growth falls below 4 percent, the rate of unemployment increases by one-third of a percent. For each percentage point of growth above 4 percent, the rate of unemployment decreases by one-third of a point.

**By models I mean not only the mathematical constructs with which economists attempt to mimic the workings of society, but also the set of conscious axioms and sub-conscious assumptions that frame and dictate their world view.

indirect and long-term consequences of growth for such qualitative concerns as the state of the environment and job satisfaction.

Also, the models are not dynamic; they do not account for such changes in the conditions of society as new technologies, new public policies, and new social values. Another problem with the economists' models is that they are based on the notion of equilibrium (that is, the idea that things will balance out nicely if we just leave them alone and wait long enough). An attendant notion is that there is a natural order or level of human affairs or behavior. Finally, the economic perspective leads to the trade-off game, in which the rule is: If you do this, you can't do that. This game leads to the framing of public policy options in painfully constrained *either/or* terms, such as job versus a clean environment. Any sensible person, however, wants both jobs *and* a clean environment.

Most dangerously, these incomplete and static equilibrium models of economics often logically and inevitably lead to overly simple and erroneous policy conclusions. For example, according to the logic on which Okun's "law" is based, the one best way to cure unemployment is to increase economic growth. The conclusion is insensitive to the fact that traditional measures designed to achieve full employment through the stimulation of economic growth have created unwanted second-order results (such as inflation and environmental degradation), while failing to provide jobs for all who want and need them. Even at the official "full-employment" level, where the unemployment rate is 4 percent or less, there are still millions of individuals who are chronically unemployed. The model does not account for the effects of changing values (such as the desire of married women for paid jobs), which have altered the very structure of the workforce. The model also assumes that there is something natural about 4 percent unemployment.

The futurist is impatient with this way of framing the analysis of important issues and with the brand of conclusions it inevitably brings. As a first step in developing more effective policies, it seems that we need to establish a new perspective of analysis, a perspective that broadens rather than narrows the range of alternatives. The goal of the futurist perspective is to identify more options for society, looking for ones that avoid politically unacceptable trade-offs. When asked if he prefers option A or option B, the futurist responds, "Let me take a look at option C."

It is this exploratory orientation that has guided the analysis of work and education in these pages. The most basic assumptions about human resources have been questioned, and other assumptions have been offered where these seemed appropriate. I have explored the available policy options and have many times suggested that more choices are called for. In so doing, I have tried to free the analysis from the traditional views of the economists, budgeteers, and professional managers who dominate decision making in the most important public and private institutions of the nation and from the bureaucratic mind-set that greets all new ideas with the following kinds of reflex reactions: "That would never work because . . ." "We've never done it like that before." "It would be too impractical." "That was tried in . . ." Most important, I have attempted to substitute the constraining vision of the economist with a world view that is dynamic, future-oriented, holistic, nondeterministic, and sensitive to qualitative concerns. Although I have not tried to develop an alternative political economy for the United States, I have tried to analyze the concerns of education and work in the broadest possible context.

At issue in this book, then, is not just work, not just education, and not even work *and* education. At issue are the complex interrelationships among human-resource concerns and such institutions as the family, community, and economy and such goals as freedom, equality, democracy, and efficiency. What is significant is how work and education influence and are influenced by other institutions of the society and how they *might* influence and be influenced by these institutions under different assumptions and policies.

This analysis was undertaken not to elevate human-resource concerns to a central place in the social order or to downplay the importance of other concerns. Rather, my purpose was to escape the narrow and specialized thinking that characterizes most contemporary analysis of work and education. This compartmentalization of disciplines, interest groups, and perspectives leads to educational proposals that are unacceptable to employers, to job-creation proposals that are unacceptable to environmentalists, and to humanistic work-design proposals that are unacceptable to trade unionists. Because current public policy analysis is a narrowing process of elimination tied to traditional assumptions, the nation seems unable to create more effective work and education policies. The traditional assumptions keep leading back to the same flawed, traditional policies. I have simply sought to reverse the process of convergence by broadening the scope of analysis.

No solutions to the difficult problems of human resources development are offered here; the aim of the book is merely to suggest how a liberal, futurist perspective would lead to *different* solutions from those arising out of the currently dominant economic perspective.

What, then, can be concluded from this exploration into the future of human resources development? My message is simply that this country need *not* accept the following kinds of widely held assumptions, assumptions that inappropriately and unnecessarily constrain our ability to create new and more effective policies relating to work and education.

Assumption 1. The current divisions of the time of our lives are rational, economically efficient, and thus "natural." The premises of economists are not wholly false, but they are only partially true. For example, economists argue that efficiency dictates the pattern in which almost everyone in the paid labor force works from nine to five, five days a week, fifty weeks a year, from the day he or she graduates from school until retirement at age sixty-five. But does the obvious necessity to provide food, clothing, shelter, and the other goods and services wanted by a modern society dictate that there is only one rational or efficient division of the time of our lives? Moreover, is there any evidence that the normative pattern is the result of the demands of workers who will not accept any other alternatives? Or is this pattern merely a tradition that has evolved because of its convenience to the needs of the industrial order, an order that "needed" men workers more than women workers, that "needed" middle-aged rather than young or old workers, that "needed" workers to man machines at specific hours if these machines were to run efficiently?

The futurist does not refute the contentions that some machines need to be manned at specific times or that some (perhaps most) workers prefer the current normative division of days, years, and lives. The futurist merely asks whether other arrangements might produce more beneficial results, not only in terms of economic efficiency, but in terms of life satisfaction, enlargement of individual choice, and flexibility. For example, offering workers many possible time configurations could lead to a higher quality of life, as well as to greater economic productivity. The economist claims that people already can choose among various kinds of native working conditions. But essentially this opportunity exists only for a privileged few, and even for these individuals, deviation from the norm has so many attendant disbenefits that in reality there is little choice at all. Although we all currently have the option to starve or be treated as pariahs, the kinds of choices the futurist advocates are real choices among real alternatives. Moreover, the futurist does not accept that order and efficiency cannot coexist with flexibility and choice. Both are possible and desirable.

Assumption 2. People work only to make money. Again, this is a partial truth. No doubt the prime needs of all people are the food, clothing, and shelter that only money can buy. Moreover, to some extent, all of us are greedy. Few people, for example, will refuse a raise. But money is not all that motivates or interests people. If surgeons were suddenly to be paid twenty thousand dollars a year, and street sweepers were paid sixty thousand, few surgeons would quit to become street sweepers, and the prestige of medicine would hardly drop at all. Ironically, the behavior of economists themselves proves the point. Many university economists can make more money in private industry, but they prefer the independence of academic life. The contradiction between the ideology and actual behavior of economists was graphically brought home to me when a young economist sat in my office and said, "People work only for money." A year later, he quit his job and, without a hint of recognition of the contradiction, told me, "I'd rather be unemployed for a little while than tolerate the demeaning attitude of the people I work for."

To get out of this bind, some economists assume that only the upper middle class cares about the intrinsic values of work, and working-class people don't care a whit about such things as

challenge and autonomy on the job. They are thus demonstrating
either simple class prejudice or an unwillingness to recognize the
enormous amount of job turnover among laboring people who
leave one average-paying job for another average-paying job because they "won't tolerate the demeaning attitudes" of their bosses.

When pushed to the wall in private, these same economists
will admit that people don't work just for money and claim that
economists would never make such a naive assumption. But the
proof is in what they do, not in what they say. All the articles in
learned economic journals and all the papers presented at professional meetings explicitly assume that people work only for money.
That economists hold to a half-truth is their problem; that their
assumptions guide the formation of public policy is a problem for
all of us.

*Assumption 3. People go to school in order to get well-paying jobs
at graduation.* This is a self-fulfilling prophecy. For the past decade,
the human-capital school of economics has argued that investments
in education pay off in higher lifetime incomes and, relatedly, also
pay off in increases in the Gross National Product. Educators,
politicians, parents, and employers took up this rational and logical
line of thinking and convinced a generation of young Americans
that "education is a good investment." Now, the market value of
education has plummeted, and the "laws" of human capitalism are
seen as merely descriptions of certain phenomena at a particular
time. Again, it is irrelevant to society that economists chose to
delude themselves. But they also deluded a generation of young
people who now feel they were stuck with a bad investment. Their
expectations for high-paying jobs were raised unrealistically, and
their expectations for learning and enjoying at college were down-
played unrealistically. Because the intrinsic rewards of learning
and the value of education as preparation for family, community,
and leisure activities were absent in the economic model of education, millions of young people are disappointed, bitter, and even
angry with schools, employers, and society.

How has society responded to this problem? By doing more
of the same. Efforts are now being made at all levels to increase
educational programs that serve solely as preparation for work.
So much are we prisoners of the economic perspective that we do

not see that the unrealizable expectations we created earlier cannot be dealt with by compounding these expectations.

Assumption 4. College graduates are overeducated. According to economists, people go to college for the rational purpose of making more money. Young people start by calculating how much the average high school graduate makes during his or her lifetime and then subtract this sum from how much the average college graduate makes; if the resulting figure is larger than the cost of a college education minus foregone income, they decide to make the four-year investment. Thus, it is perfectly rational for economists to claim that a college graduate who cannot find a well-paying job is "overeducated." Clearly, he has made a bad investment. But the economists do not stop there. From the viewpoint of public policy, educational expenditures have also become "uneconomical," because they are not producing increases in the Gross National Product. Ergo, the rational thing for government to do is to curtail educational expenditures.

Such economic rationality runs roughshod over the American commitment to free choice and equality of opportunity. It ignores the noneconomic benefits of education, such as a literate and responsive citizenry. It ignores the public benefits of a responsible citizenry in favor of the private benefits of money making. Thus, limiting educational expenditures and opportunities is economically rational. But it throws the baby out with the bath water. It optimizes the work element of the system, while throwing other and more important parts into chaos.

Assumption 5. People are unemployed because they lack skills. This is not a half-truth; this is a complete falsehood. People are unemployed because of a shortage of jobs not because of a shortage of skills. Not only is the average skill level required on the job low (about a tenth-grade education will suffice in most entry-level jobs), employers are looking for workers with specific attitudes and aptitudes, not specific skills. In a few weeks, a willing and adaptive high school graduate can be trained to do the typical entry-level job in industry. Since vocational education does not create jobs, it merely alters the order of individuals in the job queue. Thus, public money is invested to give some individuals an advantage over others, an "advantage" that is itself questionable: the vocational training often encourages senseless and invidious credentialism among employers, leads to the hardening of social-class distinctions, reduces the lifelong mobility of vocational graduates, and increases social and political alienation. Moreover, skill-training efforts distract national attention from job-creation efforts.

Assumption 6. The choice is vocational education vs. liberal education. When given a choice between pneumonia and a cold, the sensible person will ask for a third option. And many good alternatives are available. For example, fusing the best of practical and theoretical education not only avoids offensive class distinctions, but helps all people (men and women, black and white, blue-collar and white-collar) to learn more effectively. Education that integrates experience and abstraction seems to have a lasting effect on students and is an appropriate form of education for family, leisure, and community activities as well as for work.

Assumption 7. The way to solve unemployment is for the government to create jobs. The most perennially popular actions for achieving full employment are: (1) federal stimulation of economic growth; (2) increased manpower training, and (3) public-service employment. As we have seen, although the first of these is a successful policy in many respects, it also generates certain social and environmental costs while leaving pockets of people chronically unemployed. The second policy is most often a case of self-deception; the problem is too few jobs, not skills. Public-service employment is a different order of beast. It is an appropriate but insufficient solution for the following reasons: (1) most-public service jobs go to the middle class and not to those who really need them; (2) measured by challenge, meaningfulness, and the opportunity to grow and to learn, private-sector jobs are usually better than public-sector jobs; (3) alternative forms of federal expenditures produce more jobs per dollar spent; (4) public-service jobs expand the portion of the work force engaged in less productive white-collar jobs, thus creating some inflationary pressures; and (5) the palliative nature of public service jobs reduces pressures to act on the root causes of unemployment, and, consequently, the damaging problems of subemployment, low-level employment, and involuntary employment remain and grow worse.

Assumption 8. Workers are responsible for the low productivity of

American industry. American economists, industrial engineers, and managers basically believe that workers are lazy. This view leads to the conclusion that work tasks should be organized to inhibit the natural tendencies of workers to goof off, procrastinate, and engage in overt work restriction. Good management, then, is management that controls the behavior of workers in much the same way as a kindergarten teacher controls the behavior of her pupils. If the efforts and activities of the workers can be controlled and channeled, they will presumably be more productive. Although the current group of job enrichers and redesigners differs with the economists over the methods used to get workers to work harder (the new school advocates more humane and sophisticated forms of job design), they nevertheless agree that workers are directly responsible for productivity. The problem with this widely held notion is that it assumes nineteenth-century working conditions in which labor was the crucial factor in productivity.

Today, if all the workers in America were to labor five times faster and five times harder, the effect on national productivity would be negligible. Productivity in a postindustrial society depends primarily on technology, knowledge, and managerial decision making: the pace of assembly lines is determined by technology; the value of services is determined by quality and not quantity; even the price of products is determined more by marketing and financial costs than by production costs.

But if all workers in America (including professionals and managers) were to work five times *smarter,* there would be more than a fivefold increment in national productivity. The better use of brain power would increase the productive potential of technologies, improve the quality of services rendered, and improve managerial performance in planning, marketing, finance, and distribution. Future gains in productivity will come from the fuller development and use of the skills, training, intelligence, and education of workers. To more fully tap these human resources will require a new set of assumptions about labor, capital, technology, and productivity.

Assumption 9. The substitution of capital for labor increases productivity. Of course, it is as close to fact as one can get to assert that economic growth *has occurred* through the substitution of capital for labor. Historically, such growth has been at the core of much of mankind's social and political progress and economic developments. But in the future a counterargument may run as follows: the further substitutions of capital for labor may lead to greater pollution, the inefficient use of energy and other scarce resources, increased inflation, unemployment, and dissatisfying jobs for those lucky enough to find employment.

Indeed, for humankind to progress further, it may be necessary to substitute some labor for capital. This process will not involve simply the replacement of middle-range, assemblyline kinds of technology by the individual, craftsmanlike low technologies that E.F. Schumacher is developing and advocating. The process will also require highly productive, labor-intensive high technologies (such as those being created in the fields of energy production, communications, transportation, cybernetics, health care, and food production). But whether industry moves to the high productivity of high technology or the high quality of low technology, the development of the human resource will be of singular importance. Tapping the human resource will be the most thoroughly effective way of increasing gross national productivity in the future, because human resources development does not entail such side effects as the waste of energy and natural resources and the creation of pollution, unemployment, and low-quality goods.

Assumption 10. Socialism is the answer. There is widespread agreement that serious problems exist at the nexus of work and education. Unemployment, underemployment, job dissatisfaction, credentialism, and discontent with the value of education are all real and growing problems. Many Americans have analyzed and evaluated the current policies for meeting these problems and have concluded that they are inadequate, ineffective, and even counterproductive. And many of these people are despairing of finding traditional free-market solutions. The current decision-making process seems hopelessly chained to outmoded economic assumptions that keep rekindling the same outmoded policies. If the problems are to be solved, these chains must be broken, they argue. The only answer, then, is socialism.

But socialism also suffers from the trade-off mentality (freedom must be sacrificed to gain equality), and it introduces a score of other problems that are not found in a free-market system. The 130 or so socialistic nations of the world all demonstrate at least some tendency toward being bureaucratic, inefficient, dogmatic, and insensitive to the problems of personal liberty. Even Swedish socialism now tolerates unannounced raids on the homes of citizens to see whether they are cheating on their taxes.

I do not wish to imply that the best models of socialism will deteriorate into authoritarianism. For example, both Swedish socialism and Schumacher socialism are essentially democratic. Moreover, they offer impressive responses to the problems of employment. I am concerned simply with the social costs that are associated with even the most benign and attractive forms of socialism. If these costs were to be borne only by the privileged, society should be willing to pay them. But they are borne by all workers in advanced socialistic societies, as was illustrated by the experiences of a group of American auto workers who recently worked in Sweden. These workers spent a fortnight at the Saab-Scania Company in a widely publicized experiment to see if the Swedish system of industrial democracy would be attractive to Detroit's auto workers. It is fascinating that these American trade union members found Swedish society and workplaces to be paternalistic, coercive, and even a bit repressive. These rather typical auto workers sensed that it was easier and more socially acceptable to go one's own way in America (including thumbing one's nose at the system, if that was what one desired to do). The pluralistic, informal, and unpredictable American system—for all its inequalities and risks—was preferred by these workers over the homogeneous, formal security of European socialism. Like Huck Finn, American workers apparently find their own brand of security in knowing that they can "light out for the Territory" if conditions at work or in the community ever become intolerable. Although they could not fully articulate the problem (they talked about "fear" in Sweden), they sensed that there was no "territory" to light out to in a system with one completely dominant set of values and norms of behavior. All systems of socialism must eventually rest on community-induced conformity. There is no room for individualistic workers in Sweden, entrepreneurs in Yugoslavia, or conspicuous consumers in Schumacher's utopia. One simply can't opt out of the established pattern of behavior. In an *effective* socialist state, there is no room for pluralism. (Socialist Britain and Italy, still pluralistic, pay the price of being ineffective, and thus they offer the worst of both worlds.)

To preserve the kinds of intangible freedoms protected by a plurality of values and behaviors, I have thus stressed nonsocialistic responses to the problems of employment. In responding to the inequities and inefficiencies of the messy, chaotic, and undisciplined market system, I have argued that we should attempt to preserve its best social aspects—flexibility, choice, autonomy, and voluntary cooperation and participation.

But we should be careful: the trade-off mentality is at work again. The choice is *not* socialism or a totally free-market economy. There are other possibilities. The challenge is to find one in which the problems of work and education can be solved without sacrificing freedom, efficiency, quality or democracy. To identify such an alternative or alternatives we must first liberate policy analysis from the crippling constraints of the anachronistic economic paradigm to which it is currently tied.

The futurist's perspective taken here does not offer a new paradigm, it merely helps us to explore for new and more effective work and education policies. It simply frees us to see that we have more choices than we had previously assumed—a small contribution, perhaps, but essential to the future development of human resources and to the achievement of a Quality Society.

Bibliography

ADLER, M. J. *The Time of Our Lives.* New York: Holt, Rinehart and Winston, 1970.

ADLER, M. J. "Old Truths about Education and New Insights." New York: Aspen Institute for Humanistic Studies, Occasional Paper, 1971.

APPEL, J. D. "Law as a Social Science in the Undergraduate Curriculum." *Journal of Legal Education,* 1957, *10,* 485–90.

BABSON, S., AND BRIGHAM, N. *What's Happening to our Jobs?* Sommerville, Massachusetts: Popular Economics Press, 1976.

BAILEY, J. S. "Career Education and Competency-Based Credentialism." In L. McClure and C. Buan (Eds.), *Essays on Career Education.* Washington, D.C.: U.S. Government Printing Office, 1975.

BECKER, G. *Human Capital.* New York: Columbia University Press, 1964.

BELL, D. "The Corporation in the 1970s." *The Public Interest*, 1971, no. 24 (Summer), 5–33.

BELL, D. *The Coming of Post-Industrial Society*. New York: Basic Books, 1973.

BENNIS, W. *Beyond Bureaucracy*. New York: McGraw-Hill, 1966.

BERG, I. *Education and Jobs: The Great Training Robbery*. Boston: Beacon Press, 1971.

BERG, I. "Education and Training: Measuring the Payoff." *Manpower*, 1973, *5* (Nov.), 7–10.

BERG, I. "'They Won't Work': The End of the Protestant Ethic and All That." In J. O'Toole (Ed.), *Work and the Quality of Life*. Cambridge: M.I.T. Press, 1974.

BEZDEK, R., AND HANNON, B. "Energy, Manpower, and the Highway Trust Fund." *Science*, August 23, 1974, 669–675.

BISCONTI, A. H., AND SOLMON, L. C. *College Education on the Job*. Bethlehem, Pennsylvania: College Placement Council Foundation, 1976.

BLOCK, J. H. "Mastery Learning in the Classroom: An Overview of Recent Research." Santa Barbara: University of California, 1973.

BLUESTONE, I. "Democratizing the Work Place." Unpublished paper (commissioned for J. O'Toole and others *Work in America*), June 22, 1972.

BLUMBERG, P., KAPSIS, R. E., AND MURTHA, J. M. "The Victims of Education: College Graduates and the American Dream." *Social Experience*, 1976, *1*(1).

BOLLES, R. N. *What Color Is Your Parachute?* Berkeley: Ten Speed Press, 1973.

BONHAM, G. "The World of I.B.M. Education." *Change*, Winter 1973–74, pp. 36–39.

BOWEN, H. R. "Manpower Management and Higher Education." *Educational Record*, 1973, *54*, no. 1, pp. 5–14.

BOWLES, S., AND GINTIS, H. *Schooling in Capitalist America*. New York: Basic Books, 1976.

BRONFENBRENNER, U. *Two Worlds of Childhood*. New York: Russell Sage Foundation, 1970.

BRUNO, P. "For June Graduates, a Few Words about Work." *Los Angeles Times*, May 13, 1976, Part II, p. 7.

CAPLAN, R. D., COBB, S., FRENCH, J. R. P., HARRISON, R. V., AND PINNEAU, S. R., JR. *Job Demands and Worker Health: Main Effects and Occupational Differences.* Washington, D.C.: U.S. Government Printing Office, 1975.

CARTTER, A. M. "Scientific Manpower for 1970–1985." *Science,* 1971, *172* (April), 132–140.

CLARK, L. H. "Productivity Problems." *Wall Street Journal,* June 7, 1976.

COLEMAN, J. S., and others. *Youth: Transition to Adulthood.* Washington, D.C.: U.S. Government Printing Office, 1973.

COLLEGE PLACEMENT COUNCIL. "Liberal Arts Students and the Job Market." *The Chronicle of Higher Education,* May 5, 1975, p. 9.

COLLINS, R. "Functional and Conflict Theories of Educational Stratification." In B. R. Cosin (Ed.), *Education: Structure and Society.* Baltimore: Penguin Books, 1972.

DAVIS, L. E., AND TRIST, E. "Improving the Quality of Work Life: Sociotechnical Case Studies." In J. O'Toole (Ed.), *Work and the Quality of Life.* Cambridge: M.I.T. Press, 1974.

DEWEY, J. *Experience and Education.* New York: Macmillan, 1963.

DITTMAN, F. "Cultural Constraints on the Acquisition of Achievement Motivation." Research Note 18, Educational Policy Research Center. Menlo Park, Calif.: Stanford Research Institute, 1974.

DRUCKER, P. *Management.* New York: Harper & Row, 1974.

DRUCKER, P. *The Unseen Revolution.* New York: Harper & Row, 1976.

FETTERS, W. "National Longitudinal Study of the High School Class of 1972." Washington, D.C.: U.S. Government Printing Office, 1974.

FINLEY, G. J. *Business and Education: A Fragile Partnership.* New York: The Conference Board, 1973.

FREEMAN, R. *The Overeducated American.* New York: Academic Press, 1976.

FRIEDMAN, M. *Capitalism and Freedom.* Chicago: University of Chicago Press, 1962.

FRIEDMAN, M., AND ROSENMAN, R. H. *Type A Behavior and Your Heart.* New York: Knopf, 1974.

FURSTENBERG, F. F. "Work Experience and Family Life." In J.

O'Toole (Ed.), *Work and the Quality of Life.* Cambridge: M.I.T. Press, 1974.

GALBRAITH, J. K. "Tasks for the Democratic Left." *The New Republic,* August 16 and 23, 1975, *173* (7 and 8), pp. 18–20.

GALLAGHER REPORTS. "What Do Employers Think of College Graduates?" *Gallagher President's Report,* June 24, 1973.

GILFORD, D. "The Non-Collegiate Sector: Statistical Snapshots of Adult Continuing Education." Address before the American Association for Higher Education, March 11, 1974.

GOLDMAN, M. I. "Pollution Soviet Style." *Business and Society Review,* Summer 1973.

GOLDRING, P. *Multipurpose Man.* New York: Taplinger, 1974.

GOLDSTEIN, H., and others. "Projections for Use in Making Decisions on Education and Manpower." Staff paper. Washington, D.C.: The Manpower Institute, 1973.

GORZ, A. *Socialism and Revolution.* Garden City, N.Y.: Anchor Books, 1973.

GORZ, A. *Strategy for Labor.* Boston: Beacon Press, 1968.

GRASSO, J. T. "The Contributions of Vocational Education, Training and Work Experience to the Early Career Achievements of Young Men." Columbus: Center for Human Resource Research, Ohio State University, 1975.

GREDE, J. F. "The Role of Community Colleges in Career Education." In L. McClure and C. Buan (Eds.), *Essays on Career Education.* Washington, D.C.: U.S. Government Printing Office, 1975.

GREEN, T. F. *Work, Leisure and the American Schools.* New York: Random House, 1968.

GREEN, T. F. "Career Education and the Pathologies of Work." In L. McClure and C. Buan (Eds.), *Essays on Career Education.* Washington, D.C.: U.S. Government Printing Office, 1975.

HARRIS, L. "Psychology Graduate Is Winner in Race for Unskilled City Job." *Los Angeles Times,* August 6, 1976, Part II, p. 1.

HARRISON, B. "Training for Nowhere." The *Washington Post,* November 19, 1972.

HIELBRONER, R. L. *The Worldly Philosophers.* New York: Simon & Schuster, 1961.

HERMAN, W. R. *Conflicting Expectations: Conservative and Liberal Goals for Education*. Washington, D.C.: National Institute of Education, 1974.

HOFFMAN, N. "Teaching Change." *Working Papers,* 1975, *3* (Spring), 37–43.

HOLT, C. "Manpower Programs to Reduce Inflation and Unemployment: Manpower Lyrics for Macro Music." Washington, D.C.: Urban Institute, 1971.

HOUSE, J. "The Effects of Occupational Stress on Physical Health." In J. O'Toole (Ed.), *Work and the Quality of Life*. Cambridge: M.I.T. Press, 1974.

HOYT, K. B. "Toward a Definition of Career Education." Unpublished paper. University of Maryland, n.d.

HOYT, K. B. "An Introduction to Career Education." Memo dated May 22, 1974. Washington, D.C.: U.S. Department of Health, Education and Welfare, 1974.

HUSEN, T. *Strategies for Educational Equality*. Paris: Organization for Economic Cooperation and Development, 1975.

JACKSON, D., AND MARSDEN, D. *Education and the Working Class* Middlesex, England: Penguin Books, 1966.

JAQUES, E. "Death and the Mid-Life Crisis." *International Journal of Psychoanalysis,* October 1965, p. 502.

JENCKS, C., and others. *Inequality.* New York: Basic Books, 1972.

KAHN, R. L. "The Work Module: A Proposal for the Humanization of Work." In J. O'Toole (Ed.), *Work and the Quality of Life*. Cambridge. M.I.T. Press, 1974.

KELSO, L. O., AND ADLER, M. J. *The Capitalist Manifesto*. New York: Random House, 1958.

KIERNAN, O. B. *American Youth in the Mid-Seventies*. Washington, D.C.: National Association of Secondary School Principals, 1972.

KOHN, M. *Class and Conformity: A Study in Values*. Homewood, Ill.: Dorsey, 1969.

KRISTOL, I. "Is the American Worker Alienated?" *Wall Street Journal,* January 18, 1973.

LANDES, D. S. "Industry, Skills and Knowledge." In B. R. Cosin (Ed.), *Education: Structure and Society*. Baltimore: Penguin Books, 1972.

LIEBOW, E. *Tally's Corner*. Boston: Little, Brown, 1967.

LIPSET, S. M., AND LADD, E. C. "College Generations—From the 1930s to the 1960s." *The Public Interest,* 1971, no. 25 (Fall), 99–113.

LOEBL, E. *Humanomics.* New York: Random House, 1976.

McCLURE, L., AND BAUN, C. (Eds.) *Essays on Career Education.* Washington, D.C.: U.S. Government Printing Office, 1975.

MACCOBY, M. "Changing Work: The Bolivar Project." *Working Papers,* 1975, *3* (Summer), 43–55.

McLUHAN, M. "Learning a Living." In F. Best (Ed.), *The Future of Work.* Englewood Cliffs, N.J.: Prentice-Hall, 1973.

MacMICHAEL, D. C. "Occupational Bias in Formal Education and Its Effect on Preparing Children for Work." In J. O'Toole (Ed.), *Work and the Quality of Life.* Cambridge: M.I.T. Press, 1974a.

MacMICHAEL, D. C. "Career Education Meets the Recession." Menlo Park: Stanford Research Institute, Educational Policy Research Center, 1974b.

MANKIN, D. "Work and Leisure in a Zero-Growth Society." Paper presented at the Eighty-First Annual Convention, American Psychological Association. Montreal, 1973.

MARIEN, M. "Credentialism in Our Ignorant Society." *Notes on the Future of Education,* 1971a, *2* (Summer).

MARIEN, M. *Essential Reading for the Future of Education.* (Rev. ed.) Syracuse, N.Y.: Syracuse University Research Corp., 1971b.

MILLER, A. *Occupations of the Labor Force According to the Dictionary of Occupational Titles.* Statistical Evaluation Report No. 8. Washington, D.C.: Office of Management and Budget, 1971.

NATIONAL PLANNING ASSOCIATION. "U.S. Employment Shifts Through 1985." *Projection Highlights,* 1974, *3* (Feb.).

NEWMAN, F., and others. *The Second Newman Report.* Cambridge: M.I.T. Press, 1974.

O'TOOLE, J., and others. *Work in America.* Cambridge: M.I.T. Press, 1973a.

O'TOOLE, J. *Watts and Woodstock: Identity and Culture in the United States and South Africa.* New York: Holt, Rinehart and Winston, 1973b.

O'TOOLE, J. (Ed.) *Work and the Quality of Life.* Cambridge: M.I.T. Press, 1974a.

O'TOOLE, J. "Education, Work, and the Quality of Life." In D. W. Vermilye (Ed.), *Lifelong Learners—A New Clientele for Higher Education*. San Francisco: Jossey-Bass, 1974b.

O'TOOLE, J. "Work and Family Life." In *American Families: Trends and Pressures, 1973*. Washington, D.C.: U.S. Government Printing Office, 1974c.

O'TOOLE, J. "Work in America and the Great Job Satisfaction Controversy." *Journal of Occupational Medicine*, 1974d, *16* (Nov.), 710–715.

O'TOOLE, J. "Lordstown, Three Years Later." *Business and Society Review*, 1975a, *13* (Spring), 64–71.

O'TOOLE, J. "Planning for Total Employment." *The Annals* of the American Academy of Political and Social Sciences, 1975b, *418* (March), 72–84.

O'TOOLE, J. "The Reserve Army of the Underemployed." *Change*, May 1975c, pp. 26–33, 63.

O'TOOLE, J. "The Reserve Army of the Underemployed: The Role of Education." *Change*, June 1975d, pp. 26–33, 60–63.

O'TOOLE, J. "On-the-Job Learning." *Worklife*, 1976a, *1* (Jan.), 2–6.

O'TOOLE, J. *Energy and Social Change*. Cambridge: M.I.T. Press, 1976b.

ORGANIZATION FOR ECONOMIC COOPERATION AND DEVELOPMENT. *Educational Statistics Yearbook*, vol. 2, Country Tables. Paris: OECD, 1975.

PARNES, H. S. "Improved Job Information: Its Impact on Long-Run Labor Market Experience." In S. L. Wolfbein (Ed.), *Labor Market Information for Youths*. Philadelphia: Temple University Press, 1975.

PIORE, M. J. "Jobs and Training." In S. H. Beer and R. E. Barringer (Eds.), *The State and the Poor*. Cambridge, Mass.: Winthrop, 1970.

PORTER, S. "Why We Can't Afford Smog." *San Francisco Chronicle*, Nov. 14, 1975, p. 62.

POWERS, T. "Planning Occupational Curricula in a Changing World." In T. Powers (Ed.), *New and Emerging Careers*. University Park: Pennsylvania State University Press, in press.

PREDIGER, D., ROTH, J., AND NOETH, R. "A Nationwide Study of Student Career Development: Summary of Results." Research Report No. 61. Iowa City: American College Testing Program, 1973.

QUINN, R., AND SHEPPARD, L. *1972–1973 Quality of Employment Survey.* Washington, D.C.: Employment Standards Administration, U.S. Department of Labor, 1974.

RAINWATER, L. "Work, Well-Being, and Family Life." In J. O'Toole (Ed.), *Work and the Quality of Life.* Cambridge: M.I.T. Press, 1974.

REUBENS, B. G. "Manpower Training in Japan." *Monthly Labor Review,* 1973a, *96* (Sept.), 16–24.

REUBENS, B. G. "German Apprenticeship: Controversy and Reform." *Manpower,* 1973b, *5* (Nov.), 12–20.

REUBENS, B. G. "Occupational Preparation in Education and Training." Paper prepared for a conference on "New Options Beyond Compulsory Education." Paris: Organization for Economic Cooperation and Development, 1974a.

REUBENS, B. G. "Vocational Education for *All* in High School?" In J. O'Toole (Ed.), *Work and the Quality of Life.* Cambridge: M.I.T. Press, 1974b.

RIGBY, L. "The Nature of Human Error." Albuquerque: Sandia Laboratories, 1970.

ROGERS, D. "Vocational and Career Education: A Critique and Some New Directions." *Teachers College Record,* 1973, *74* (May), 471–511.

ROSOW, J. Address before Western Assembly of the American Assembly. University of California, Berkeley: May 30, 1974.

SCHRANK, R., AND STEIN, S. "Yearning, Learning, and Status." In S. Levitan (Ed.), *Blue Collar Blues.* New York: McGraw-Hill, 1972.

SCHULTZ, T. W. *Investment in Human Capital.* New York: Free Press, 1970.

SCHUMACHER, E. F. *Small Is Beautiful.* New York: Harper & Row, 1973.

SHEPPARD, H., AND HERRICK, N. *Where Have All the Robots Gone?* New York: Free Press, 1971.

SHORE, M. F. *Youth and Jobs: Educational, Vocational, and Mental Health Aspects.* Washington, D.C.: National Institute of Mental Health, 1971.

SIMON, K., AND FRANKEL, M. M. "Projections of Educational, Vocational Statistics to 1980–81." Washington, D.C.: U.S. Government Printing Office, 1972.

SOLOMON, L. D. "Toward a Federal Policy on Work: Restructuring the Governance of Corporations." *The George Washington Law Review,* 1975, *43* (Aug.), 1263–1342.

SPEER, A. *Inside the Third Reich.* New York: Avon, 1971.

STRAUSS, G. "Is There a Blue-Collar Revolt against Work?" In J. O'Toole (Ed.), *Work and the Quality of Life.* Cambridge: M.I.T. Press, 1974.

STRINER, H. *Continuing Education as a National Capital Investment.* Washington, D.C.: W. E. Upjohn Foundation, 1972.

SURVEY RESEARCH CENTER. *Survey of Working Conditions.* Washington, D.C.: U.S. Department of Labor, August, 1971.

TERKEL, S. *Working.* New York: Pantheon, 1974.

THEROUX, D. *The Great Railway Bazaar.* Boston: Houghton Mifflin, 1975.

THUROW, L. "Educational and Social Policy." *The Public Interest,* No. 28, Summer, 1972.

THUROW, L. "Technological Unemployment and Occupational Education." In T. Powers (Ed.), *New and Emerging Careers.* University Park: Pennsylvania State University Press, in press.

TROMBLEY, W. "College Freshman Wealthier, Job Oriented, Survey Finds." *Los Angeles Times,* February 11, 1974.

TROW, M. "The Democratization of Higher Education in America." *European Journal of Sociology,* 1962, *3* (2).

U.S. BUREAU OF LABOR STATISTICS. "The United States Economy in 1985: An Overview of BLS Projections." *Monthly Labor Review,* 1973, *96* (Dec.), 3–42.

U.S. DEPARTMENT OF LABOR. *Employment of High School Graduates and Dropouts.* Special Labor Force Report 145. Washington, D.C., October, 1971.

U.S. DEPARTMENT OF LABOR. *Employment of Recent College Graduates.* Special Report 151. Washington, D.C., 1973a.

U.S. DEPARTMENT OF LABOR. *Handbook of Labor Statistics.* Washington, D.C.: U.S. Government Printing Office, 1973b.

U.S. DEPARTMENT OF LABOR. *Manpower Report of the President.* Washington, D.C.: U.S. Government Printing Office, 1973c.

U.S. DEPARTMENT OF LABOR. *Manpower Report of the President.* Washington, D.C.: U.S. Government Printing Office, 1974a.

U.S. DEPARTMENT OF LABOR. *Occupational Outlook Handbook 1974–75.* Washington, D.C.: U.S. Government Printing Office, 1974b.

WALKER, J. W. "Evaluating the Practical Effectiveness of Human Resource Planning Applications." *Human Resource Management,* 1974, *13* (Spring), 19–27.

WALL STREET JOURNAL "The Public Employment Bill." January 29, 1976, p. 10.

WALTON, R. E. "Alienation and Innovation in the Workplace." In J. O'Toole (Ed.), *Work and the Quality of Life.* Cambridge: M.I.T. Press, 1974.

WHITEHEAD, A. N. *An Anthology.* Selected by F. S. C. Northrop and M. W. Gross. New York: Macmillan, 1961.

WILMS, W. *Public and Proprietary Vocational Training: A Study of Effectiveness.* Berkeley: Center for Research and Development in Higher Education, University of California, 1974.

WIRTH, A. G. "Job and Work: Two Models for Society and Education." In T. Powers (Ed.), *New and Emerging Careers.* University Park: Pennsylvania State University Press, in press.

WIRTZ, W. *The Boundless Resource.* Washington, D.C.: New Republic Book Co., 1975.

WOLFBEIN, S. L. (Ed.) *Labor Market Information for Youths.* Philadelphia: Temple University Press, 1975.

WOOL, H. and others. "The Labor Supply for Lower Level Occupations." Washington, D.C.: National Planning Association, June, 1973.

YANKELOVICH, D. *Changing Youth Values in the 70's.* New York: McGraw-Hill, 1974.

Index

233